FROM THE
COOLEST CORNER
Nordic
Jewellery

Widar Halén (ed.)

FROM THE COOLEST CORNER
Nordic Jewellery

Liesbeth den Besten
Knut Astrup Bull
Widar Halén
Love Jönsson
Charlotte Malte
Päivi Ruutiainen
Jukka Savolainen
Harpa Thórsdóttir
Jorunn Veiteberg

ARNOLDSCHE Art Publishers

CONTENTS

PREFACE

From the Coolest Corner: Nordic Jewellery presents an exciting and broad range of the contemporary studio jewellery created in the Nordic countries. This book will be accompanied by a touring exhibition and an international symposium, all casting new light on the importance of this art in the 'coolest corner' of Europe. The artists and images included correspond to the objects exhibited; this book is also intended as an exhibition catalogue. *From the Coolest Corner: Nordic Jewellery* has a three-fold aim: to present the newest and most advanced contemporary Nordic jewellery, to intensify the discourse on today's jewellery and strengthen the knowledge about this field, and to consolidate Nordic jewellery's position in national and international arenas.

The organising committee consists of Widar Halén and Knut Astrup Bull from The National Museum – The Museum of Decorative Arts and Design in Oslo, Ingjerd Hanevold from the Oslo National Academy of the Arts, Elisabeth Sørheim from the Norwegian Association of Arts and Crafts, and Martina Kaufmann as project coordi-

nator. In addition, local project groups in each of the Nordic countries comprise representatives of the artists, artists' organisations, museums and universities.

Artists from all the Nordic countries, Estonia included, have been asked to send their suggestions to an international jury consisting of Liesbeth den Besten (the Netherlands), head of the jury, Widar Halén (Norway), Love Jönsson (Sweden), Päivi Ruutiainen (Finland) and Jorunn Veiteberg (Denmark). They have selected 156 works from sixty-one artists out of 219 applicants and invited five honorary guest artists: Kim Buck, Helena Lehtinen, Konrad Mehus, Kadri Mälk and Tore Svensson. The exhibition design has been undertaken by the jewellery artist Sigurd Bronger.

This book features chapters and artists contributions by all the jury members as well as by Knut Astrup Bull, Charlotte Malte, Jukka Savolainen and Harpa Thórsdóttir. The editing committee comprises Widar Halén (chief editor), Marianne Yvenes and Reinhold Ziegler. We would like to thank all these individuals and all the participating artists as well as our associated organisers in the Nordic museums of design and decorative arts, the Nordic crafts associations and the national colleges of art and design as well as, of course, our sponsors Nordic Culture Point and Nordic Culture Fund, Arts Council Norway, David-Andersen AS, Thune AS and, last but not least, Arnoldsche Art Publishers for producing this beautiful book.

An international symposium, including workshops and seminar and artist presentations at the Oslo National Academy of the Arts, will contribute to launching the exhibition and this publication. The touring exhibition will be shown at The National Museum – The Museum of Decorative Arts and Design in Oslo, the Designmuseum Danmark in Copenhagen, the Design Museum in Helsinki, The Röhsska Museum for Fashion, Design and Decorative Arts in Gothenburg, the Estonian Museum of Applied Art and Design in Tallinn, and at Galerie Handwerk in Munich during the event *Schmuck* in 2015.

We hope that this book will contribute to reinforcing the image of contemporary Nordic jewellery as expressive, reflexive and 'cool'.

Widar Halén, Knut Astrup Bull, Ingjerd Hanevold, Martina Kaufmann and Elisabeth Sørheim

JEWELLERY FROM THE COOLEST CORNER

Widar Halén

While the status and acceptance of jewellery as art has increased over the years, it is still a rather unknown field and excluded from several major museums around the world. However, this is not the case in the coolest corner of Europe, in Nordic countries, where art jewellery is thriving and being exhibited in all larger museums. It is treated entirely on par with other art expressions, and it is contributing to the development of the wider art scene. It is important to remember though that this jewellery is different from the semi-industrial or commercial samples, and therefore it is often called art jewellery, studio jewellery or author jewellery. The value is not determined by the material it is made of but rather by its artistic expression and content. It is not merely decorative but intended to be accepted as a serious and unique artistic statement.

However, the practice of the jeweller is also related to that of the designer, considering new techniques and materials as well as functional aspects. It is a hybrid practice operating at the interface of design on the one hand and fine art on the other.

Today jewellers, like other visual artists, contribute to blurring the borders between craft, fine art and design, incorporating non-precious materials, found objects and ready-mades as well as installation, performance and digital expressions. For a long time jewellers have stressed their art status, but art historian Liesbeth den Besten recently claimed that this is no longer needed, since they have 'discovered the power of their own trade'.[1] This may seem like a paradox, but it clearly shows that the old hierarchy of the various art fields has become irrelevant. Art historian Marjan Unger recently emphasised that the art aspect in fact may have contributed to isolating contemporary jewellery and that it should relate more expressively to the wider context of society, such as urbanism, sustainability, gender, sociology, medicine and biotechnology.[2] Indeed, much of the jewellery in this exhibition relates to these very aspects and sets it apart from previous Nordic exhibitions of this kind.

Tone Vigeland, CAP, 1992, oxidised silver, 150 x 210 mm
The National Museum of Art, Architecture and Design, Oslo

Paying tribute to this relatively small but important field, two major exhibitions have been presented over the last twenty years: *Nordisk Smykkekunst – Nordic Jewellery* in 1995/1997[3] and *Nordisk Smycketriennal – Nordic Jewellery* in 2001/2002,[4] organised respectively by Danish and Swedish jewellery artists in collaboration with the Nordic Design and Decorative Arts Museums. This time, with the aid of an international jury, it is Norway's turn to act as organisers.

As in previous years, the jury has focused on the most recent and groundbreaking jewellery in the Nordic countries: Denmark, Estonia, Finland, Iceland, Norway and Sweden.

In 2003 Nordic contemporary jewellery was included in the exhibition *Scandinavian Design Beyond the Myth*, which toured fourteen different countries in Europe.[5] Evidently the myths around Nordic jewellery should also be more thoroughly debated. Today jewellery artists are fascinated by the history of jewellery and its myths, stories and legends. The numerous ways in which jewellery is developing, in dialogue with both its own history as well as with other visual disciplines, ought to be constantly discussed and questioned.[6] Are there any common features in Nordic jewellery and is it possible to identify national characteristics? Probably not since Nordic jewellery today is part of the global art movement, but we may still detect certain ways of communicating Nordic ideas. It seems that the notions of democratic, affordable and wearable have to a certain degree survived in the North, and there is a great revival in the interest in nature and basic materials like wood, for instance. As art historian Jorunn Veiteberg has underlined, jewellery still offers a language we can use to tell the world who we are, what we stand for and what we would like to become.[7] In a time of globalisation it is important to look at certain entities like Nordic and Scandinavian notions which still have a meaning to people around the world.

Nordic jewellery as an art form is a relatively recent phenomenon, which originated in the 1980s. Its roots may be detected in the avant-garde European and American movement of the

Kim Buck, rings PUMPOUS COLOR, 2012, 999 silver, powder coated, various sizes

1960s and 1970s, which Peter Dormer and Ralph Turner in 1985 coined 'New Jewelry' (or 'New Jewellery' in British English).[8] They defined three different categories in jewellery: controlled expressionism, exaggerated expressionism and design-based, so-called good taste jewellery. Their most important contribution, however, was to define the jewellery scene as international, diverse and pluralistic. This broad emancipation of jewellery led to a new artistic awareness, and it eventually developed into the global movement we experience today.

During the 1980s the American and English concept of wearable objects, which had already been launched in the 1960s, became a household term in Europe. Jewellery also began to be more international, and urbanism along with the lifestyle of larger cities like New York, London and Tokyo was brought into focus. City life and technology formed a basis for new shapes and materials. Aluminium combined with plastic and rubber entered the scene. Some of the 1980s' jewellery was large and sculptural, conveying the

wearable object concept to the extreme. These daring and unconventional pieces were far removed from Nordic Functionalism and Scandinavian Design ideas. In 1980 a group of Norwegian designers and craft artists had arranged a mock funeral for Scandinavian design, which had dominated the crafts and design milieus in Nordic countries for thirty years. They had finally had enough and drove through the city with a funeral casket marked 'Scandinavian Design', which they lowered at sea in front of Oslo City Hall. With this and other powerful statements, Nordic crafts and design entered the period of postmodernism.[9] In the late 1970s Nordic craft artists established their national societies and collectives. They were fighting for their artistic and social rights, which eventually gave them a strength and freedom never previously seen in Nordic countries.

New Jewellery brought about a marked focus on the body, which came to play an entirely new role in jewellery. By the early 1990s 'body design' (cosmetic surgery and transformations) had come into focus, and surgical steel as well as space-age materials, such as niobium and titanium, became a popular material. It gave a new dimension to jewellery, but these 'high-tech' pieces were also questioned and debated. They were infused with ideas and materials which many felt were alien to the 'aesthetics of slowness' often associated with the crafts ideology. 'Great crafts should be scratched out of the heart-roots', quoted museum director Jan-Lauritz Opstad of the Museum of Decorative Arts in Trondheim in 1989,[10] recalling some of the fierce debates that had taken place.

A new generation of craft artists had manifested themselves by the 1990s. They had witnessed the political years of the 1970s, and readymades and recycled materials were important to them. The autonomy and independence of jewellery was emphasised – the so-called objectifying of the jewel. Jewellery had finally become an object for storytelling and content, thus enhancing the relationship between the artist, the user and the viewer.

For jewellery artists, the postmodern movement gave way to a freer play with historical forms and ornaments frequently juxtaposed with humorous or ironic touches. Ornament had fully returned as a symbol that was being reinterpreted and used in various new ways.

In addition, highly conceptual creations with anthropomorphic ideas inspired by genetic manipulation entered the scene. Combined with totally unconventional materials, this inspired fetish-like and provocative jewellery, sometimes bordering on the line of sculpture and performance art, which could be seen in the pieces by Kim Buck, Torben Hardenberg, Christer Jonsson, Kadri Mälk, Olli Tamminen and Tone Vigeland, to mention a few.

During the last twenty years this tendency has accelerated. Sculptural shapes and the most unconventional materials have been used to create contemporary jewellery. In this way jewellery has challenged what was regarded as suitable and acceptable in crafts. Evidently the making and wearing of studio or art jewellery remains a counterpoint to luxury status jewels. In the late 1990s and onwards ceramics, glass, felt, plastics, rubber, wax, wood and found objects, such as pieces of soap, teabags, and the like, became a main feature. These pieces now focus more on artistic content than on craft techniques, and they convey an ultimate scepticism to the old-fashioned hierarchy of the arts. New materials and new concepts have challenged traditional art jewellery, but some artists have also reacted against this trend.

We still have a large group of artists working in a way more related to goldsmiths, although a gradual disintegration of traditional crafts methods have been detected. Today most jewellers are educated in the metalwork departments of art schools and colleges and lack proper training as gold- or silversmiths. Previously this training was compulsory, but this is no longer so. It was precisely this aspect, the skills of the crafts and their revitalisation as a contemporary expression, that was debated in 2012 at a seminar in connection with the Saatchi Gallery's crafts fair *Collect* in London.[11] The participants were concerned with the question of what skills we need and want to preserve for future craft artists and whether or not art schools should provide adequate teaching and intangible know-how, a timely concern now that handicraft skills are being superseded by automation and outsourcing has become a household word.[12]

Today jewellery, like art in general, reflects the vital ideas and developments of our time and it is an amazingly diverse art scene we are experiencing, from the traditional material-based pieces to trash, found objects, and interactive and digitalised expressions. However, in the art of jewellery, communication is mostly about materials, form and identity. In a global perspective, identity is constantly being questioned in the arts, and many of the Nordic jewellery artists occupy themselves with these existential questions. They debate 'the perfect body syndrome', sustainability, nature, gender issues, racism, and national myths and stereotypes as well as the purely decorative and aesthetic. It is a highly reflexive approach, which also embraces the domestic and ritual in everyday life. Thus it will continue to give meaning in the lives of people – making

Kadri Mälk, brooch BLACK MENHIR, 2012, jet, silver, coral, 75 × 58 × 14 mm

Nordic contemporary jewellery 'cool' and enticing for many years to come.

1   Besten, Liesbeth den, 2011. *On Jewellery: A Compendium of International Contemporary Art Jewellery*. Stuttgart: Arnoldsche, p. 129.
2   Unger, Marjan, 2012. *Freedom has its limitations: Jewellery today, seen from a Dutch perspective*, lecture held on 18 Mar 2012 at Die Neue Sammlung – The International Design Museum Munich.
3   Funder, Lise and Lohman, Jan (eds.), 1995. *Nordisk Smykkekunst: Nordic Jewellery*. Copenhagen: Arnold Busck.
4   Funder, Lise (ed.), 2001. *Nordisk Smycketriennal 2 – Nordic Jewellery*. Copenhagen: Arnold Busck.
5   Halén, Widar and Wickman, Kerstin (eds.), 2003. *Scandinavian Design Beyond the Myth: Fifty Years of Design from the Nordic Countries*. Stockholm: Arvinius/Form.
6   Halén, Widar, 2002. 'Neo-Tradition: A Nordic Case Study', in Greenhalg, Paul (ed.), 2002. *The Persistence of Craft*.
     London: A & C Black, pp. 138–48.
7   Funder 2001 (see note 4), p. 24.
8   Dormer, Peter and Turner, Ralph, 1985. *New Jewelry: Trends and Traditions*. London: Thames and Hudson.
9   Halén, Widar, 2003. 'Fifty Years of Scandinavian Design – and After', in Halén/Wickman 2003 (see note 5), p. 7.
10 Opstad, Jan-Lauritz, 1989. *En Ny Bevissthet: Norsk Kunsthåndverk 1970–1990* [A New Consciousness: Norwegian Crafts 1970–1990]. Oslo: C. Huitfeldt, p. 9.
11 *Museum for Skills* seminar, organised by Art Projects and Solutions, Art Quest, and the Norwegian Association for Arts and Crafts at the British Council, London, 10 May 2012.
12 Bugge, Erling Moestue, 2012. 'Diagnosing Skills', www.norwegiancrafts.no, issue 3/2012.

HOW COOL IS THE COOLEST CORNER?

Liesbeth den Besten

It is a tricky endeavour to observe the Nordic countries as a whole. Although there are connections obviously, which are reflected in the mutual Nordic jewellery exhibition project, there are also differences between the individual countries, and maybe these differences are even stronger than a simple outsider can ever discover without visiting each country. It may be that the connection is only a practical one, that it is just a cooperation of some countries in some part of Europe which share some history together and whose people even understand each other's language quite easily (at least the Danes, Norwegians and Swedes). For an outsider from the Netherlands (by the way, a country that for unknown reasons is often located within Scandinavia by people outside Europe) there are a lot of questions for although there is an affinity, it is also a different world. Jewellery from the Nordic countries shares a mystery within the minds of other Europeans. It took a very long time before Europe became aware of contemporary jewellery from the Nordic countries, and it only happened when other countries had already reached some kind of maturity in contemporary jewellery. The outbreaks of radical and freaky jewellery were already history in central and Western Europe when it became clear that something was moving in the northern countries as well.

Today we can witness a Nordic eagerness to join the international contemporary jewellery scene. Various facts indicate a new Nordic ambition in contemporary jewellery, like the innovation of jewellery education at Konstfack University College of Arts, Crafts and Design in Stockholm, which started in 2004 with the appointment of the Dutchman Ruudt Peters as a professor and continues under his successor Karin Pontoppidan. The exhibition *The State of Things* in Die Neue Sammlung in Munich (2012) presented an 'interim report' of a jewellery school in a state of flux. The *Koru* international jewellery triennial in Finland, organised in 2012 for the fourth time with workshops, exhibitions, catalogues and a symposium, and the organisation of attractive international jewellery exhibitions and

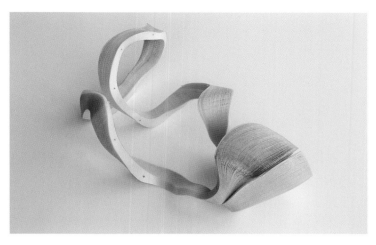

Janna Syvänoja, necklace UNTITLED I, 2012, paper, steel wire, 300×170×90 mm

publications in Estonia (*Nocturnus*, 2002; *Just Must*, 2008; *õhuLoss/Castle in the Air*, 2011), show the importance of the Nordic contribution to contemporary jewellery – also in the well-organised and enduring mutual effort. The *Nordic Jewellery* exhibitions of 1995, 2001 and 2013 and the fact that *From the Coolest Corner* will end its tour in Munich during *Schmuck* 2015 are further proof of the new Nordic self-confidence and ambition. This chapter aims to offer an appreciation of contemporary jewellery from the northern European countries within the broader perspective of international contemporary art jewellery and its history.

Pinning down movements or styles in art history to fixed dates and names is a habit that needs scrutiny. Yet there seems to exist a certain *communis opinio* among those who are knowledgeable about the fact that the history of contemporary jewellery starts during the course of the 1960s, when a reaction against jewellery as a status symbol became visible and accumulated in an international movement known as 'New Jewelry' – a name coined by Peter Dormer and Ralph Turner,

who published a book under the same title in 1985. 'Contemporary' means that the work is an expression of today and is global or, as it is defined in fine art discourse, 'that which is being made now – wherever'.[1] Therefore the term 'contemporary' indicates awareness of what is being made elsewhere and what has been made previously. 'Contemporary' is constantly changing, increasing, is flexible. The term does not describe a specific style or practice though. In the case of jewellery we can add two other conditions: that there is a breach with tradition (the passing from the gold standard to the artist's standard, and from skilfulness to experiment[2]) and that it is not the customer who decides how a piece will look.

HOW DID THE EUROPEAN NEW JEWELLERY MANIFEST ITSELF?

The Dutchman Gijs Bakker is notorious for being a jewellery designer who made radical pieces of jewellery that had an obvious anti-character

Märta Mattsson, brooch FOSSILS, 2011, cicadas, crushed pyrite, resin, silver, 150 × 150 mm

ironic and socially aware. The heavy aluminium neckpieces from 1967, designed for a jewellery show in the Stedelijk Museum in Amsterdam, are referred to in sources from that time as 'anti-status necklaces'. These pieces, made and designed in close collaboration with his wife Emmy van Leersum, were big in order to convince, all the while enclosing the head and shoulders. The reception of these pieces varies from 'torture instruments' (press comment, 1967) to 'a concern for armouring the body'.[3] Bakker's transparent Perspex *Circle in Circle* bracelet of the same year expressed the opposite extreme: it was a minimalist statement, a reversal of the idea of jewellery. Six years later Bakker designed his *Shadow Jewellery*, reducing jewellery's presence to the temporary imprint of a gold wire that had been fixed to the body for a period of time – here Bakker arrived at the full dematerialisation of jewellery. Other radical jewellery was made in Austria, also in the 1970s. Manfred Nisslmüller formulated ideas about 'anonymous and non-anonymous jewellery. ... Positive and negative phenomena appear as

jewellery, a position, a state, a situation, an incident, a moment, something. ... Jewellery can happen.'[4] He exhibited a torn-up photo showing the encircled head of a man and also a drawing showing a military tank from the side, front, back and above, together with technical details. This was in Galerie am Graben, Vienna, 1977, where Inge Asenbaum, one of the first protagonists of contemporary European jewellery, organised an exhibition on Austrian jewellery and tableware. The exhibition also included Peter Skubic's famous *Jewellery under the Skin*, presented through two X-rays of his upper forearm showing the steel implant that had been inserted on 4 November 1975 – another example of disfigured and dematerialised jewellery. In Switzerland, at the end of the 1970s, Bernhard Schobinger started to use the detritus of our consumer society, using a bottle cap, a can opener or glass shards, often combined with precious materials, to make jewellery with an aggressive aesthetic. In England the wearable art movement of the 1960s and 1970s, characterised by the use of flexible and colourful materials, revealed a sculptural approach towards the body. Susanna Heron's *Light Projections* of 1979 integrated photography as a medium to document temporary light projections that worked like ornaments on the body. The German formal and material innovations of the 1960s and 1970s eventually gave way to Otto Künzli's conceptual and minimal jewellery, including unforgettable works like *Drawing Pin Brooches* (1980), *Gold Makes You Blind* (1980) and *Swiss Gold: The Deutschmark* (1983), which investigated serial work and traditional values in jewellery, making use of photography and performance as additional media to transmit the work.

These fluctuations and experiments were the result of a congenial affiliation with the fine arts – some artists, like Gijs Bakker, Emmy van Leersum and Peter Skubic were part of a fine arts circle. The growing awareness of the creative individuality in the arts was underscored by an ideology of the avant-garde, a phenomenon that exerted an attraction on those craftspeople who looked for a renewal and emancipation of their practice.

Looking back at these infant days of contemporary jewellery, one is struck by the clearness of ideas, by the radical positioning of the artists and by the international network that soon developed. However, a slight feeling of despair can also come over: everything has been done before, every material has been tried, every medium, what's left for younger generations? Another question is what has this movement actually brought us? One thing stands out: the ideology of the creative individual. 'New Jewellery' has turned into 'author jewellery' – made by an author, meaning a creator, a maker, someone who has a discernable 'voice' or 'handwriting'. This appears to be a blessing and a disadvantage at the same time: a blessing because it brought makers freedom of creation, a disadvantage because contemporary jewellery now suffers under the same alienation from those who do not belong to the inner circle, as fine art does.

Only at the end of the 1980s did the Nordic countries begin entering the scene, as can be traced back in exhibition catalogues.[5] The Scandi-

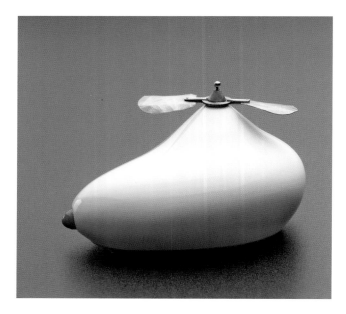

Sigurd Bronger, brooch/pendant NO MORE FEAR OF FLYING,
1995, hard foam, silver, 18 ct gold, micro motor, 60×50×110 mm
The National Museum of Art, Architecture and Design, Oslo

navians just skipped the rebellious New Jewellery phase; twenty years later their work fitted seamlessly into the general playful and colourful international trend at the time. On the basis of exhibition research we can conclude that first the Danes (Anette Kræn, Per Suntum, Kim Buck), then the Norwegians (Liv Blåvarp, Sigurd Bronger) and the Finns (Janna Syvänoja, Tarja Tuupanen, Terhi Tolvanen, Anna Rikkinen, Nelli Tanner) and finally the Swedes (Pia Åleborg, Hanna Hedman, Märta Mattsson, Agnes Larsson) became manifest as national entities in the international arena.

The reason why Scandinavia was not involved in the international New Jewellery movement may be the fact that Scandinavian jewellery for a long time was under the spell of modernist and functionalist design. Its triumph became like a diktat: there was no other way than the modernist way. The worldwide success of industrial Scandinavian manufacture reached from the period between the world wars until far into the 1980s (and still lives on in the minds of many). Exhibitions showcasing Scandinavian design travelled successfully in the United States for years in succession. And modernist interior design, cutlery and jewellery sold all around the world in the better interior and jewellery shops. The Danish jewellery and silver company Georg Jensen developed from a small Copenhagen-based jewellery workshop in 1904 into an international business with flagship stores in the United States, Asia and Dubai. Modernist Scandinavian design was perceived as 'good design'. There was no room, nor reason, for fiddling around, for experiment and adventures (although some individuals did). After all, design was in the right. Finland is the exception; this country witnessed the emergence of a 'bronze revival' in the 1950s to the 1970s. Jewellery designers such as Pentti Sarpaneva, Björn Weckström, Jorma Laine and Seppo Tamminen discovered bronze as an easily available material for casting jewellery and sometimes combined it with precious or glass stones. Their experiments ended in a kind of hippie cult aesthetic, individual, informal and playful. Marita Kulvik experimented with body-related

Pentti Sarpaneva, necklace, c.1965, silver, bronze, spectrolite, c.95 × 38 mm; chain c. 710 mm

forms and materials, working with coloured fibres, leather, fur and sisal combined with brass and silver organic elements, while other designers had been using acrylic since the early 1960s.[6] Clearly Finland's contemporary jewellery history differs from that of the other Nordic countries as well as from New Jewellery.

Only some individuals in the Nordic countries managed to break with the modernist diktat. Tone Vigeland (b. 1938) is one of them. As Norway's pioneering protagonist of contemporary jewellery, who today is dedicated to sculpture, she had to go through a modernist phase until she was able to liberate herself and find her own style, which was immediately recognised as 'typical Nordic' (or Viking) because of the black metals she used and the small linked parts that were associated with mesh and chainmail. As she once stated, she found more inspiration in the studio work of Torun Bülow-Hübe than in the industrial jewellery of Georg Jensen, testifying to a more individual and sensitive approach, away from the rather clean, functional and impersonal

Scandinavian jewellery design. Alexander Calder's simple treatment of metal wire also showed her a way out of the modernist paradigm.[7] Vigeland was in search of more expression and for a more 'natural' connection with the body, and in the 1970s she started experimenting with flexible and tactile structures. By linking small little rings and other parts to flexible mats, she finally found her direction. Her first solo exhibition in years (1978) also became the starting point for an international positioning of her jewellery – she went to London and presented her work to Barbara Cartlidge at Gallery Electrum in London, at that time one of the few galleries that was presenting New Jewellery. In 1981 she was offered a solo exhibition at Electrum, through which she became accepted by and part of the international contemporary jewellery network. She succeeded without losing her own identity and her commitment to 'classical' metals and their treatment. Vigeland's history shows that being 'contemporary' has to do with an eagerness to be part of an international scene instead of a local one, a will to 'get

Tone Vigeland, neckpiece, 1985, steel, gold 14–18 ct, inner dia. 120 mm, outer dia. 240 mm
The National Museum of Art, Architecture and Design, Oslo

out of one's shell' and a confidence to establish yourself. Although Vigeland embarked on her international adventure rather insecure about where it would end up, she had the guts to just try and do it. However, courage is exactly what many jewellers in the Nordic countries seem to be missing. There seems to be a general Nordic morality of acting normal, being average not extraordinary, a feeling of human equality, which may hold people back from moving forward and forcing unwritten laws.

From the Coolest Corner proves that today's Nordic jewellery has become international and contemporary. Sweden, Finland and Estonia all profit from good educational institutions, where the teaching is on an international level. The output of these schools is steadily growing, and the importance of these centres in Stockholm, Imatra and Tallinn is reflected in their impressive contribution to the exhibition. The Finnish school is rooted in a stone-cutting school, a characteristic that is slowly tending to become blurred by other approaches. Estonian jewellery has a spe-

cific mysterious, gloomy and poetic character; here, natural materials, minerals and stones are the preferred materials, while Swedish jewellery tends towards excess, dwelling on the one hand on ornamentation and exaggeration and on the other hand on the assembling of abstract elements and waste materials. Icelandic jewellery is the most unknown within the Nordic context. Tradition has held strong in this remote country, but it was also the place where Swiss Fluxus artist Dieter Roth (1930–98) settled in 1957 and made some of his famous art work and poetry, and – not very widely known – cutting-edge experimental jewellery as early as 1957.[8] It is unclear, however, if this jewellery appealed to local goldsmiths at all, or if jewellery artists in central Europe were aware of his efforts in this field. Today's Icelandic jewellery has overcome traditional goldsmith values that still set the tone in the previous Nordic jewellery exhibitions and publications: now jewellers use driftwood, porcelain, rope and rusted chain to make expressive wearable pieces.

Besides this, there is also room for the more restrained and classical goldsmith's work – for instance, in Denmark and in Norway. There is still a lot of excellent work by gold- and silversmiths made in Scandinavia that combines good craftsmanship with a rather inexpressive and diminutive character. The Scandinavian jewellery infrastructure is one of the causes. There are very few contemporary jewellery galleries in the Nordic countries, and yet they have a different aim and origin than jewellery galleries in other countries. Nordic jewellery galleries are workshop-rooted, based on individual workshops. The rigorous separation in many countries between the goldsmith and the jewellery artist, which was the result of the rebellious movements of the 1960s and 1970s, is not the reality of contemporary jewellery in the Nordic countries. Here, craftsmanship is held in high esteem. There are only a few collectors of contemporary jewellery, and so jewellers must work for customers: this is why there are so many beautifully equipped jewellery shops with annexed workshops in Copenhagen, Oslo,

Stockholm and elsewhere in northern Europe, where individual or collaborations of goldsmiths sell and make their jewellery. Only the youngest generation dares to jump in the deep end and tries to survive as jewellery artists. They rely on sales through jewellery galleries in different countries and aim to have their work in as many international jewellery shows as possible. By going global they don't choose the easy way. In fact, the galleries offer a lower income for their artistic work than their own workshop would do.[9] Supported by a good education, ambitions and talent, they took a barrier that was unassailable for many years, providing Nordic jewellery with an international appeal: Nordic jewellery has become cool.

1   Gillick, Liam, 2010. 'Contemporary Art does not account for that which is taking place', e-flux journal no. 21, December 2010 (accessed 27.08.2012).
2   Note that in fine arts these steps had already been made in the nineteenth century, and that the great Art Nouveau jewellers' work, which introduced new materials, authorship and formal experiment, did not set a new – generally accepted – modern standard.
3   Pavitt, Jane, 2008. *Fear and Fashion in the Cold War*. London: V&A, p.70.

4   Galerie am Graben, Kunst des zwanzigsten Jahrhunderts, 1977. *Schmuck: Tischgerät aus Österreich 1904/08–1973/77*. Vienna, unpaginated. Translated from German by LdB.

5   During the 1970s and 1980s the number of international contemporary jewellery exhibitions increased at high speed. The first of these exhibitions that included a considerable amount of Scandinavians was *Joieria Europea Contemporània* held in Barcelona in 1987. Among the four Scandinavians were three Danes: Anette Kræn, Mikala Naur and Per Suntum. Kim Buck started exhibiting abroad during the same period.

6   Willcox, Donald, 1973. *Body Jewelry: International Perspectives*. Chicago.

7   Brundtland, Cecile Malm, Drutt English, Helen W., Holzach, Cornelie, 2003. *Tone Vigeland: Jewellery + Sculpture. Movements in Silver*, Stuttgart: Arnoldsche, p. 22.

8   In 2008 the Musée de design et d'arts appliqués contemporains in Lausanne made the exhibition *Dieter Roth's Rings*, showcasing his early experimental metal rings (1957) and rings designed in the early 1970s in collaboration with his fellow countryman goldsmith Hans Langenbacher, who also lived in Iceland. They collaborated until Roth's death, making playful jewellery that wearers could modify according to their own taste and wishes.

9   I would like to thank Sofia Björkman of the gallery Platina in Stockholm for taking the time to explain me the Swedish situation, and also the many Danish goldsmiths whom I met and visited while being in Copenhagen for the Skt. Loye Smykke & Korpus Event in August 2012.

BETWEEN COMMON CRAFT AND UNCOMMON ART – ON WOOD IN JEWELLERY

Jorunn Veiteberg

Traces of Function is the thought-provoking title of a series of jewellery objects by the young Swedish artist Tobias Alm. In this context, the word 'function' is ambiguous. These objects are made from pieces of wood that are either assembled using carpentry joints or tied together with cotton. Many of the elements have holes drilled through them, some of which are plugged with small protruding dowels. A cord can be threaded through the holes, allowing the object to be hung around the neck, although it is questionable whether this is what the holes were originally made for. Some of the joints are reminiscent of pegs, others of familiar methods used to connect pieces of wood in furniture and buildings. The slots and stubs of carpentry joints are a common feature of wooden artefacts, and in the world of furniture making their function needs no justification – it is self-evident. In the context of jewellery, however, their purpose is less obvious. But as is often the case when artists employ materials or objects from other walks of life and treat them as raw materials for more expressive statements,

the aim is to draw attention to practices outside the sphere of art. In effect, Alm is creating a visual language from techniques that were never meant to serve as art. Things from the realm of everyday life that we tend to overlook are highlighted and given new value. These jewellery objects juxtapose the carpenter with the artist, the utilitarian or practical with the 'superfluous' and aesthetic. They demonstrate that one and the same technique can serve a variety of purposes. Or could it be that their function is simply unclear, and that they capture the tension that arises when a perceived functionality conflicts with prevailing notions of what is beautiful? To quote the press release issued by Galerie Rob Koudijs in Amsterdam when Alm exhibited this series there in early 2012: 'Keen to see when doubt might set in, when the obvious would give way to uncertainty. Alm makes necklaces and brooches with shapes that are suggestive, but elucidate little.'[1] Evidently the ambiguity is deliberate, even if these objects are confirmed as jewellery by being presented in a jewellery exhibition.

Tobias Alm, brooch TRACES OF FUNCTION XVII, 2012, wood, steel, 70 × 40 × 40 mm

I begin with Alm's work because of its relevance to the discussion about new trends in Nordic jewellery. Alm plays with conventions that many people regard as typical of the design one finds in this part of the world, particularly that of the Scandinavian Design period. The defining features of such design are the use of wood as the main material, the facts that the wood is unpainted and the methods of construction are clearly visible, and the format is intimate and aimed at 'ordinary people'. Taken together, these qualities represent a 'sympathetic respect for the natural materials and a concern for their "proper" use by the designer and consumer,' as the English craft expert Jennifer Opie has put it.[2] In this aesthetic, beauty – which jewellery is always concerned with at some level – is synonymous with the natural.

Alm is not the only contributor to *From the Coolest Corner* who uses wood as his main material. In fact, it is so prominent that one could almost speak of a trend, which is why I want to dwell on its use here.

THE TRADITION OF WOOD

It should come as no surprise that 'nature' and 'natural' are key words in discussions about art and design in the Nordic countries. Scandinavian towns are small compared with the big international metropolises, and most people in the region live close to nature. The climate is conducive to outdoor activities in the mountains, on the sea, and in forests and fields. Large parts of Norway, Sweden and Finland are covered by woodland, making wood an obvious material to use for house construction, furniture and other artefacts. But wood has never been the favourite material of the jeweller. If we look back at the first touring exhibition of Nordic jewellery in 1995/97, wood featured only to a modest extent – with a few exceptions. Admittedly, Anette Kræn from Denmark and Juhani Heikkilä from Finland have combined wood with other materials in their work, while wood was also employed to eloquent effect in the creations of another Finn, Helena Lehtinen, one of the doyens in *From the Coolest*

Helena Lehtinen, brooch from the series LANDSCAPES, 2009, wood, thread, silver, stone, 155 × 60 × 20 mm

Corner: 'Rejecting metal, she has begun to use wood and various objects, found in a natural state,' to quote the catalogue of the earlier exhibition.[3] This revealing comment implies that wood carries connotations that are contrary to those of metal. But it was in the Norwegian section of the show that the exceptions abounded, in the jewellery of Konrad Mehus, Lillan Eliassen, Elsie-Ann Hochlin and Liv Blåvarp. The latter in particular, who is also represented in *From the Coolest Corner* alongside two of the other artists named here, has focused on wood ever since her breakthrough in the late 1980s.

Back then, no one was surprised that it was primarily the Norwegian artists who had adopted this material. 'Every source indicates that wood is part of the Norwegian national character,' claims the American jewellery designer and writer Marjorie Simon in an article about Blåvarp.[4] Or to quote the press release for a general-interest book on wood: 'Most Norwegians have an affinity for wood. We live in wooden houses, dream of wooden boats, and have woodwork benches in

our basements.'[5] Although many today would wince at terms like 'national character', the fact remains that woodcarving and carpentry are deeply rooted in Norwegian culture. From the era of the Viking ships to the present, woodworking has endured as a thriving and popular tradition. And the choice of wood signals an awareness of that tradition in a way no other material could before. Both Blåvarp and Mehus have often cited folk art as an important source of inspiration, although not without a note of caution: 'When using traditional materials in art, you find yourself balancing on a knife-edge,' says Mehus.[6] The balance he is referring to is the difficulty of living in your own day and age rather than in the past and of maintaining an international outlook as opposed to one that is national and parochial; it is about refusing to romanticise and keeping one's gaze critical. As Mehus says in the same interview: 'It's alarming when tradition obscures your view. But as a *foundation* for having a view, tradition is brilliant.'[7] It was this sense of tradition coupled with a free and undogmatic approach,

Liv Blåvarp, necklace BLACK BEAUTY II, 2008, wood,
whale tooth, outer dia. 270 mm

which in the 1980s allowed Mehus and Blåvarp
to align themselves with the postmodernist trend
in Norwegian crafts. And it is this so-called *neo-
tradition*[8] that we can now thank for the radical
renewal and revitalisation of wood as a medium.

On the other hand, the strong linkage between
tradition and folk practices might also explain
why many other jewellers have considered wood
unsuitable as a material. For, if anything, Nordic
jewellery art before the 2000s was characterised
by the absence of wood. In the second major touring exhibition of Nordic jewellery, which took
place in 2001/02, wood featured even less than it
did in its forerunner.[9] The exceptions this time
were the works of guest artists from Estonia: Piret
Hirv, Maria Valdma and, not least, Eve Margus-
Villems, who contributed a number of distinctive
neck pieces.

THE WOOD REVIVAL

In *From the Coolest Corner* wood or wooden elements can be found in works by jewellers from
each of the participating countries. One can only
speculate as to the reasons for this revival of
wood as a material. But in a time of economic
crisis, when the price of gold and other precious
metals and stones are at record highs, wood
certainly represents an affordable alternative.
It is also much more readily available. Moreover,
in recent years people have become far more
concerned about where materials come from and
whether they have been produced and refined
in ways that are ethically defensible and environ-
mentally sustainable. Here again, wood is a win-
ner. Thus we get a list of words that sum up the
connotations of wood as a material: traditional,
rustic, affordable, readily available, sustainable,
organic. Other things that we associate with its
organic quality are life and growth. Wood frequently figures in central creation myths, and it
is a widespread custom to plant a tree to mark

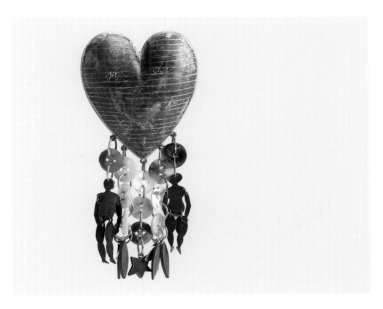

Konrad Mehus, brooch MARIA'S HEART, 1995, silver,
buttons, painted wood, 137 × 55 × 17 mm
The National Museum of Art, Architecture and Design, Oslo

turning points in life, such as a birth or a death. All these symbolic meanings are there for jewellery artists to draw upon.

The works on show in *From the Coolest Corner* exemplify great variety in the handling of wood as a physical and connotational material. Some have made jewellery from driftwood, found pieces shaped and smoothed by the sea. Another has collected wooden lolly sticks and given them new and enduring life as a pendant. Some wooden elements are left untreated, others are painted; some have been cut by hand, others using laser cutters. Despite the sheer variety of practices, all these works apply a hands-on approach. Artists can be drawn to a particular material for many reasons: aesthetic, emotive and intellectual. At the same time, it is tempting to ask whether this renewed interest in wood among jewellery artists has anything to do with the revival of craft techniques and natural materials that could also be seen in other branches of the visual arts in recent years.[10]

DEFAMILIARISATION

The most widespread preconception about Nordic and Baltic art is that it is romantic and closely associated with nature.[11] This is true whether we are talking about painting or furniture, sculpture or jewellery. The use of wood can easily be interpreted as a confirmation of this basic assertion, but, as I have sought to show here, wood has had little prominence as a material in jewellery until relatively recently. As far back as 1987, in a catalogue essay for the exhibition *Scandinavian Craft* in Japan, the Swedish critic Ulf Hård af Segerstad claimed it was difficult to identify not just common *Nordic* but even common *national* characteristics among the great diversity of individual idioms contained in the exhibition.[12] I, too, find it difficult to identify a common Nordic style or quality in *From the Coolest Corner*, yet this does not make it irrelevant that all the works on display were produced in the Nordic countries or by Nordic jewellers. What it does mean is that the Nordic dimension finds expression in very different ways from one work to the next, and from one artist to another. In some cases, local materials or an appreciation of nature have influenced the design or the choice of motif; in others, the key to the work lies in some very different factors, such as the artist's gender, age or social background. One thing that becomes clear when we consider the diversity of jewellery art in the Nordic and Baltic countries is that the actual appearance of much of the work is better explained with reference to the variety of local traditions than it is by appealing to factors such as nature, climate and mentality.

There is much to suggest that distinctions between the Nordic countries have, if anything, increased since the 1980s. Educational institutions have developed in different directions, while differences in financial support schemes have produced differences in working conditions. Increased internationalisation has further weakened the feeling of a shared Nordic identity and the notion of some uniquely Nordic qualities. When the art magazine *Flash Art* turned its attentions to the Nordic region in spring 2012, they wanted to know what was distinctive about Nordic art today. All the art historians, museum directors and curators they interviewed gave the same answer: it can no longer be defined. The art world has become global. Artists rarely stay put in one place but travel, train and work in many different countries. And neither, they argue, can one pin down a specifically Nordic interest in, for example, nature.[13]

Even so, the regional community remains meaningful in other ways. The geographical proximity of these countries to each other stimulates cooperation. And even if their inhabitants do not cultivate a shared romantic view of nature or a common design language, they do share a desire to develop jewellery as an art form. This purpose is served by an openness to new materials and techniques, by exploring new combinations of familiar methods, motifs and functions and by introducing new forms of distribution. Not least, it is served by shaking up conventions that we regard as so self-evident that we hardly even think about them. This is what happened internationally in

Eve Margus-Villems, neckpiece UNTITLED, 2001, engraved bone, painted wood, 200 × 150 mm
Estonian Museum of Applied Art and Design, Tallinn

the field of jewellery making in the 1960s and 1970s, helping to take the art form in new directions. Our habitual ways of looking at and using jewellery were challenged by a process of defamiliarisation, to borrow a term coined by the literary theorist Viktor Shklovsky. This is one of the most important techniques art has at its disposal; by giving a new twist to familiar things and representing them in unusual ways, we 'may recover the sensation of life; [art] exists to make one feel things,' to use Shklovsky's words.[14] Alm's ambiguous jewellery objects offer precisely this kind of experience. His use of wood and familiar woodworking methods in the unfamiliar context of jewellery produces new meaning. A common type of work is defamiliarised, thereby rendering the uncommon nature of art clear for all to see.

1   Schrijver, Ward, www.galerierobkoudijs.nl/site.php?xs=exhibitionsDetail&id=91&mode=archive.
2   Quoted from Davies, Kevin M., 2003. 'Marketing Ploy or Democratic Ideal?', in Halén, Widar and Wickman, Kerstin (eds.), 2003. *Scandinavian Design Beyond the Myth: Fifty Years of Design from the Nordic Countries.* Stockholm: Arvinius/Form, p. 101.
3   Aav, Marianne, 1995. 'The Triennale: Finland', in Funder, Lise and Lohman, Jan (eds.), 1995. *Nordisk Smykkekunst: Nordic Jewellery.* Copenhagen: Arnold Busck, p. 105.
4   Simon, Marjorie, 2001. 'A Hand to Wood: The Work of Liv Blåvarp', in *Liv Blåvarp: Jewellery/Smykker 1984–2001.* Kristiansand: The Art Museum of South Norway/Liv Blåvarp, p. 28.
5   Press release 17.10.1999 for Kuccera, Bohumil and Næss, Ragnar M., *Tre: naturens vakreste råstoff*, Oslo: Landbruksforlaget 1999.
6   Skre, Arnhild, 1991. 'Skrått blikk på tradisjonen', in *Dag og Tid*, 19 December 1991, p. 14.
7   Ibid.
8   Halén, Widar and Lium, Randi, 1997. *Gift of the Forest – Gifts of the Loom. Norwegian Women in Contemporary Wood and Textile Art.* Oslo: Museum of Applied Art and Ministry of Foreign Affairs, p. 5; see also Schou-Christensen, Jørgen, 1994. 'The Presence of Past and the Presence of Now', in *In Touch.* Oslo: De norske bokklubbene/Kulturprogrammet for de XVII Olympiske Vinterleker på Lillehammer.
9   Funder, Lise (ed.), 2001. *Nordisk smycke triennal 2: Nordic Jewellery.* Copenhagen: Arnold Busck.
10 This phenomenon is discussed in Manco, Tristan, 2012. *Raw + Material = Art. Found, Scavenged and Upcycled.* London: Thames and Hudson, p. 24.
11 See Arrhenius, Sara, 2012. 'Life after the Miracle: Art in the Nordic Countries', in *Flash Art*, no. 283, March–April, pp. 62–3; Veiteberg, Jorunn, 2000. 'Fins det en nordisk kunst?', in *Blue. 10 Scandinavian Experts.* Middelfart: Danmarks Keramikmuseum.
12 Segerstad, Ulf Hård af, 1987. 'What is Scandinavian about Scandinavian Crafts?', in *Scandinavian Craft Today*, Tokyo: The Seibu Museum of Art, p. 10.
13 Politi, Giancarlo, 2012. 'A Nordic Light', in *Flash Art*, no. 283, March–April, pp. 60–2.
14 Shklovsky, Viktor, 1998. 'Art as Technique', in Rivkin, Julie and Ryan, Michael (eds.), 1998. *Literary Theory: An Anthology.* Oxford: Blackwell, p. 18.

EXISTING AND NON-EXISTING BOUNDARIES

Päivi Ruutiainen

What does art jewellery look like and how is it viewed? What characteristics are typical for contemporary jewellery? Jewellery is a complex concept because it is used to refer to so many different things. The etymology of the word has connotations to playfulness, while people in general have adapted many understandings of jewellery based on historical perspectives. Jewellery can be named on the basis of its type or how it is used – for example, a brooch– or it can be used to signify belonging to a particular tradition of craftsmanship – for instance, unique jewellery, design jewellery, costume jewellery or fine jewellery.

Jewellery has always been about strong personal preferences, which in turn just add to the complexity regarding jewellery. Jewellery stores memories – some related to personal history, some to status – and they have formed several layers of different meanings around them. Due to these reasons most people have an opinion of what jewellery is. Our perception of jewellery consists of a mix of personal definitions which result in conflicts in the general definition. A piece can be a pendant made by a child, a souvenir bought at a street market, valuable jewellery that has been inherited or a decoration bought from a cheap store intended to last for only a moment. Pieces that resemble works of art – for instance, installations – cause confusion. Each piece is defined by its user, who views it from a personal perspective. This also allows users to exclude such elements that they find insignificant in regard to its essence. Jewellery makers and researchers also form definitions.

These ways of discussing jewellery are important because they define and locate the piece. What is considered a piece of jewellery and how is it regarded? Is a piece a consumer product, decoration or art? Naming is one way of structuring the appearance of jewellery: 'trash jewellery' is obviously seen as a cheap disposable object, but what about the definition for contemporary jewellery? All definitions include some significance while excluding others. Such is the case, too, when defining a piece as contemporary jewellery; it builds intertextuality to contemporary art.

Simultaneously it is separated from the traditional definition.

So how can we define contemporary jewellery when the definition for contemporary art is just as vague and varied? The 1960s are often considered the start of the contemporary art era. By now the term 'contemporary jewellery' has been used for quite a while, primarily to link it with other art forms. During the past twenty years it has gained additional content: a contemporary piece now includes varied styles and methods of creation, just like contemporary art does. What is really interesting is observing what sort of general art definitions we apply to art jewellery and seeing whether it can be structured and defined in the same way as art. In more general terms, it is interesting to see what theoretical framework is applicable to jewellery. How adequate are, for instance, terms such as conceptual jewellery or Minimalism when discussing jewellery? In jewellery literature very few definitions on new styles are found. Can we therefore speak of Arte Povera or transavantgardism when discussing art jewellery? Is there a need for new terminology to define style within art jewellery or can we borrow these from the art scene?

IN THE ART FIELD

Art and jewellery share work methods and structures, both in regard to similarities and differences. If we accept, like Pierre Bourdieu, that the art scene is a field with its own laws, it also means we have to expound the working practices in this field. According to Bourdieu the field is characterised by a constant fight about who rules the scene: who has most accredited capital to define the rules and borders for the work practices in the art field? Those who control the capital also decide who can and cannot enter the scene. In the art scene, museums and galleries are considered to be those who have the most significant capital to define it, while those who research and write about art construct an image of respectable art. In regard to art jewellery we have fewer institutions, researchers and writers. The structure of

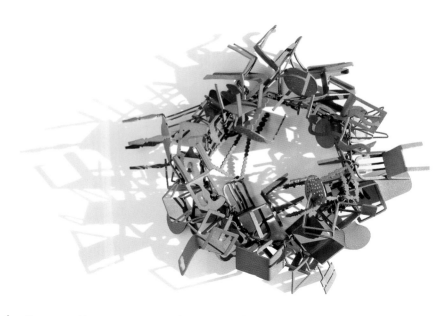

Åsa Elmstam, necklace THINGS I, 2010, brass, plastic, 200×200×50 mm

ruling is what separates the two scenes, and jewellery artists have risen to the position of those who define their field. Jewellery artists constantly re-evaluate jewellery just by the way they work and by the way they form the field and its dominating values. By presenting the exhibition *From the Coolest Corner: Nordic Jewellery* in respected museums and influencing who writes about it, we raise the status of art jewellery.

BOUNDARIES AND ABOUT TOUCHING BOUNDARIES

It is interesting to study within which *boundaries* jewellery has generally been regarded. By doing that we simultaneously define what is acceptable as jewellery. These definitions deal with *body*, *scale*, *size*, *materials*, *techniques*, *content*, and *themes* and specifically *what sort* of art is affiliated with jewellery. By setting boundaries we place the jewellery in a certain tradition, but is art jewellery renewing this tradition or are we prepared to abandon it totally? In addition, it is intriguing to see how strictly these boundaries are set and if there is room for expansion. Art jewellery has, however, been subject to strong winds of change for the past two decades.

The strong connection to the body is indisputably central and has a certain stigmatising character, yet the jewellery genre has also been associated with decorative art objects. For several decades the sculptural elements in jewellery have been a subject for discussion. In the Nordic countries this aspect has been represented by such artists as Björn Weckström, Kristian Nilsson, Torben Hardenberg and Konrad Mehus. The sculptural forms as such are not in any way new, but the ways these sculptural elements are used and implemented, however, are. *Family Portrait* by Janne Hirvonen is a set of sculptural figures that cannot be worn in practical ways at all, while *Things* by Åsa Elmstam consists of tiny furniture that can be worn as jewellery. The pieces made by Sigurd Bronger are, in contrast, apparatus-like devices.

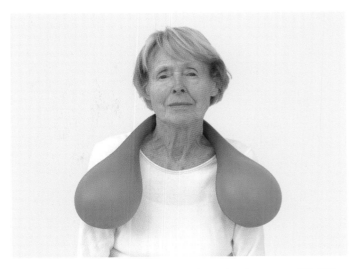

Lillan Eliassen, neck piece COURAGE, 2012, casting clay, copper, 430 × 360 mm

Nowadays jewellery can be worn in different ways than it was in the past: in unusual ways and in order to decorate parts of the body that traditionally have not been highlighted by jewellery. Some makers have made strong comments to this relation to the body, such as the significance of the senses and their opposites: preventing the use of senses. A piece of jewellery can be an extension of the body, which possibly completes the body or empowers it. The massive jewellery pieces by Lillan Eliassen, intended to be hung around the neck, are like punchbags. They emphasize the carrier's strength of personality. In the union between body and jewellery the construction of identity becomes a relevant characteristic.

The numerous ways in which jewellery is supposed to be worn can be illustrated with photographs, especially if it has a complex structure. It is said that a piece is completed only when worn on the body, but some jewellery seems to live a totally independent life. Its relationship to the body becomes multifaceted and ambiguous. The body becomes a stage for the jewellery, but sometimes it is more like a tool. This relation to the body has been put to test by both art and jewellery; during the past two decades the size of jewellery has occasionally varied. It seems that testing the bodily boundaries is no longer of the same interest as it was in the past.

The revolution in materials used for jewellery began with the acceptance of non-precious materials. For the past few decades we have seen quite an array in the choice of materials. It seems that anything will do, and traditional materials are used to diffuse the elementary non-precious nature. Various techniques have developed in the same way and become manifold. The application of photography as a technique in creating jewellery is nowadays just as acceptable as it is within other artistic expressions; it is now one technique among many others. A possible polemic relationship to precious materials is part of the trade. An everyday object in a recyclable material, such as the plastic hip flask by Paula Lindblom, is made just as precious as a gold piece. The focus on materials has been replaced by a focus on ideas.

Paula Lindblom, brooch THE ESSENCE OF NATURE, 2012, everyday plastic objects/flea market findings, glass beads, glue, 925 silver, c. 80×50 mm

The exhibition highlights the whole range of diversity related to contemporary jewellery and its idiom. Some jewellery is plainly simplistic, such as that belonging to the series *New Places* by Karin Johansson. Åsa Lockner's *Crown Jewels* on the other hand are as decorative as one might expect by their name. Liv Blåvarp's works are simple and confident yet multifold, and *Kissmekiss-mekissme* by Anna Talbot is kitschy in a decorative way. The jewellery by the master of stylish simplicity Janna Syvänoja is contrasted by the rough jewellery with an untreated look by Nicolas Cheng.

When comparing art jewellery from different countries, we often look for defining national traits. In the Nordic cultures we find that many overarching elements find similarities in their themes. Nature is traditionally considered a significant theme, animals and plants especially. The relation to the untamed and indigenous nature has from time to time indisputably become somewhat ironic. For instance, Paula Lindblom's jewellery is a statement on ecological matters. The array of varied themes in art jewellery is fascinating: the political has become personal statements which can be small and daily themes, but we also witness bigger and larger themes living parallel to them. These themes can be intertextual and can comment on matters related to society or art. In this way the emphasis on jewellery's capability to communicate contents to the viewer has been increasingly underlined.

What about the relation to history? The exhibition contains jewellery that in many ways is strongly anchored to the tradition and history of jewellery, despite a seeming distance to these themes. Re-evaluation of a traditional piece and its relation to history are elements that characterise art jewellery. Although we use types of jewellery that lean on tradition, the expression is usually different in contemporary jewellery. Various traditional forms are exhibited in, for example, the Norwegian artists Konrad Mehus's and Gunnhild Tjåland's jewellery. Here we can sense traces of a reinterpretation of vernacular jewellery. *Prelude* by Anna Léger indisputably brings

to mind the Jugendstil art movement and its idioms; only these pieces are constructed in ways that differ to the old ones. Kim Buck brings alive an ironic statement in shiny gold, highlighting how the value of a certain material is in some way inconceivable.

Contemporary art has broadened its boundaries and has incorporated and accepted many new ways of making art: graffiti and cartoons are nowadays presentable forms of art. One might wish to see that one day contemporary jewellery will also become a presentable form of art, as we've seen happen with photography as an art form. Photography art is a respected part of contemporary art; by broadening the boundaries of contemporary jewellery we can make it more attractive and appreciated.

Some jewellery pieces are utility articles and some have clear contact surfaces to art. History and apprehensions of jewellery have affected the way we view jewellery today. Talk of vanity can be found as far back as the Bible and is part of the undesired baggage and presentation of jewellery because decoration diminishes the respect for jewellery. Is a piece of jewellery merely a decoration or does it have an independent value as such like works of art have?

Discourses regarding jewellery can contribute to constructing boundaries and placing specific pieces in their respective places. A piece may be seen in its traditional place or it may be an object for a desire to renew it. If a piece is tied to history, it is difficult to change its meaning, but the truth is it can be renewed in delicate ways and with respect for tradition. Renewal means infinity, yet boundaries to some are both real and important. The significance of the body as a profound element within art jewellery divides opinions: does the body only function as a platform on which to hang jewellery or is it sufficient in itself as a platform from which the art jewellery can set off?

In this ensemble contemporary jewellery appears as a varied and prism-like compilation. There is no single contemporary piece, but a range of them, setting off from the tradition and breaking boundaries. We see a display of beauty and

Konrad Mehus, brooch RIKSVEI 3 from the series NORWEGIAN ROAD SILVER,
1991, silver, iron, wood, copper, 145 × 60 mm
The National Museum of Art, Architecture and Design, Oslo

glamour but also of the very opposite: statements,
playfulness, a sense of humour, daily life, ugliness
and, foremost, a partaking in the discourse
regarding jewellery itself. The very words we use
also tell of how we judge and appreciate things:
do we place the jewellery in the box in which it
has been kept or do we accept it as a mobile object
and part of the action in the art field?

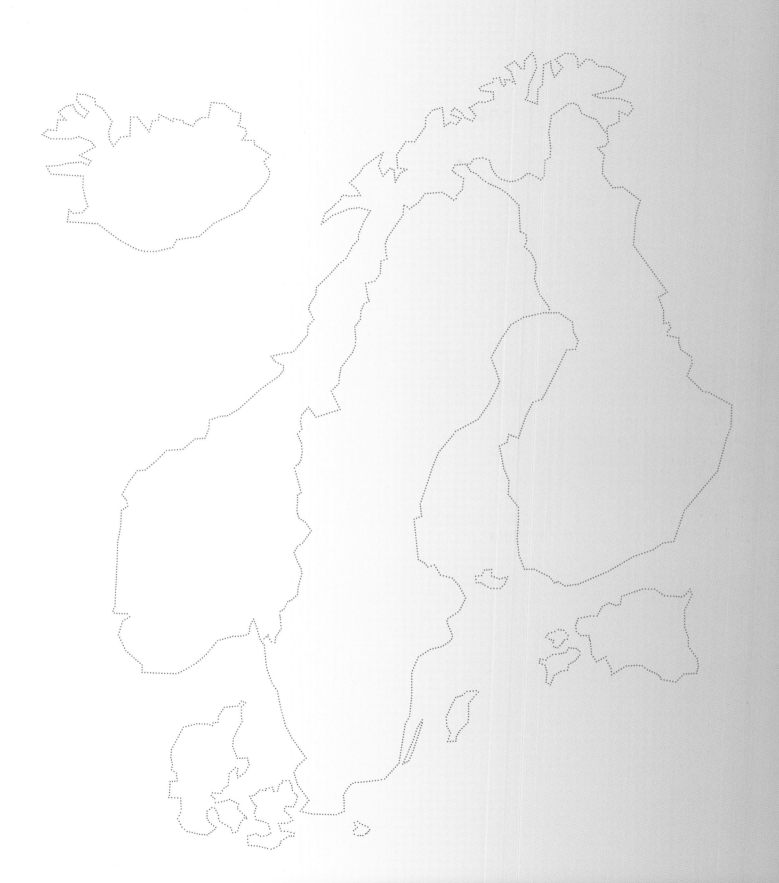

KIM BUCK [GUEST OF HONOUR]

JULIE BACH

ANNETTE DAM

KAORI JUZU

MARIE-LOUISE KRISTENSEN

THORKILD HARBOE THØGERSEN

JOSEPHINE WINTHER

DENMARK

KIM BUCK

GUEST OF HONOUR

Born 1957

EDUCATION
1982 Qualified goldsmith
1983–85 Institute of Precious Metals, Copenhagen, Denmark

PUBLIC COLLECTIONS
The Danish Arts Foundation, Denmark
Designmuseum Danmark, Copenhagen, Denmark
Museet på Koldinghus, Kolding, Denmark
Collections of Aberdeen Art Gallery & Museums, Aberdeen, Great Britain
The Röhsska Museum for Fashion, Design and Decorative Arts,
Gothenburg, Sweden
Museum of Art and Design, New York, USA

In 2003, Kim Buck was invited to contribute to an exhibition called *Smykkeskrin* [Jewellery Box]. The title prompted him to reflect on the range of items usually found in a jewellery box: some of them heirlooms, some purchases, some presents, some craftsman-made, others mere costume jewellery. The result was a series of brooches consisting of negative casts of classic jewellery designs ranging from pearl earrings to a solitaire ring. A cast tells us about something that was once there – a trace or memory now preserved in a new form.

Kim Buck's works are characterised by a fond but critical attitude towards the varied creations of the jewellery industry. As in the series *Bonsai*, this sometimes results in jewellery that cannot be worn but serves instead as objects for contemplation. Bonsai is the Japanese art of cultivating miniature trees in pots. The pieces in Buck's series are rings made from blocks of wood using a CNC router. The established opinion in Japan is that one can only succeed at bonsai by taking it very seriously and investing maximum love and care. Only then will a tree have a long life. Buck's works can be viewed as ironic commentaries on much of the jewellery produced today, which rarely exemplifies the care and attention it ought to have received.   J.V.

Kim Buck, PUMPOUS RINGS II–VI, 2011, 24 ct gold, silver, paint, various sizes (see also p.39)

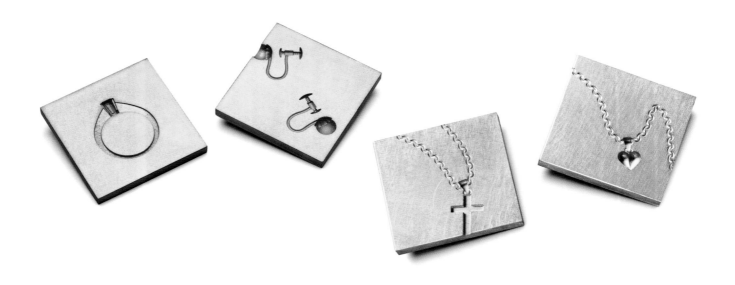

Kim Buck, brooches SOLITAIRE RING, PEARL EARRINGS, CROSS IN ANCHOR CHAIN and HEART IN ANCHOR
CHAIN, 2003, gold 750, 40 × 40 × 4 mm each
Designmuseum Danmark, Copenhagen, Denmark (1, 3, 4)

>>   Kim Buck, BONSAI I–II, 2012, series of five trunks ending in a carved ring, birchwood, c. 150 mm each

JULIE BACH

Born 1979

EDUCATION
2002 BA Fashion Design, Kolding School of Design, Kolding, Denmark

Julie Bach is a trained fashion designer and currently lives and works in Aarhus, where she designs jewellery and works with sculptures with the design organisation Højkant. Her background as a fashion and costume designer has provided her with the desire to work with unconventional materials and has therefore made it easier for her to create new types of jewellery and accessories. Her work is characterised by an aspiration to explore life and transform the stories that inhabit it. Bach explores psychological extremes and contrasts whilst at the same time being humorous and playful and communicating poignant narratives. She frequently experiments with various forms of expression. Bach works closely with handmade techniques and her style often results in exciting, modern pieces.

The work for *From the Coolest Corner* comprises two leather bracelets, which are part of a series inspired by berries and a homage to late summer abundance.   C.M.

44

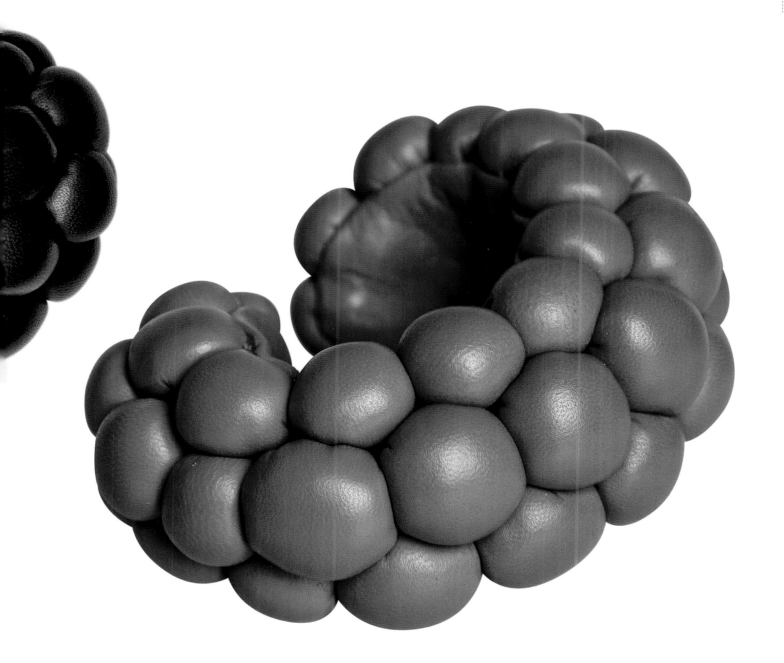

Julie Bach, BIG BERRY BRACELET, black and pink, 2010, Japanese calfskin, lamb nappa, cotton stuffing, 60 × 100 × 120 mm each

ANNETTE DAM

Born 1972

EDUCATION
1994–99 Metal Art and Jewellery, Oslo National Academy of the Arts,
Oslo, Norway

PUBLIC COLLECTIONS
Danish Arts Foundation, Copenhagen, Denmark
Skt. Loye Collection, Goldsmith's Guild, Copenhagen, Denmark

Annette Dam graduated in art and works as a professional artist creating beautifully aesthetic
items as a traditional goldsmith. Her choice of materials is often unconventional and as such
their unique properties form an important part of the design process. Through her jewellery,
Annette Dam often confronts the common values that permeate a democratic nation and the
codes of conduct that underpin a well-functioning society. The jewellery is often characterised
by Dam's desire to 'integrate abstract concepts … and frame [her]self and others within both
the senses, humour and the mind.'

In her work *84.5 karat* for *From the Coolest Corner*, she has utilised goldsmith techniques but
with a humorous dimension and with updated materials. The stones in the work are set in the
type of boxes that goldsmiths traditionally would buy the stones in but here are used as a frame
for a necklace.   C.M.

Annette Dam, necklace 84.5 KARAT, 2011, silver, precious stones, pearls, white corals, plastic boxes, 400 × 300 × 20 mm

KAORI JUZU

Born 1978

EDUCATION
2002 Jewellery Line, The School of Design, Bornholm, Denmark
2003 Trainee at the studio of the Danish jewellery artist Per Suntum
2004 Apprenticeship to Per Suntum
2008 Goldsmith

PUBLIC COLLECTIONS
The Danish Arts Foundation, Denmark
Designmuseum Danmark, Copenhagen, Denmark
Museet på Koldinghus, Kolding, Denmark
Fondazione Cominelli, Contemporary Jewellery Collection, Brescia, Italy

Kaori Juzu is a Japanese goldsmith who lives and works in her own studio in Tejn, Bornholm. Her work is characterised through its high artistic quality, perfectionism and its complex technical composition.

Kaori Juzu works with classical enamel techniques but does not want her work to be conceived as merely traditional jewellery. She seeks to challenge the public's perception of jewellery. The surfaces of her works are comprised of multiple layers of enamel to create textures that enhance its expression and provide a depth that resembles naturally occurring geological structures. Her work transforms the nature of the materials and enables the works to tell their own story.

The jewellery series *Field of Interference* is a range of unique brooches from 2011 which form one collection. The brooches are made from enamel, copper, gold, silver and stainless steel. The brooches are created using an open process whereby the shapes, colours and sizes interact and influence one another. The result is a dialogue between the hand, metal and enamel. Kaori Juzu hopes that the audience is drawn into the interactions that the range encapsulates.   C.M.

<<   Kaori Juzu, brooch INTERFERENCE III from the series FIELD OF INTERFERENCE, 2011, enamel, copper, 14 ct gold, 75 × 53 × 20 mm

Kaori Juzu, brooch INTERFERENCE I from the series FIELD OF INTERFERENCE, 2011, enamel, copper, 14 ct gold, 83 × 57 × 15 mm

Kaori Juzu, brooch INTERFERENCE IV from the series FIELD OF INTERFERENCE, 2011, enamel, copper, silver, 58 × 58 × 30 mm

Kaori Juzu, brooch INTERFERENCE V from the series FIELD OF INTERFERENCE, 2011, enamel, copper, 14 ct gold, 82 × 48 × 40 mm

MARIE-LOUISE KRISTENSEN

Born 1971

EDUCATION
2004 Institute of Precious Metals, Copenhagen, Denmark

PUBLIC COLLECTIONS
Smykkeskrinet – The Danish Arts Foundation, Denmark

Marie-Louise Kristensen works with jewellery from an 'ambition to unite a certain critical precision with a humorous caricature that says more than 100 words.' Her work is often grouped into themes such as reflection on self-promotion and transformation of everyday objects, with the jewellery usually accompanied with an ironic subtitle emphasising the theme.

Marie-Louise's collection for the 2012 St. Loye Prize featured jewellery that was about to be melted but was granted a new lease of life as a multifaceted object representing both the original status of the jewellery and also a love letter to the more traditional and romantic values from communal gardens and classic designs. The series for *From the Coolest Corner* represents a link between the private and public spheres, whereby personal experiences and feelings interact with physical and recognised urban features, such as scaffolding, lakes, park benches and, in the case of Copenhagen, the traditional bathing spot Helgoland.   C.M.

<< Marie-Louise Kristensen, brooch CPH: FAIRE LA FÊTE – ET APRÈS, 2011, second-hand gold ring, brass, 40 × 22 × 25 mm

Marie-Louise Kristensen, brooch CPH: PARK BENCH, 2011, brass, wood, 60 × 70 × 20 mm

Marie-Louise Kristensen, brooch CPH: RECONSTRUCTION, 2011, *silver*, *wood*, plastic, 110 × 85 × 20 mm

Marie-Louise Kristensen, brooch CPH: HELGOLAND, 2011, silver, wood, plastic, 80 × 60 × 30 mm

THORKILD HARBOE THØGERSEN

Born 1964

EDUCATION
1985–88 Diploma in Jewellery Design and Manufacture, Durban Institute of Technology, Durban, South Africa
1989–91 Precious metal designer, Institute of Precious Metals, Copenhagen, Denmark

PUBLIC COLLECTIONS
Montreal Museum of Decorative Arts, Montreal, Canada
The Danish Arts Foundation, Denmark
Designmuseum Danmark, Copenhagen, Denmark
Ringen, Museum for Moderne Dansk Smykkekunst, Grenå, Denmark
Cooper-Hewitt National Design Museum, New York, USA

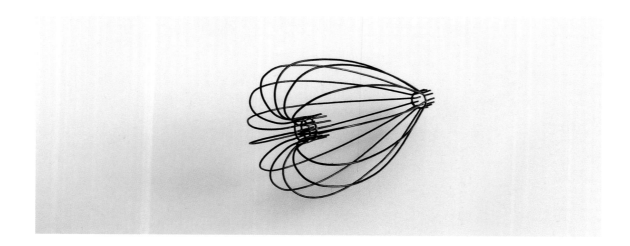

Thorkild Thøgersen is a Danish goldsmith and jewellery designer who was raised in South Africa and currently lives and works in Islands Brygge, Copenhagen. His work in recent years has focused on the use of metal wires in complex and contrasting jewellery forms. His reticulated structures are inspired by the geometric expressions of ancient cultures combined with textile weaving, digital patterns, feather structures and organic forms.

In *From the Coolest Corner*, he presents a series of brooches and pendants from April 2012. In this range, Thøgersen has utilised a completely new approach to the use of metal wires in jewellery. He has reduced his complexity and uses only a simple black floral design. Despite the fact that he is a highly proficient and skilled craftsman who can draw upon his perfectionist ingenuity to create intricate creations, he has opted to focus on a more minimalist theme. The results are delicate shapes which appear vulnerable as they depict fleeting moments in an attempt to find the balance between the simple and the chaotic.

Although the works often have a similar starting point and share a similar basic structure and design expression, their titles indicate their unique characters and individual narratives. His inspiration stems from a minimalist expression of emotions and from capturing fleeting moments.   C.M.

<<   Thorkild Harboe Thøgersen, pendant THE DREAM TRAP, 2012, iron binding wire, 60 × 40 × 60 mm

Thorkild Harboe Thøgersen, pendant DEFLATED, 2012, iron binding wire, 75 × 35 × 35 mm

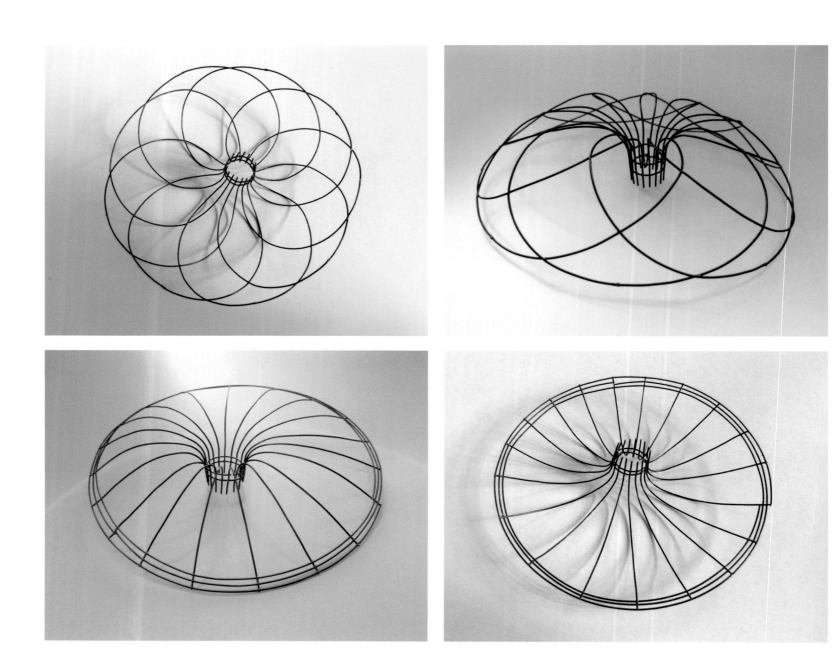

Thorkild Harboe Thøgersen, brooch THERE AND BACK AGAIN, 2012, iron binding wire, dia. 100 mm

Thorkild Harboe Thøgersen, brooch BLACK HOLE, 2012, iron binding wire, dia. 100 mm

Thorkild Harboe Thøgersen, brooch FRAIL HOPE SEED POD, 2012, iron binding wire, dia. 120 mm

JOSEPHINE WINTHER

Born 1964

EDUCATION
1997–99 Institute of Precious Metal, Copenhagen, Denmark
2008–10 MA, Royal College of Art, London, Great Britain

PUBLIC COLLECTIONS
Royal College of Art, London, Great Britain
Smykkeskrinet, Jewellery Box, The Danish State Art Collection of Jewellery
Skt. Loye Collection, Goldsmith's Guild, Copenhagen, Denmark
Designmuseum Danmark, Copenhagen, Denmark

Josephine Winther has previously focused on rings as a subject of her jewellery. They consist of a simple design that surrounds the finger and creates an interaction with the body. Rings have long been the subject of inquiry into a work that both compliments and contradicts the body's contours. Winther's work with rings features vivid, pure colour palettes that contrast the body but evoke a sense of natural movement through their amorphous form.

 In recent years, Josephine Winther has worked with sound and the effect of sound on the body and mind. *Ding*, exhibited at *From the Coolest Corner*, is a collection of forty-five individual necklaces with bells, each with a separate character and unique sound. This encourages people to use different senses when choosing their jewellery. The different sounds associated with each necklace are created through altering the alloy compositions and their hand-crafted manufacture. The sounds are based on Winther's personal recollections.   C.M.

Josephine Winther, necklaces DING, 2011, 45 bells, five different bronze alloys, silver, gold/copper alloy, porcelain, amber, agate, 30 x 25 x 25 mm to 40 x 20 x 20 mm

KADRI MÄLK [GUEST OF HONOUR]

JULIA MARIA KÜNNAP

MAARJA NIINEMÄGI

KRISTI PAAP

ANNA-MARIA SAAR

TANEL VEENRE

ESTONIA

KADRI MÄLK

GUEST OF HONOUR

Born 1958

EDUCATION

1981–86 Department of Metal Art, Estonian State Art Institute,
Tallinn, Estonia
1993/94 Gemology and stone cutting, Lahti Institute of Design,
Lahti, Finland
1994 Atelier Bernd Munsteiner, Stipshausen, Germany

PUBLIC COLLECTIONS

Estonian Art Museum, Tallinn, Estonia
Tallinn Art Hall, Tallinn, Estonia
Collection de la ville, Cagnes-sur-Mer, France
Kunstgewerbemuseum Hamburg, Germany
Museum of Decorative Arts, Berlin, Germany
Royal College of Art, London, Great Britain
Museum of Decorative and Applied Arts, Moscow, Russia
The Museum of Fine Arts (The Helen Williams Drutt Collection),
Houston, USA

Kadri Mälk can be observed as the 'grand old dame of Estonian jewellery', although she is only
in her fifties. Yet, Kadri breathed new life into Estonian jewellery: she renewed education,
brought it to an international level, created a coherent Estonian jewellery community and organised inspiring exhibitions and publications. In a lecture (*Chroma / Monochroma*, Tallinn 2006)
Kadri Mälk made a crucial observation when she said: 'The piece of jewellery in your mind,
in your imagination is always correct and beautiful. Resistance starts when you try to convert
it into material. Materials are like elementary particles – charged, heavily charged sometimes,
but indifferent. They don't tell you much, you have to tell them the truth.'

Kadri Mälk, like many Estonians, prefers to work with natural materials, stones, minerals,
wood, and materials from the sea, such as coral or sepia. Her jewellery has a gloomy atmosphere
because of its dark colours and its imagination. There's an aspect of hope and entrancement
in her jewellery (*Yehudi Menuhin*), but also mystery (*Black Menhir*) and despair and sorrow (*Very
Guilty, Medusa V*). Her jewellery talks about the struggles and passions of life, in a highly individual, poetic and seductive way.   L.d.B.

<<   p. 63 Kadri Mälk, brooch VERY GUILTY, 2010, Siberian jet, black rhodium plated with white gold, spinel, tourmalines, 115 × 66 × 12 mm

Kadri Mälk, brooch MEDUSA V, 2004, darkened silver, rubber, 118 × 63 × 27mm

Kadri Mälk, brooch YEHUDI MENUHIN, 2011, painted wood, black precious coral, cordierite, aquamarine, almandine, silver, 128 × 62 × 14 mm

Kadri Mälk, brooch BLACK MENHIR, 2012, jet, silver, coral, 75 × 58 × 14 mm

>>   Kadri Mälk, necklace FATA MORGANA XXV BURKINA FASO, 2006, painted Cibatool, darkened silver, haematite, black jade, almandines, 690 mm

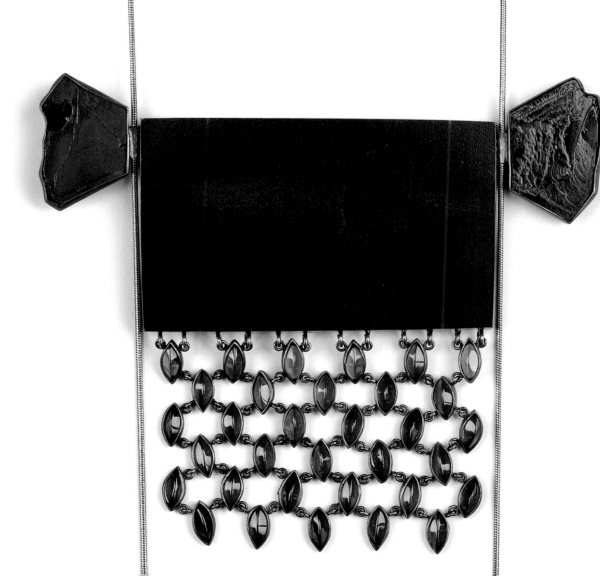

JULIA MARIA KÜNNAP

Born 1979

EDUCATION
1997–2004 Department of Jewellery and Blacksmithing, Estonian
Academy of Arts, Tallinn, Estonia
1999 Konstfack, Stockholm, Sweden

PUBLIC COLLECTIONS
Estonian Museum of Applied Art and Design, Tallinn, Estonia
Tallinn Art Hall, Tallinn, Estonia

Julia Maria Künnap works as a freelance jewellery artist, designer of accessories and furniture, and filmmaker (her *The Penguin Parade* animation film and *Mari* high chair are award winning). Movement and the dream of flying have been important aspects of Julia Maria Künnap's jewellery. She has produced silver rings and brooches with electronics, or integrating mechanics, such as antennas, ventilation tubes, wheels, screws, blades or gears.

Her recent work is quite different; she now dedicates herself to the basic materials and simple techniques, such as grinding and polishing. All her jewels are grinded from a single piece of mineral, obsidian or smoky quartz. The stones, cut sharply on one side, seem to become liquid on the other side, dripping down in thick transparent tears or melting in a black and oily pool.   L.d.B.

Julia Maria Künnap, brooch IS THIS THE HAPPINESS, 2012, smoky quartz, gold, 35×35×20 mm

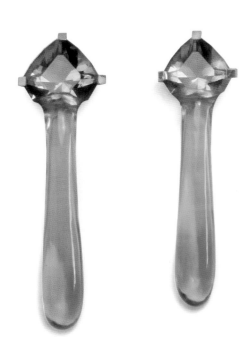

Julia Maria Künnap, earrings A GRAND DAY OUT, 2012, smoky quartz, gold, c. 40 mm

Julia Maria Künnap, brooch FROM THE MIDDLE OF A DREAM, 2010, obsidian, gold, 50×20×10 mm

MAARJA NIINEMÄGI

Born 1979

EDUCATION
1997–99 Department of Arts, Painting, University of Tartu, Tartu, Estonia
1999–2008 Department of Jewellery and Blacksmithing, Estonian Academy of Arts, Tallinn, Estonia
2007–2010 Gemstone Design and Engraving, Trier University of Applied Sciences, Idar-Oberstein, Germany

PUBLIC COLLECTIONS
Estonian Museum of Applied Art and Design, Tallinn, Estonia

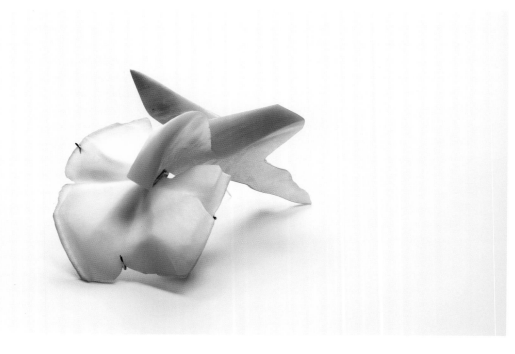

Maarja Niinemägi likes to work with stones because of the colours, the relief and the surfaces she finds in them. Her recent jewellery collection is called *Spring*. It is concerned with the movement of the body, engraved in stone. To avoid too obvious human characteristics and identifications she chooses to take the monkey as its deputy. *Little White-Ear on a Float* presents a macaque, his head turned away, silently sitting on a flowering, floating branch. Besides the monkey theme, Niinemägi also took the flower as a subject in her *Spring* collection, transforming opal into abstract flowers. The stone is cut in such a way that the flower becomes like a floating image, subtly moving in an imaginary river. As Maarja states: 'The idea of *Spring* is influenced by water'.   L.d.B.

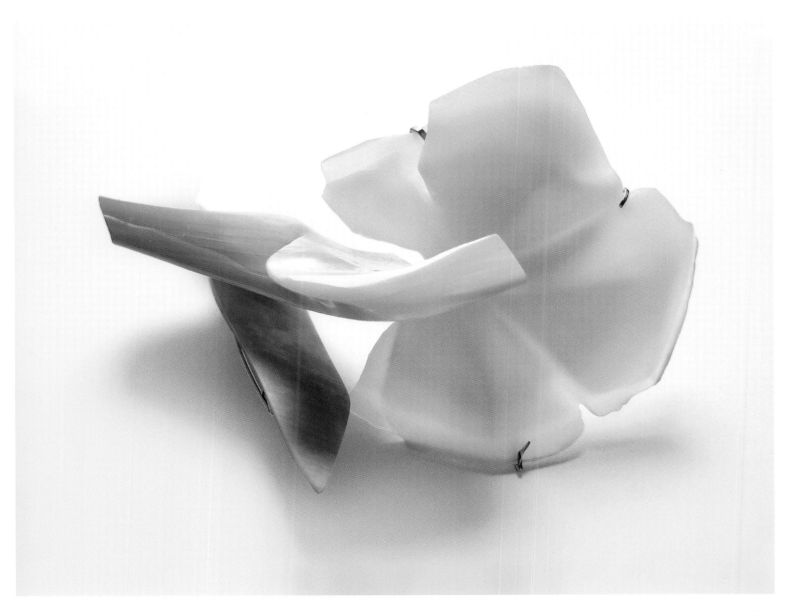

Maarja Niinemägi, brooch WAVE CREST, 2011, opal, mother of pearl, silver, gold, 120 × 100 × 70 mm

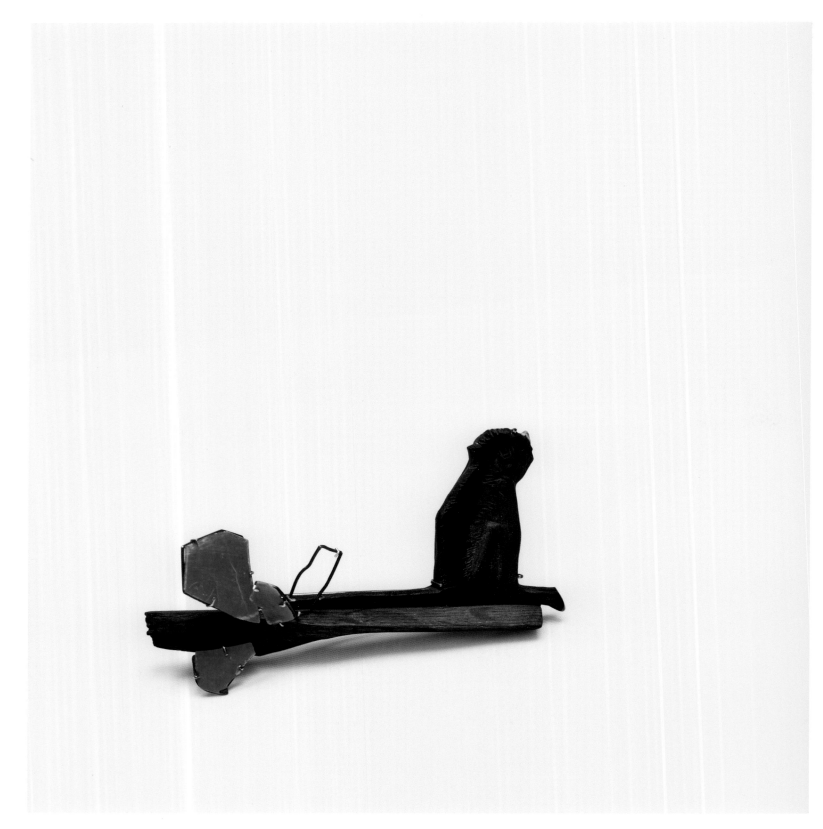

Maarja Niinemägi, brooch LITTLE WHITE-EAR ON A FLOAT, 2011, opal, agate, black oak, silver, gold, 70×100×50 mm

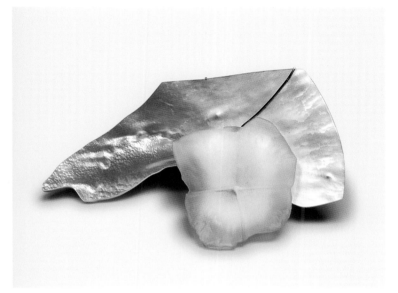

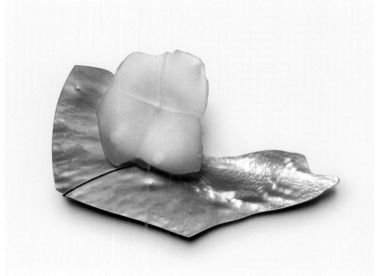

Maarja Niinemägi, brooch FLOATING, 2011, opal, mother of pearl, silver, gold, 100×140×40 mm

KRISTI PAAP

Born 1973

EDUCATION
1992–96 Department of Metal Art, Tallinn Art University, Tallinn, Estonia

PUBLIC COLLECTIONS
Art Museum of Estonia, Tallinn, Estonia
Estonian Museum of Applied Art and Design, Tallinn, Estonia

By using natural materials, such as cherrywood, lilac wood, cherry stones and plum stones, Kristi Paap's jewellery produces delicate sounds when it moves. This way she is searching for – as she calls it – 'the sound of nature: leaves rustling in the wind, the drone of insects, and waves leaping against the shore.' She sees her jewellery as being '. . . part of nature's low-key sound or loud silence'. Her jewellery, when put in motion, makes quite some noise – it makes you aware of the silence as in nature when the crickets suddenly start chirping, or when a heavy blast of wind makes the reed sing. It makes the wearer a performer, aware of the rhythm of his movements and intervals.   L.d.B.

Kristi Paap, brooch FIRST *VIEW* IN *WHITE*, 2010, lilac *wood*, jasper, tombac, silver, 85 × 80 × 20 mm

Kristi Paap, brooch RISTIK, 2012, cherry stones, cherrywood, paint, thread, 205 × 50 × 20 mm

Kristi Paap, brooch *TWELVES VIEW*, 2011, cherrywood, thread, silver, 170 × 70 × 20 mm

ANNA-MARIA SAAR

Born 1988

EDUCATION
2007–11 Department of Jewellery and Blacksmithing, Estonian Academy
of Arts, Tallinn, Estonia

Anna-Maria Saar combines object and photography in work that is situated around the body.
Her work comments on experiences in her own life and human relationships in general.
Suffering Interruptions is a necklace made from her hair that she lost one day, within an hour,
after a quarrel. She states 'that even when the memory may be lying, the body always remembers'.
In her work she uses foreign carriers to evoke remembrances and bodily experiences. In her
images a well-chosen model acts as an intermediary between the object and the observer. Her
work is characterised by a powerful approach, a result of her education as a blacksmith and being
used to work on another scale and with heavier tools than a goldsmith. Her installation *Golden
Brooch Ornament* magnifies the transparent and ornamental potency of traditional Estonian
folk jewellery.   L.d.B.

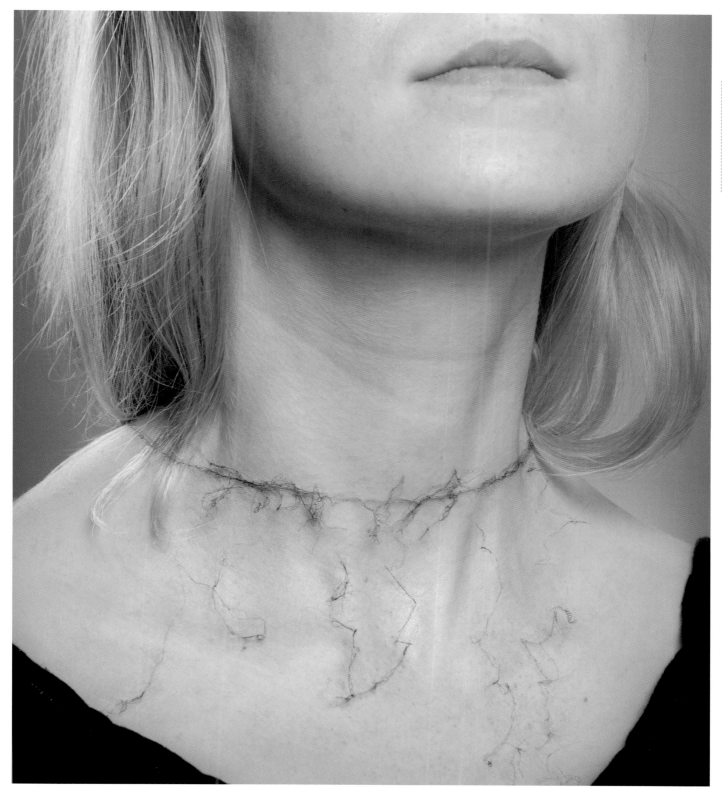

<<   Anna-Maria Saar, *wearable object* FOR THE SURVIVOR: CROWN, 2009, forged iron, 220 × 180 × 150 mm

Anna-Maria Saar, *wearable object* SUFFERING INTERRUPTIONS, 2012, photograph and object, 135 hairs, 4800 mm

Anna-Maria Saar, *wearable object* PERSISTENCE, 2010, stone, *wood*, hair, 1070 × 80 × 250 mm

TANEL VEENRE

Born 1977

EDUCATION
1995–2005 Department of Jewellery and Blacksmithing, Estonian Academy
of Arts, Tallinn, Estonia
1997/98 Jewellery Department, Gerrit Rietveld Academy, Amsterdam,
the Netherlands

PUBLIC COLLECTIONS
Estonian History Museum, Tallinn, Estonia
Estonian Museum of Applied Art and Design, Tallinn, Estonia
Collection de la ville, Cagnes-sur-Mer, France
Rotasa Collection Trust, Mill Valley, USA

Tanel Veenre is a versatile artist, working in the field of contemporary jewellery, photography and fashion. As part of a group of six Estonian artists called õhuLoss, he has produced various exhibitions and publications (including *õhuLoss/Castle in the Air*, Stuttgart 2011, together with Kadri Mälk).

Tanel Veenre's statement reads: 'I believe in the power of imagination and archetypes'. His jewellery is characterised by the use of ornaments, contrasting natural, fabricated and re-used materials and a fabulous imagery. In his recent work *In the Beginning Was the Word*, Tanel portrays himself wearing a book by Romanian-French philosopher Emile Cioran, Estonian writer and historian Karl Ristikivi and French philosopher Jean-Paul Sartre – whose writings were highly effected by the whimsicalities of modern history. To wear a book as a necklace is like a subversion of the object; however, the medium of photography helps to transfer the observer's gaze to what is behind the object.   L.d.B.

<<   Tanel Veenre, neck piece SCREAMINGLY SILENT, 2012, balsawood fishing floats, oak, silver, cosmic dust, 300 × 200 × 70 mm

Tanel Veenre, neck piece BEFORE LIGHTNESS AND AFTER DARKNESS, 2012, balsawood fishing floats, silver, cosmic dust, 170 × 170 × 60 mm

Tanel Veenre, neck piece IN THE BEGINNING WAS THE WORD, 2011, jet, textile, 130 × 100 × 20 mm

Tanel Veenre, self-portraits as Emile Cioran, Karl Ristikivi and Jean-Paul Sartre

HELENA LEHTINEN [GUEST OF HONOUR]

AMI AVELLÁN

AINO FAVÉN

CLARICE FINELL

JANNE HIRVONEN

SIRJA KNAAPI

MERVI KURVINEN

MIRJA MARSCH

ANNA RIKKINEN

JANNA SYVÄNOJA

MONICA WICKSTRÖM

FINLAND

HELENA LEHTINEN

GUEST OF HONOUR

Born 1952

EDUCATION
1977 Silversmith, Bachelor of Crafts and Design, Lahti University of Applied
Sciences, Lahti, Finland

PUBLIC COLLECTIONS
Design Museum, Helsinki, Finland
Die Neue Sammlung – The International Design Museum, Munich (permanent
loan from the Danner Foundation, Munich), Germany

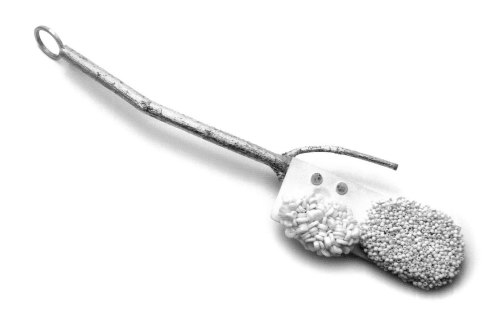

Helena Lehtinen's diversity as a jewellery artist is visible in her uncompromising style adapted consistently during her long career. Although she's changed the use of material in her production – she's moved from using silver to using wood, and later on she combined silver with recyclable materials – her signature style has, however, always been prominent, and from time to time it has also been rather surprising. In her oeuvre we find traces of Minimalism, although her works are never simple or cold. Lehtinen has been accustomed to working with an array of themes, such as those we see in the series *Family, Gardens* and *Temperatures*. The works belonging to these thematic series are tied together through the sharing of certain similar elements; in *Gardens* we find forms that remind us of plants, and the glass beads form a sort of conjunctive material and a common thread throughout the series. Due to their bright colours, these works differ from her previous ones. In her series called *Temperatures* Lehtinen has illustrated the cold winter by using cool silver, and the snow by using various shades of white.

　　Lehtinen's oeuvre is characterised by her precise, but never boring, compositions which we are able to witness in her series. Her jewellery pieces are like paintings or sculptures, always consisting of heterogeneous forms: the soft and round meet the hard and angular.　P.R.

<<   p. 91 Helena Lehtinen, necklace BREAKING UP OF THE ICE, 2012, silver, reconstructed stone, 140 × 90 mm

<<   Helena Lehtinen, necklace GARDENS, 2012, wood, silver, beads, 130 × 60 mm

Helena Lehtinen, necklace GARDENS, 2012, wood, leaf gold, silver, beads, 190 × 50 mm

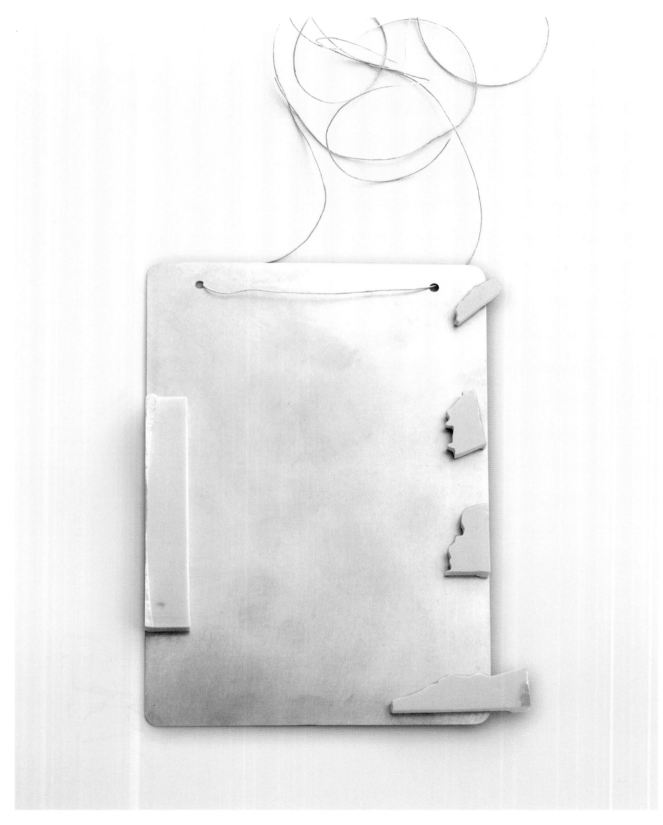

Helena Lehtinen, necklace ICE, 2012, silver, gold, 140 × 90 mm

Helena Lehtinen, necklace FIRE, 2012, silver, leaf, gold, reconstructed stone, 100 × 140 mm

AMI AVELLÁN

Born 1978

EDUCATION

2002–05 BA, HDK School of Design and Crafts, University of Gothenburg, Gothenburg, Sweden

2011/12 MA, Saimaa University of Applied Sciences, Lappeenranta, Finland

Ami Avellán's archaic necklace echoes back in time to the early days of man. The use of natural materials, such as birch root and reindeer leather, in a very primitive way raises the issue of jewellery not only as decoration but also as a hunting trophy and as a sign of status. Ami Avellán searches for new materials and 'hunts for treasures'.   J.S.

Ami Avellán, necklace FOLIUM from the series SPRING TIME, 2012, birchwood, reindeer leather, silver, pillow filling, silk, paper, string, 660 × 240 × 70 mm

Ami Avellán, necklace FOLIUM from the series SPRING TIME, 2012, birchwood, reindeer leather, silver, pillow filling, silk, paper, string, 660 × 240 × 70 mm

AINO FAVÉN

Born 1957

EDUCATION
1980–85 MA, University of Art and Design, Helsinki, Finland

PUBLIC COLLECTIONS
Design Museum, Helsinki, Finland
Finnish Museum of Natural History, University of Helsinki, Finland
The Finnish State Art Collection, Finland
Ev. luth. parish of Kauniainen, Finland
Salo Art Museum, Finland

Aino Favén often uses recycled materials and trash in her works. Her love for nature is a strong element in her pieces, and she moves between art and jewellery in her expression of it. She is inspired by contrasts and feels a need to use materials that have been touched by others and are not new. On the one hand she dislikes throwing used bottles or plastic bags into the trash, but on the other hand she falls in love with the material and its subtle expression in its own right.

The pieces made of translucent plastic bags are subtle comments on the large trash islands floating in our oceans and endangering our nature and wildlife. They are also memorial garlands for birds and other animals that have died from eating plastic waste.   J.S.

Aino Favén, necklace GARLAND, 2010, used plastic bags, polyester cloth, dia. 350 mm

CLARICE FINELL

Born 1977

EDUCATION
1996–99 Seamstress, Östra Nylands Yrkesskola, Borgå, Finland
1999/2000 Art Jewellery, Borgå Hantverks- och konstindustriskola, Borgå, Finland
2004–06 Art Jewellery, Lahti University of Applied Sciences, Lahti, Finland

For Clarice Finell many works start with an idea or a thought. First the works are named, and then they are made. Most of her works are wearable, but that doesn't mean they are comfortable or easy to wear. About her work methods, she stresses that the working times are stolen moments in the evenings or at night.

The selected works, *The Pessimist* and *The Optimist*, are paintings as much as they are jewellery. The works are commentaries on her own life, and the names are translations of song titles.   J.S.

Clarice Finell, *wall pieces/pendants* THE OPTIMIST AND THE PESSIMIST, 2012, silk, embroidery, *wood, paint, dia. 120 mm each*

JANNE HIRVONEN

Born 1965

EDUCATION
2001 MA, University of Art and Design, Helsinki, Finland

Janne Hirvonen's jewellery pieces comment on the world around us. Hirvonen himself states that the objects in the pieces selected are trying to manifest themselves and point out the four mortal sinners of our times. The work consists of four characters: individualist, nationalist, economist and lawyer. The work thus comments on religion, socialist realism, violence, societal problems, greediness and justice; the frailness of the pieces prophesise the demise of Western culture.

Hirvonen is an industrial designer by education. In his jewellery he builds bridges between the worlds of the individual and the surrounding environment, taking advantage of the very personal experience a piece of jewellery gives to the wearer.   J.S.

<< Janne Hirvonen, brooch INDIVIDUALIST from the series FAMILY PORTRAIT – CAPITALISTIC REALISM, 2011, copper, 120 × 70 × 30 mm

Janne Hirvonen, brooch JURIST from the series FAMILY PORTRAIT – CAPITALISTIC REALISM, 2011, copper, 120 × 70 × 30 mm

Janne Hirvonen, brooch ECONOMIST from the series FAMILY PORTRAIT – CAPITALISTIC REALISM, 2011, copper, 120 x 70 x 30 mm

Janne Hirvonen, brooch NATIONALIST from the series FAMILY PORTRAIT – CAPITALISTIC REALISM, 2011, copper, 120 x 70 x 30 mm

SIRJA KNAAPI

Born 1985

EDUCATION
2001–12 MA Cultural Entrepreneurship, focus jewellery, Saimaa
University of Applied Sciences, Imatra, Finland
2004–08 BA Stoneware and Jewellery Design, South Karelia University
of Applied Sciences, Lappeenranta, Finland

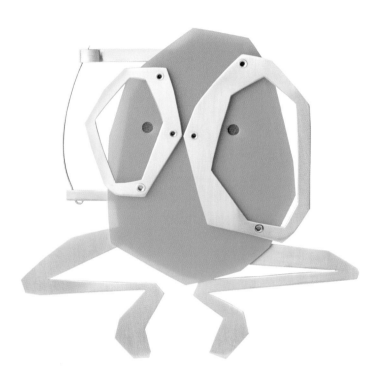

With her jewellery work, Sirja Knaapi wants to bring joy to the wearer. Through her studies she has become familiar with a variety of materials and techniques, enabling her to transform her thoughts and ideas into reality and to mix new materials with more traditional jewellery materials and techniques.

The selected works in their pictorial message challenge the user and viewer to concentrate and pause for a moment. The forms are very familiar and natural but at the same time unrecognizable. The viewer can see a frog, a dog or some mystical animal that only exists in the imagination.   J.S.

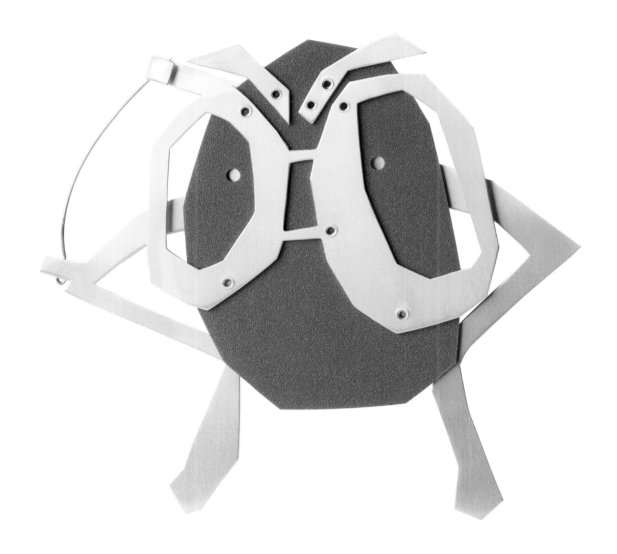

<< Sirja Knaapi, brooch UNTITLED, 2011, aluminium, plastic, steel, 200 × 110 × 6 mm

Sirja Knaapi, brooch UNTITLED, 2011, aluminium, plastic, steel, 140 × 155 × 6 mm

MERVI KURVINEN

Born 1974

EDUCATION
1994 University of Joensuu, Finland
1996 Lappeenranta College of Arts and Crafts, Finland
1997–2001 South Carelia Polytechnic, Lappeenranta, Finland
1999 Jewellery Design, Gerrit Rietveld Academy, Amsterdam,
the Netherlands
2003 Advanced studies of jewellery, South Carelia Polytechnic,
Lappeenranta, Finland

In many of Mervi Kurvinen's works the inspiration comes from popular culture, such as films, books, everyday observations and experiences. In her jewellery she uses powerful contradictions and combinations. Her treasures are found from rubbish skips, flea markets, even from Easter eggs.

In her works, ready-made objects are carefully and skilfully combined with valuable and cheap materials alike. Mervi Kurvinen quotes Dr Seuss: 'In my world, everyone's a pony and they all eat rainbows and poop butterflies'.   J.S.

Mervi Kurvinen, necklace FREEWHEEL, 2012, silver, steel, porcelain, hand painted by Tarja Häsästell, 260 × 110 mm

MIRJA MARSCH

Born 1976

EDUCATION
2000–04 BA, Textile Design, EVTEK Institute of Art and Design, Vantaa, Finland

Mirja Marsch uses materials freely in her art jewellery, experimenting with the combination and interaction of techniques, materials and subject matter. Her background in textile design gives her a variety of skills and explains why she prefers to use textile and embroidery in her works and thus challenges the traditional materials of jewellery. Her choices of subject matter give her works a profound artistic meaning that question the traditional role of jewellery and follow its topical discussion.

The pieces selected are wearable brooches, and for Mirja Marsch it is always important that her jewellery is not just conceptual art but comprises true jewellery pieces that can be worn by anyone and used every day. The use of embroidery is supported by the subject matter, commenting on the near past and the stereotypes of Finnish society and culture.   J.S.

<<   Mirja Marsch, brooch EVERY SELF-RESPECTING WOMAN SHOULD HAVE A ROLLING PIN, 2012, heat transfer picture, textile, 95 x 75 mm

Mirja Marsch, earrings SEARCHING FOR MY INNER JUSTIINA, 2012, heat transfer picture, textile, 100 x 110 mm

ANNA RIKKINEN

Born 1976

EDUCATION
2002 BA, Jewellery and Stonework, South Carelia Polytechnic,
Lappeenranta, Finland
2004 BA, Jewellery Design, Gerrit Rietveld Academy, Amsterdam,
the Netherlands

PUBLIC COLLECTIONS
Korutaideyhdistys Collection, Helsinki, Finland

Anna Rikkinen often questions the role of jewellery in her works. How does a piece of jewellery change in meaning when it is worn and touches the body of the user? Does a piece of jewellery leave a mark on the body or its surroundings? Can a piece of jewellery be a piece of jewellery even if it is not worn?

In the works selected for this exhibition, Anna Rikkinen finds inspiration from Dutch portrait paintings from the seventeenth century, where white emotionless faces are counterbalanced by the dark background and big lace collars. Anna's necklaces are big and heavy, rendering the wearer uncomfortable and static and thus changing the meaning of the necklace from an ornamental addition to a dominating force. The photographs in the series *A Dutch Encounter* are by Markus Henttonen.   J.S.

Anna Rikkinen, necklace A DUTCH ENCOUNTER II, 2011, painted wood, textile rope, 500 × 400 × 120 mm
Anna Rikkinen, A DUTCH ENCOUNTER II, 2011, digital photograph, 800 × 600 mm

Anna Rikkinen, necklace A DUTCH ENCOUNTER VII, 2011, painted wood, textile, 500 × 400 × 120 mm
Anna Rikkinen, A DUTCH ENCOUNTER VII, 2011, digital photograph, 800 × 600 mm

Anna Rikkinen, *A DUTCH ENCOUNTER V*, 2011, digital photograph, 800 × 600 mm

Anna Rikkinen, necklace A DUTCH ENCOUNTER V, 2011, lacquered wood, paper yarn, 600 × 500 × 120 mm

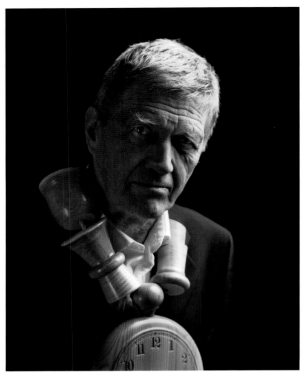

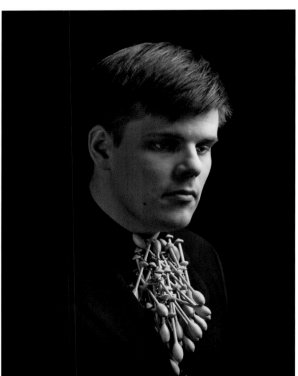

Anna Rikkinen, A DUTCH ENCOUNTER I, 2011, digital photograph, 800 × 600 mm
Anna Rikkinen, necklace A DUTCH ENCOUNTER I, 2011, lacquered wood, rope, 500 × 400 × 120 mm

Anna Rikkinen, A DUTCH ENCOUNTER III, 2011, digital photograph, 800 × 600 mm
Anna Rikkinen, necklace A DUTCH ENCOUNTER III, 2011, bobbins, silver, cotton ribbon, 250 × 150 × 80 mm

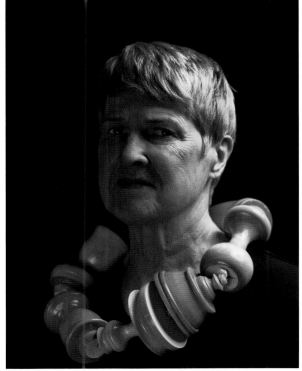

Anna Rikkinen, necklace A DUTCH ENCOUNTER IV, 2011, lacquered wood, rope, 500 × 400 × 120 mm
Anna Rikkinen, A DUTCH ENCOUNTER IV, 2011, digital photograph, 800 × 600 mm

Anna Rikkinen, necklace A DUTCH ENCOUNTER VI, 2011, lacquered wood, rope, 500 × 400 × 120 mm
Anna Rikkinen, A DUTCH ENCOUNTER VI, 2011, digital photograph, 800 × 600 mm

JANNA SYVÄNOJA

Born 1960

EDUCATION
1982–93 MA Furniture and Interior Design, University of Industrial Arts,
Helsinki, Finland

PUBLIC COLLECTIONS
Design Museum, Helsinki, Finland
State of Finland
National Museum of Scotland, Edinburgh, Great Britain
National Museum of Art, Architecture and Design, Oslo, Norway
Nationalmuseum, Stockholm, Sweden
The Röhsska Museum for Fashion, Design and Decorative Arts,
Gothenburg, Sweden
Museum of Arts and Design, New York, USA

 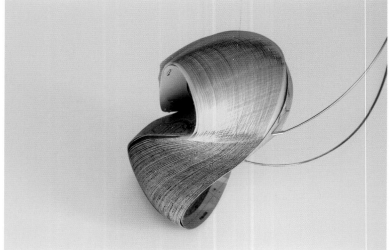

Janna Syvänoja's works not only comment on the role of jewellery, materiality and their value, but they also reflect her personal aesthetic language that finds beauty from found materials and recycled everyday objects, such as phone books, maps, dictionaries and catalogues. The pieces become vessels for cultural messages and hidden worlds that are created by using printed paper, which conceal parts of the message from the viewer. Her use of a processed natural material raises the question of ecology and responsibility.

Syvänoja's works are on the borderline between art and design. On the one hand they are miniature sculptures in their own right; on the other they are elaborate pieces of jewellery that are very comfortable to wear and that find new meanings when they interact with the user in everyday situations.   J.S.

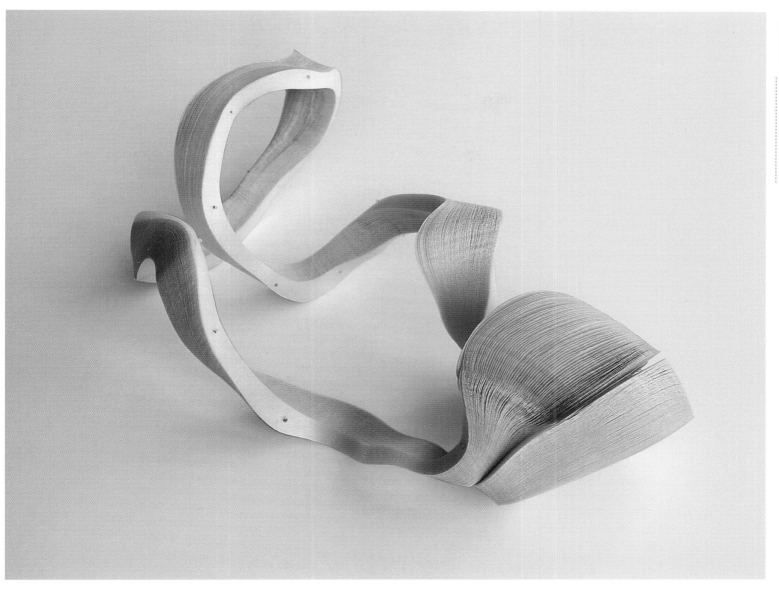

<< Janna Syvänoja, necklace UNTITLED, 2012, paper, steel wire, 100×150×70 mm

Janna Syvänoja, necklace UNTITLED I, 2012, paper, steel wire, 300×170×90 mm

MONICA WICKSTRÖM

Born 1955

EDUCATION
2000–03 School of Arts and Crafts, Porvoo, Finland

Monica Wickström often combines precious materials with trash and found items, thus giving a heightened emphasis to the precious natural resources we tend to waste. She works and moves very freely between art, handicraft and design.

The *Medals of Decadence* narrates the public spirit of Europe today and the economic crisis. The materials chosen for the work may mislead the user or viewer into gender issues and commentary on women's lives, but here the material symbolises a strong person, whether it be a man or a woman. The framing of the stocking holes was not easy, as Wickström comments. She also points out that going through an economic crisis is not easy either.   J.S.

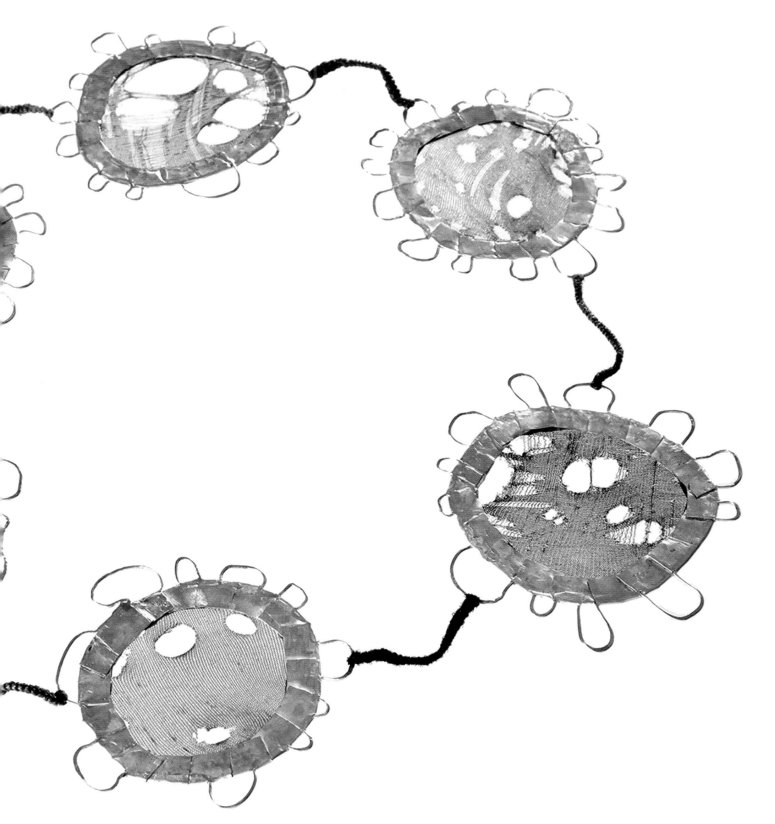

Monica Wickström, necklace MEDALS OF DECADENCE, 2009, silver, textile, 280×280×2 mm

HILDUR ÝR JÓNSDÓTTIR

HULDA B. ÁGÚSTSDÓTTIR

HELGA RAGNHILDUR MOGENSEN

ÁSTÞÓR & KJARTAN FOR ORR

ICELAND

HILDUR ÝR JÓNSDÓTTIR

Born 1976

EDUCATION
1999/2000 Design Department, Vocational School of Hafnarfjörður, Iceland
2002–06 BA, Jewellery Department, Gerrit Rietveld Academy, Amsterdam, the Netherlands

PUBLIC COLLECTIONS
Die Neue Sammlung – The International Design Museum, Munich (permanent loan from The Danner Foundation, Munich), Germany
International Ceramics Studio, Kecskemét, Hungary
The Riga Porcelain Museum, Riga, Latvia

Hildur Ýr elected to study at the Jewellery Department at the Gerrit Rietveld Academy because of the freedom it allowed students to work with diverse materials. Since then her works have been characterised by a rich need to experiment with everything she lays her hands on and by testing every material to its limits. She has worked with a range of materials, including fish skin, aluminium, iron and wood, and in her works she often takes a stance on environmental issues.

The porcelain necklaces are made from knotted string dipped in liquid porcelain. A climax is reached after high firing when the unexpected form has taken shape. Hildur Ýr's struggle with the porcelain is manifested with particular clarity in the contradiction intrinsic to this fragile material, in the form that she imposes on the substance. The porcelain necklaces are at the very limit of enduring the friction and wear that their purpose demands. The sculptural quality of her work reveals an ambiguity towards its role, awakening urgent questions about aesthetics and the tolerance of form for purpose.   H.T.

<<   p.125 Hildur Ýr Jónsdóttir, necklace BEAUTY OR A BEAST, 2012, Herend porcelain (high fired), plaster, rusted chain, c. 420 × 150 × 100 mm

Hildur Ýr Jónsdóttir, necklace NO TITLE 1, 2012, Herend porcelain, cotton rope, c. 420 × 225 × 50 mm

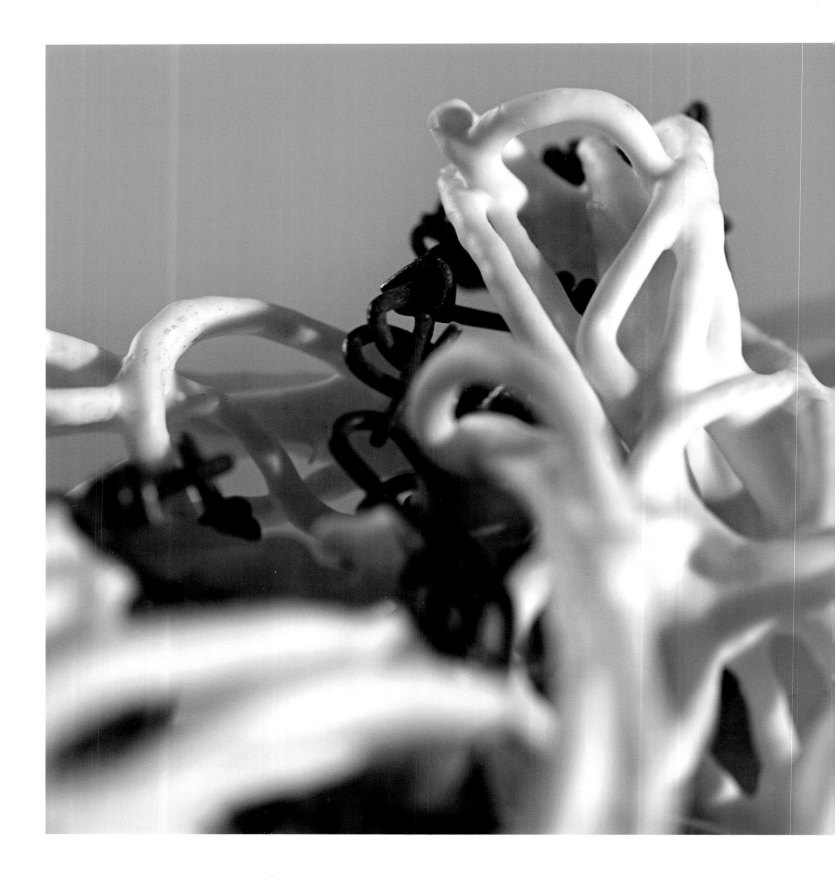

Hildur Ýr Jónsdóttir, necklace KNOTS, 2010, Herend porcelain, rusted iron chain, 310 × 210 × 40 mm

HULDA B. ÁGÚSTSDÓTTIR

Born 1952

EDUCATION
1974–78 Department of Painting, École des Beaux-Arts, Aix-en-Provence, France
1980/81 Department of Experimental Art, Icelandic School of Arts and Crafts, Reykjavik, Iceland

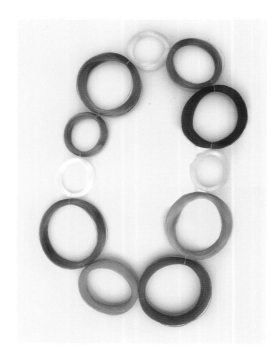

Hulda studied painting in France and proceeded to unravel those studies in the Experimental Art Department of the Icelandic School of Arts and Crafts. Concept art dominated within the school at the time, and the teaching methods of instructors such as Dieter Roth and Magnus Palsson inspired a whole generation of artists. Since completing her studies, Hulda has emphasised her jewellery design and is best known for the plastic and rubber jewellery she began working on in 1996.

This choice of material made Hulda one of the pioneers in a more liberal approach to raw materials than Icelandic jewellery design had seen before. She gave norms of beauty and value a new platform, with necklaces and bracelets comprising assembled bolts and painted plastic tubes in cheerful colours. Colour combinations arise from endless experiments in a process Hulda describes as a chain reaction: a drop ripples the water, a rhythm forms on the surface. Effortlessly, it seems.   H.T.

Hulda B. Ágústsdóttir, neck piece ROUND&ROUND, 2000, dyed nylon threads, 700 × 500 × 20 mm

HELGA RAGNHILDUR MOGENSEN

Born 1980

EDUCATION
2003–07 BA, Jewellery and Silversmithing, Design and Applied Arts,
Edinburgh College of Art, Edinburgh, Great Britain

Helga draws on memories and places to bring a highly personal touch to her works. Driftwood from the remote Strandir coast in northern Iceland forms the basis for most of her jewellery and plays an important symbolic role: it is taken from the place where Helga preserves the core of the memories that inspire her.

Helga does not take a refining approach to form in her work, which is roughly polished just like when the driftwood was washed onshore. In both works she draws subjective portraits of people: in the first work, family members, who run like a common thread through her life, are amplified with intimacy by their positioning on the chain; in the second, the imagery is far more open to divergent interpretations. The sincerity of the symbolism she captures so artistically with her material is not commonly observed in Icelandic jewellery. In the few years since her graduation, Helga has set sail and made landfall on a new shore, one she describes only through her works.   H.T.

Helga Ragnhildur Mogensen, neck piece THE RED THREAD, 2010, driftwood, thread, sterling silver, 510 × 210 mm

Helga Ragnhildur Mogensen, neck piece ARE WE REALLY THAT DIFFERENT?, 2009, driftwood, sterling silver, dia. 950 mm

ORR

KJARTAN ÖRN KJARTANSSON

Born 1967

EDUCATION
2000 Goldsmith, Technical College Reykjavik, Reykjavik, Iceland

ÁSTÞÓR HELGASON

Born 1975

EDUCATION
1998 Goldsmith, Technical College Reykjavik, Reykjavik, Iceland

Goldsmiths Kjartan and Ástþór, collectively called Orr, immediately carved themselves a niche when their collaboration began over a decade ago with a daringly opulent take on classical forms. A set of rings with large, polished zircons set in coarse 'melted' silver claws attracted particular attention. Today the stones in many of their pieces are even larger and more dominant. Their creations have burst into a more three-dimensional world than jewellery commonly occupies.

'Collaboration gives us freedom,' they say. These words are key to the method behind their fertile creativity. The necklace *Mengi* is everything at once: jewellery for the neck, an accessory to the clothes on which it forms a coordinate system, a bracelet, or even a ring you could wind around your neck and finger. Such humble grandeur lies not least in the freedom of plentiful raw material. Nothing is started without an ample supply of silver. *Mengi* began as a ring, but grew into a necklace, typifying the playful spirit of these partners who resist the notion that creating jewellery demands a fixed conclusion.   H.T.

Ástþór & Kjartan for Orr, necklace, ring bracelet, a thing to *wear* in 1000 different *ways*, MENGI, 2012, silver, 3100 mm

KONRAD MEHUS [GUEST OF HONOUR]

LIV BLÅVARP

SIGURD BRONGER

LINNÉA BLAKÉUS CALDER

LILLAN ELIASSEN

ELISE HATLØ

ANNE LÉGER

ANNA TALBOT

GUNNHILD TJÅLAND

NORWAY

KONRAD MEHUS

GUEST OF HONOUR

Born 1941

EDUCATION
1967 Master certificate as goldsmith
1967 Statens lærerskole i forming, Oslo, Norway
1970–72 Sculpture, Oslo National Academy of the Arts, Oslo, Norway

PUBLIC COLLECTIONS
Art Museums of Bergen, Norway
MiST – Nordenfjeldske Kunstindustrimuseum, Trondheim, Norway
National Museum of Art, Architecture and Design, Oslo, Norway
The Röhsska Museum for Fashion, Design and Decorative Arts,
Gothenburg, Sweden

Søljer, silver brooches of a special kind, are an integral part of Norwegian folk costumes. For many years now, Konrad Mehus has been creating contemporary versions of these traditional ornaments. He frequently uses coins, buttons and pottery shards as baubles or decoration. More recently, he has also used food tins as storage boxes for his brooches. In Norway, Mehus was a pioneer in the use of found items as materials for jewellery. The transformation of remnants or waste from industrial processes into unique, handmade objects with a different meaning and a new beauty indicates a close relationship to the artefacts of everyday life and a corresponding scepticism to the pressures and excesses of consumerism. The objects that feature in his works have crossed social and economic boundaries, reminding us that art is about questioning entrenched ideas and established values.

Among Mehus's works inspired by folk art we also find several bridal crowns. Collectively, these pieces carry the ambiguous title *Krona på Verket*. As a fixed expression, 'krona på verket' means 'crowning glory' (literally, 'the crown on the work'), but the title also plays on the name of the place where Mehus lives: Verket.   J.V.

<< p.139 Konrad Mehus, brooch POT SØLJE (WITH BOX), 2012, copper, silver, wood, tin can, 95 × 61 × 19 mm; box: 101 × 31 mm

Konrad Mehus, bridal crown KRONA PÅ VERKET 2 – BIRD'S NEST, 2003, silver and twigs, dia. 165 × 130 mm

MiST – Nordenfjeldske Kunstindustrimuseum, Trondheim

Konrad Mehus, brooch BOLESØLJE (WITH BOX), 2012, silver, potsherd, coins, mother-of-pearl buttons, tin can, 86 × 27 mm; box: 101 × 34 mm

Konrad Mehus, brooch BOLESØLJE, BLACK (WITH BOX), 2012, silver, wood, 63 x 29 mm; box: 85 x 31 mm

LIV BLÅVARP

Born 1956

EDUCATION
1979–83 Department of Metalworking, Oslo National College of Art
and Design, Oslo, Norway

PUBLIC COLLECTIONS
Designmuseum Danmark, Copenhagen, Denmark
Museum of Decorative Arts, Berlin, Germany
National Museum of Scotland, Edinburgh, Great Britain
Art Museums of Bergen, Norway
The Art Museum of Northern Norway, Trømso, Norway
MiST – Nordenfjeldske Kunstindustrimuseum, Trondheim, Norway
National Museum of Art, Architecture and Design, Oslo, Norway
Nationalmuseum, Stockholm, Sweden
The Röhsska Museum for Fashion, Design and Decorative Arts,
Gothenburg, Sweden
Cooper-Hewitt National Design Museum, New York, USA
Museum of Arts and Design, New York, USA
Mint Museum, Charlotte, USA
Museum of Fine Arts, Boston, USA
The Museum of Fine Arts (The Helen Williams Drutt Collection),
Houston, USA

Since the 1980s, Liv Blåvarp has worked mainly with neck pieces, exploring and perfecting the sculptural possibilities of this jewellery genre. She chose wood as her material, which was at the time unusual in Norwegian jewellery circles. Throughout history, jewellery has been associated with precious materials, such as gem stones, a convention Blåvarp rejected in opting for wood. As one of the first Norwegian jewellery artists to break with tradition in this way, she demonstrated that jewellery was about something other than status and preciousness. A recurrent feature of Blåvarp's work is the use of wood and of natural, organic forms. In the 1980s and 1990s she used a figurative language to create neck pieces with representations of natural objects, such as banana fruits and leaves. In the late 1990s she began to treat these natural themes with greater abstraction, developing a non-figurative language of organic form with undulating shapes and a greater emphasis on shades of wood and colour. Over the years, Blåvarp has developed a distinctive and highly personal idiom that combines an exceptional sense of form with a perfected technique in jewellery that is supple and accommodating, both to wear and to look at.   K.A.B.

<<   Liv Blåvarp, necklace BAT, 2011, birdseye maple, cocobolo, ebony, dia. c. 300 mm

Liv Blåvarp, necklace SUNDANCE II, 2010, peroba rosa, amarello, amboina, whale tooth, dia. c. 350 mm

SIGURD BRONGER

Born 1957

EDUCATION
1975–79 MTS Vakschool Schoonhoven, the Netherlands

PUBLIC COLLECTIONS
Designmuseum Danmark, Copenhagen, Denmark
Design Museum, Helsinki, Finland
Die Neue Sammlung – The International Design Museum Munich, Germany
Middlesbrough Institute of Modern Art, Middlesbrough, Great Britain
Royal College of Art, London, Great Britain
Victoria and Albert Museum, London, Great Britain
Stedelijk Museum, Amsterdam, the Netherlands
Stedelijk Museum 's-Hertogenbosch, the Netherlands
Art Museums of Bergen, Norway
Art Museum of Northern Norway, Trømso, Norway
Lillehammer Art Museum, Norway
MiST – Nordenfjeldske Kunstindustrimuseum, Trondheim, Norway
National Museum for Art, Architecture and Design, Oslo, Norway
Sørlandet Art Museum, Kristiansand, Norway
Nationalmuseum, Stockholm, Sweden

At his debut exhibition in the early 1980s, Sigurd Bronger presented simple and constructivist works of a kind that had never been seen before in Norway. Bronger studied in Amsterdam, where he was in daily contact with international influences and studied under a different set of teachers than those with whom most other Norwegian craft artists trained. Rather than comment on tradition, which was at the time a popular theme among Norwegian jewellery artists, Bronger invited people to reflect on the question of what jewellery is. In his early works, he used reduction and construction to highlight this question in a series of brooches that consisted of small geometrical shapes attached to needles under tension. These pieces reduced to a minimum the notion of what a brooch could be. In the 1990s, he introduced eggs and balloons into his vocabulary. Today these airy shapes have become the hallmark of his jewellery. Any overall characterisation of Bronger's work from the past thirty years is likely to include terms such as construction, mechanics, absurdism and 'airy' humour.   K.A.B.

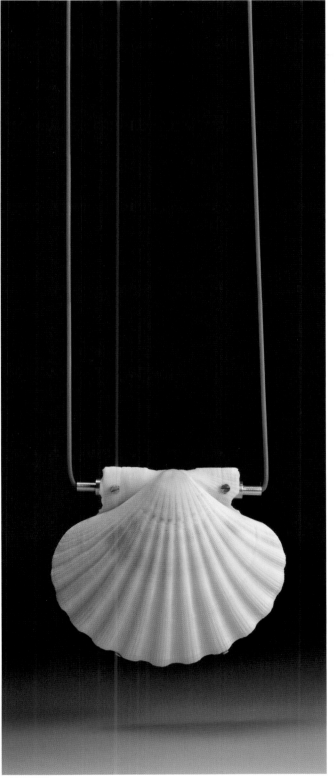

<<   Sigurd Bronger, brooch CARRYING DEVICE FOR A BLACK SEASHELL, 2011, enamel, brass, paint, steel, rubber, seashell, 60 × 50 × 25 mm

Sigurd Bronger, necklace CARRYING DEVICE FOR SEASHELL, 2011, gold-plated brass, shell, rubber cord, 100 × 100 mm

Sigurd Bronger, brooch CARRYING DEVICE FOR LIQUID FLUID, 2012, gold-plated brass, stainless steel, rubber, 90 × 40 × 30 mm

Sigurd Bronger, FAN BROOCH, 2009, gold-plated brass, steel, enamel paint, 80×25 mm

LINNÉA BLAKÉUS CALDER

Born 1955

EDUCATION
1977–79 Diploma, Institute of Precious Metals, Copenhagen, Denmark

PUBLIC COLLECTIONS
MiST – Nordenfjeldske Kunstindustrimuseum, Trondheim, Norway

Linnéa Blakéus Calder trained as a goldsmith and artist. She is, however, best known as a goldsmith and has for many years had her own workshop, where she has produced numerous jewellery collections in limited editions under her own name. She can now look back on a career of versatile creativity, for in addition to producing wearable jewellery, she has carried out many public art commissions and worked with craft objects intended for gallery spaces rather than the consumer market. In recent years Blakéus Calder has explored new territory that has taken her out of her jeweller's workshop in pursuit of new possibilities. Away from her workshop and its traditional tools, she has sought other working methods and materials. As her project *Your Trash My Treasure* indicates, Calder now works with found objects, which she casts in plaster.

These days, she finds her materials on the beaches in the area where she lives. This rich variety of objects provides the basis for her wearable objects. Her jewellery can be described as a cross between an urban visual culture and shaman-like ornaments suggestive of the ritual fetishes normally associated with practices that worship nature.   K.A.B.

Linnéa Blakéus Calder, YOUR TRASH MY TREASURE, 2012, found objects coated with plaster and painted; print on aluminium, 70×100 cm

LILLAN ELIASSEN

Born 1961

EDUCATION

1983–89 Diploma, Department of Metalworking, Oslo National College
of Art and Design, Oslo, Norway

PUBLIC COLLECTIONS

Designmuseum Danmark, Copenhagen, Denmark
Art Museums of Bergen, Norway
MiST – Nordenfjeldske Kunstindustrimuseum, Trondheim, Norway
National Museum of Art, Architecture and Design, Oslo, Norway
The Art Museum of Northern Norway, Trømsø, Norway
Sørlandet Art Museum, Kristiansand, Norway

Working in a variety of genres, Lillan Eliassen has made both small contemplative objects and large installations. She is, however, first and foremost a jewellery artist. Her first series of wearable jewellery took knives as its theme. Eliassen's knives function like buttonhole flowers. Made of metal with wooden details, they combine a figurative language with vibrant colours. Her idiom and the fact that she takes her inspiration from the ornamental knives associated with Norwegian folk costumes align her with the folkloric interests of the so-called neo-tradition of the late 1980s and early 1990s within the crafts field. Eliassen has always given her knife pieces titles that allude to interpersonal and – usually male-female – relationships. With the knife as her theme and titles that often play on words describing amorous dreams, her colourful and exuberant works from this period tend to carry disturbing overtones.

The contrast between beautiful, dreamy love and its darker side is something Eliassen returns to repeatedly in her jewellery. In the early 2000s, she took the tiara as a basis for head jewellery made of metal and perspex. Thematically, these pieces refer to women's aspirations and anxiety about what the world has in store for them. In recent years she has built her narratives around air and inflated receptacles made of durable materials.   K.A.B.

Lillan Eliassen, neck piece COURAGE, 2012, casting clay, copper, 430 × 360 mm

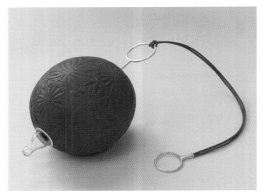

<<   Lillan Eliassen, necklace EVERY ROAD IS JUST ANOTHER WAY HOME, 2012, casting clay, silver, 140 × 240 mm

Lillan Eliassen, neck piece RUN BABY RUN, 2012, concrete, copper, steel, 420 × 320 mm

ELISE HATLØ

Born 1981

EDUCATION
2007–09 MA, Department of Metalworking, Oslo National Academy
of the Arts, Oslo, Norway

PUBLIC COLLECTIONS
Art Museums of Bergen, Norway
MiST – Nordenfjeldske Kunstindustrimuseum, Trondheim, Norway
National Museum of Art, Architecture and Design, Oslo, Norway

In recent years, many jewellery artists have dwelt on ornament as a principle feature of their work, a trend exemplified by Elise Hatlø. For her, jewellery is a medium that transports stories, and ornament in particular has historic tales to tell. Hatlø clearly reveals her background in crafts by taking as her theme the refined craft techniques of earlier generations and the values and experience associated with them. She is fascinated by textile techniques, such as crocheting, embroidery and knitting, all of which she uses as a source of visual elements for her own work. Another noticeable source of inspiration is the ornamental splendour of jewellery traditions, while her use of mounted stones is a clear case of homage to history. The appeal of Hatlø's jewellery lies in its combination of venerable handicraft, references to the history of jewellery, and of contemporary visual culture. In this sense, we can attribute an autobiographical theme to her work, in which memories are accorded a central place. Her creations can also be interpreted as a comment on the early feminist condemnation of women's crafts. Hatlø's jewellery allows us to view craft traditions with new eyes and from a post-feminist perspective.   K.A.B.

Elise Hatlø, brooch GRANDMA SINGS THE BLUES, 2011/12, silver, copper, smoky quartz, agate, silk, lacquer, 100 × 40 × 60 mm
Elise Hatlø, necklace GRANDMA SINGS THE BLUES, 2011/12, silver, copper, citrine, agate, rock crystal, silk, lacquer, 130 × 40 × 50 mm

ANNE LÉGER

Born 1966

EDUCATION
2006–08 MA, Department of Metalworking, Oslo National Academy
of the Arts, Oslo, Norway

The theme of nature is focal to the work of many contemporary jewellery artists. Anne Léger
can be seen as an exponent of this trend. With nature as her source of inspiration, she abstracts
ideas and turns them into decorative jewellery. Natural motifs have been an essential feature
of her work, from her first series based on butterflies through to her latest work with floral
designs. Like her butterfly series, her most recent jewellery also references Art Nouveau and Japa-
nesery, albeit using a rougher-edged idiom. Her creations are highly expressive in their use of
contrasting materials, colours, surfaces and themes. Expressivity is a recurrent feature in most of
her jewellery series. Her representations of nature suggest the realm of sensory experience while
also containing references to specific plants and musical compositions indicative of more personal
moods and responses to nature. They also contain contrasts between the illuminated and the
obscure, as if to warn us that something disturbing lurks beneath the beauty of even the most
captivating colours and forms.   K.A.B.

<< Anne Léger, necklace NOCTURNE, 2012, *wood*, silver, pearl, enamel, dia. 250 mm and
necklace PRELUDE, 2012, *wood*, silver, enamel, moonstone, quartz, dia. 180 mm
Detail of PRELUDE

ANNA TALBOT

Born 1978

EDUCATION
2007–09 MA, Department of Metalworking, Oslo National Academy of the Arts, Oslo, Norway

PUBLIC COLLECTIONS
Art Museums of Bergen, Norway
MiST – Nordenfjeldske Kunstindustrimuseum, Trondheim, Norway
National Museum of Art, Architecture and Design, Oslo, Norway

Anna Talbot belongs to a young generation of jewellery artists in Norway who represent a new orientation within the field. There are many references in her work to the 1980s' postmodern reaction against merely functional or ornamental jewellery, a reaction that manifested itself in the use of ready-mades and alternative materials. Unlike the postmodernists, however, who often stressed the use of non-precious or prefabricated materials, Talbot juxtaposes materials of all kinds, treating them with equal value. What she emphasises is the process of refining ready-made objects and materials. In this way she shows her commitment to forms of crafts that value knowledgeability about materials, taking this as her starting point for the creation of meaningful jewellery. Talbot's works are clear testimony to the return of ornamentation in jewellery. They exemplify what can be described as a baroque joy in ornamentation, enhanced with lively colours and a profundity of composition. Many of her necklaces are like theatrical scenes with surrounding floral arrangements, tableau settings that capture single moments from performances of fairy tales often 'peopled' with animals and human figures. These scenes could be compared to the pastoral tradition in painting, which depicted romantic and serene situations against the backdrop of nature. Even so, one notices hints of something indefinable and sinister that prick one's curiosity and invite more personal interpretations of these scenes.   K.A.B.

Anna Talbot, necklace KISSMEKISSMEKISSME, 2012, ready-mades, anodised aluminium, *wood*, silver, brass, 200 × 300 × 60 mm

Anna Talbot, necklace DON'T LEAD ME ASTRAY, 2012, ready-made, anodised aluminium, *wood*, lacquer, silver, brass, 230 × 230 × 150 mm

162

Anna Talbot, necklace OH MY DEER, 2011, ready-made, anodised aluminium, lacquer, silver, brass, 150 × 170 × 80 mm

GUNNHILD TJÅLAND

Born 1968

EDUCATION
1989–95 Department of Metalworking, Oslo National College of Art and Design, Oslo, Norway

PUBLIC COLLECTIONS
Art Museums of Bergen, Norway
MiST – Nordenfjeldske Kunstindustrimuseum, Trondheim, Norway
National Museum of Art, Architecture and Design, Oslo, Norway

Gunnhild Tjåland stands out as a versatile artist who has worked with both precious and base metals. Her repertoire ranges from brooches, rings, pendants and bracelets to hammered objects that can be categorised as sculptures. Although Tjåland shows a particular affinity for silver, she is an artist who emphasises the individual qualities of materials and allows them to speak for themselves. This fundamental sobriety is characteristic not just of her approach to materials but also of her working methods and her design language. Tjåland uses traditional techniques, such as hammering and filigree work, in designs based on geometry and the mathematical reduction of nature. Starting out from observations of her surroundings, she seeks underlying basic forms from which she can produce modules or building blocks. Through the application of geometrical and mathematical systems, she builds up three-dimensional, seemingly corporeal jewellery. Frequently perforated, her objects are like small sculptures in which material and immaterial elements generate life and contrast. Thus her forms also reduce to the mere suggestion or skeleton of a shape or object. Deriving many of her geometric building blocks from older jewellery, Tjåland is an artist who pursues an on-going dialogue with the history of jewellery and craft traditions.   K.A.B.

<< Gunnhild Tjåland, necklace TOPOGRAFI, 2011, silver, dia. 80 mm

Gunnhild Tjåland, necklace UMBILLICUS, 2011, silver, dia. 80 mm

TORE SVENSSON [GUEST OF HONOUR]

TOBIAS ALM

SARA BORGEGÅRD ÄLGÅ

BEATRICE BROVIA

NICOLAS CHENG

ÅSA ELMSTAM

DANIELA HEDMAN

HANNA HEDMAN

KARIN JOHANSSON

JENNY KLEMMING

AGNIESZKA KNAP

AGNES LARSSON

KAJSA LINDBERG

PAULA LINDBLOM

ÅSA LOCKNER

MÄRTA MATTSSON

LENA OLSON

LINA PETERSON

ANNIKA PETTERSSON

MARGARETH SANDSTRÖM

SANNA SVEDESTEDT

ANNA UNSGAARD

PETER DE WIT

ANNIKA ÅKERFELT

SWEDEN

TORE SVENSSON

GUEST OF HONOUR

Born 1948

EDUCATION

1972–74 Västerberg Art School, Gävle, Sweden

1974–78 HDK School of Design and Crafts, University of Gothenburg, Gothenburg, Sweden

PUBLIC COLLECTIONS (SELECTION)

National Gallery of Australia, Canberra, Australia

Montreal Museum of Decorative Arts, Montreal, Canada

Nationalmuseum, Stockholm, Sweden

The Röhsska Museum for Fashion, Design and Decorative Arts, Gothenburg, Sweden

The Museum of Fine Arts (The Helen Williams Drutt Collection), Houston, USA

Concentration and precision form the signature style of Tore Svensson, whose work stands out for its sophisticated use of steel as a material for jewellery and hollowware. The artist prefers to create his jewellery works in conceptually unified series in which the individual pieces show a range of subtle variations in form, texture and colour. *Portraits*, his recent body of work, is a group of small medallion-like brooches depicting human heads *en face* or in profile. Using photographs as his starting point, the artist has stylised the portraits and copied them onto steel plate using diverse techniques, such as etching, gilding, linseed oil blackening and painting.

The *Portraits* series, currently comprising some fifty different brooches, opens up a distinctly new dimension in Tore Svensson's work. The careful handling of line and proportion and the technical mastery of surface textures in these works are features that echo his previous output. What is striking as new and surprising is the personal and even intimate imagery that we encounter here. Portrayed on the brooches we see the artist himself, his family, friends and close colleagues. Some pieces even catch him in a tender embrace with his girlfriend. For a maker whose work as a rule has shied away from anything private and anecdotal, tending instead to unfold as an investigation of form based on strict geometrical formulas, these brooches are a bold and challenging step.

With an internationally recognised oeuvre and a career spanning more than four decades, Tore Svensson is a key figure in Swedish jewellery and silversmithing. Apart from being a prolific studio artist, he has held the position of professor of jewellery at his alma mater, the HDK School of Design and Crafts at the University of Gothenburg, Sweden. He was also one of the founders of Hnoss, an artists-run gallery for contemporary jewellery in Gothenburg that from 1997 through to 2011 served as a leading exhibition space in Scandinavia for those working in the field.   L.J.

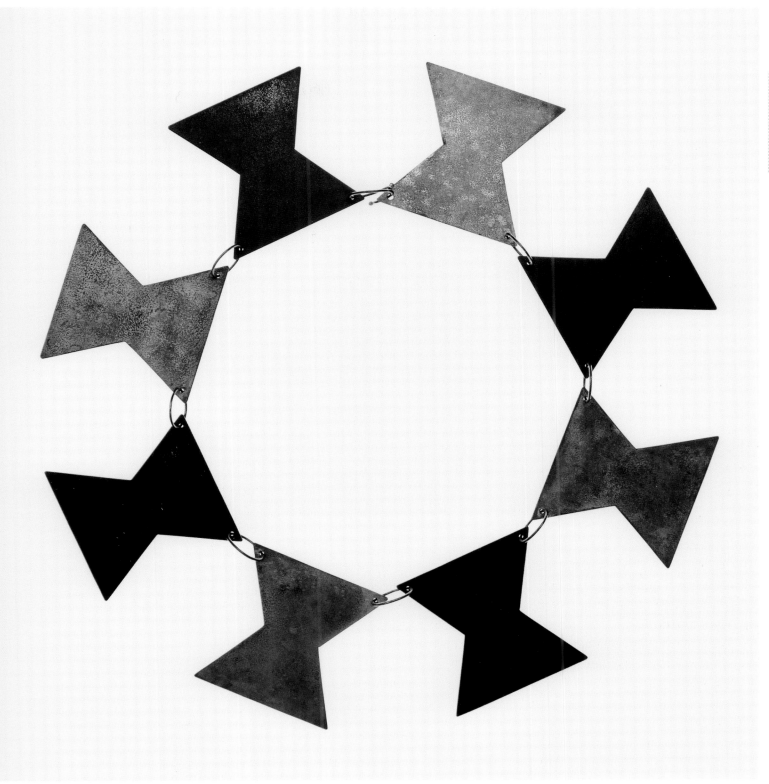

<<   p. 167 Tore Svensson, brooch MISS K, 2012, steel, 50 x 42 mm

Tore Svensson, necklace, 1999, steel, etched, silver coated, outer dia. 220 mm

Tore Svensson, brooch SH, 2012, steel, 45×35 mm

Tore Svensson, brooch COUPLE, 2011, steel, gilt, dia. 51 mm

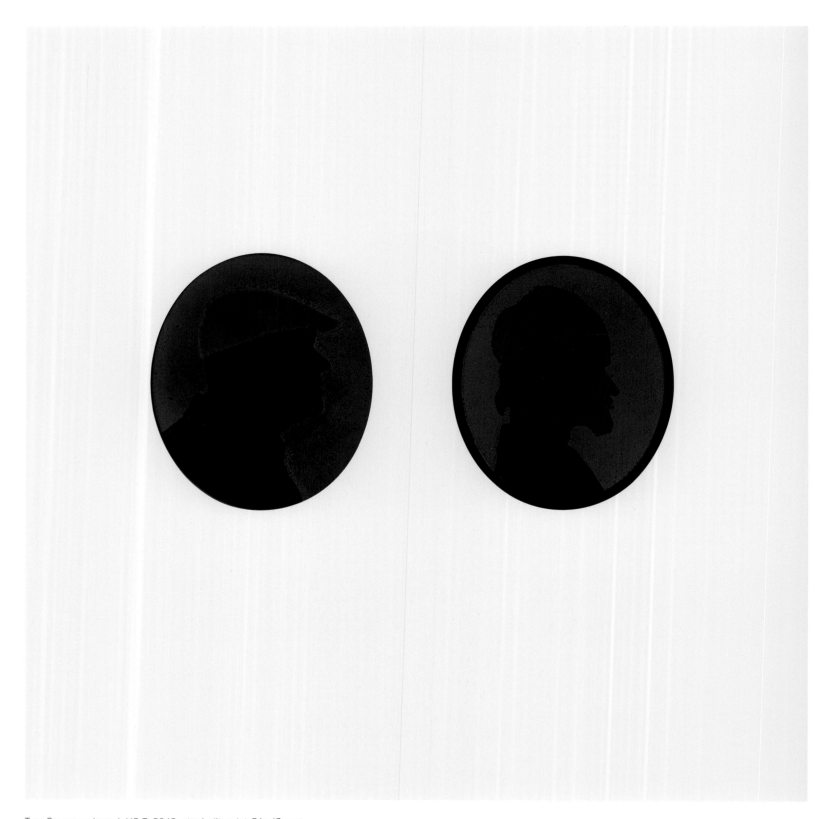

Tore Svensson, brooch MR T, 2012, steel, gilt, paint, 51×43 mm

Tore Svensson, brooch LASSE P, 2012, steel, gilt, paint, 50×42 mm

Tore Svensson, brooch ELSE, 2012, steel, gilt, 40 × 33 mm

Tore Svensson, brooch KJ, 2012, steel, paint, 50 × 42 mm

TOBIAS ALM

Born 1985

EDUCATION
2004–06 Metalsmithing, Stenebyskolan, Dals Långed, Sweden
2006–09 BFA, Ädellab, Jewellery + Corpus, Konstfack University College
of Arts, Crafts and Design, Stockholm, Sweden

The jewellery pieces included in Tobias Alm's series *Traces of Function* evoke the appearance of buttons, grip bars and coat racks, but, as things, they seem evasive and mysterious. There is a certain muteness to the forms, a lack of communication that challenges the viewer. In this connection, the artist has spoken of the interest he has developed in how a function can be perceived in an object 'without clearly knowing what it could be used for, or has been used for.' In this series, he also wants to address the question of what it is that makes something into a tool – what it is that its 'toolness' lies in. Clearly inspired by the conceptual universe of Heidegger and his famous investigation into the meaning of tools, Tobias Alm's project serves as an indicator of the ease with which today's jewellery artists bring pragmatic questions about the crafts, their function and their use, together with more high-flying abstractions of philosophy.   L.J.

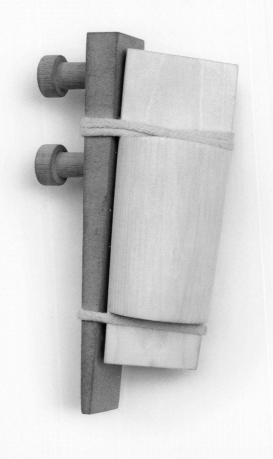

Tobias Alm, brooch TRACES OF FUNCTION XVIII, 2012, *wood, cotton, steel*, 80 × 40 × 30 mm

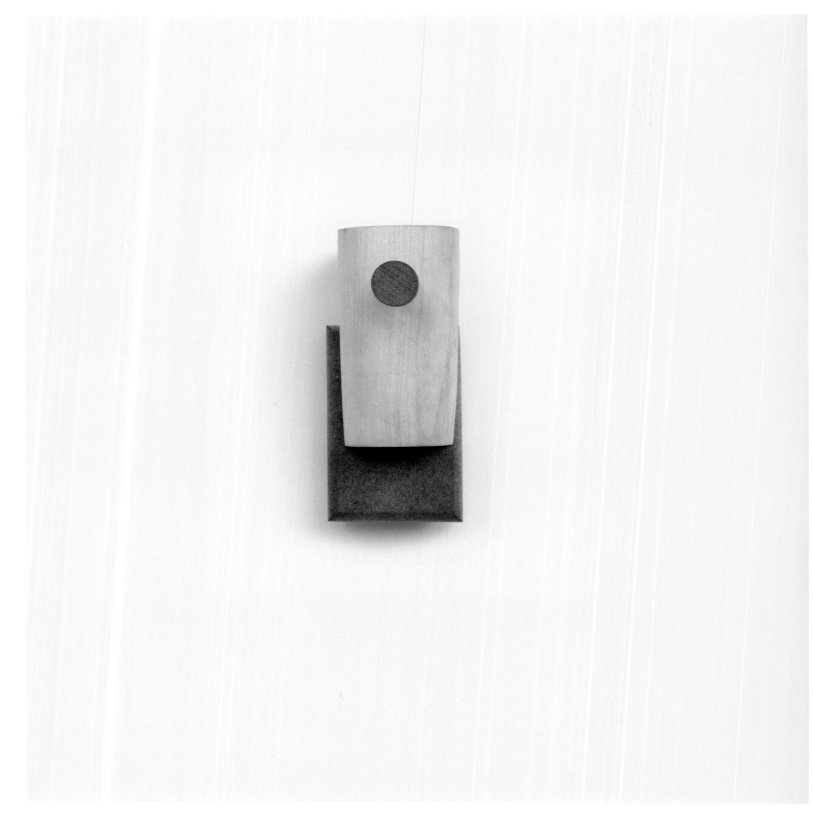

Tobias Alm, brooch TRACES OF FUNCTION XVII, 2012, wood, steel, 70×40×40 mm

Tobias Alm, neck piece TRACES OF FUNCTION XIX, 2012, *wood, cotton,* 420 × 60 × 50 mm

SARA BORGEGÅRD ÄLGÅ

Born 1976

EDUCATION
2002–07 BFA and MFA, Ädellab, Jewellery + Corpus, Konstfack
University College of Arts, Crafts and Design, Stockholm, Sweden

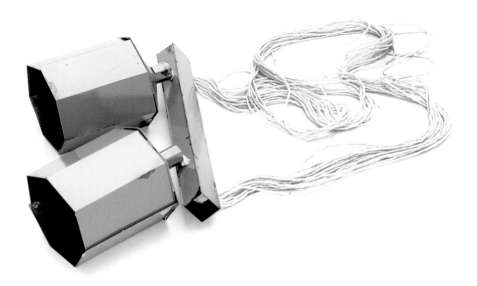

In Sara Borgegård Älgå's jewellery pieces, fragments and remainders of the industrial society often turn up and make their presence felt. Their individual details can direct thoughts to factory buildings, mine shaft towers and silos. Some of the pieces make use of wood and adhesive tape, at times to a sketch-like effect, but most often it is iron coated with a layer of protective, monochrome colour that provides the artist with her primary material. Not uncommonly, the spray-painted surfaces come in light pastel colours that create a contrast to the heavier and rougher impression produced by the iron plates joined together by soldering. Closest to the edges, the colour, as a rule, has rubbed off as if through abrasion, a reference to wear and tear and the passing of time that gives the pieces a certain elegiac quality. At the same time as these works can be interpreted as paying homage to the aesthetics of modern technology and architecture, they also suggest an understanding of themselves as a contemplation on its unavoidable decline and fall.   L.J.

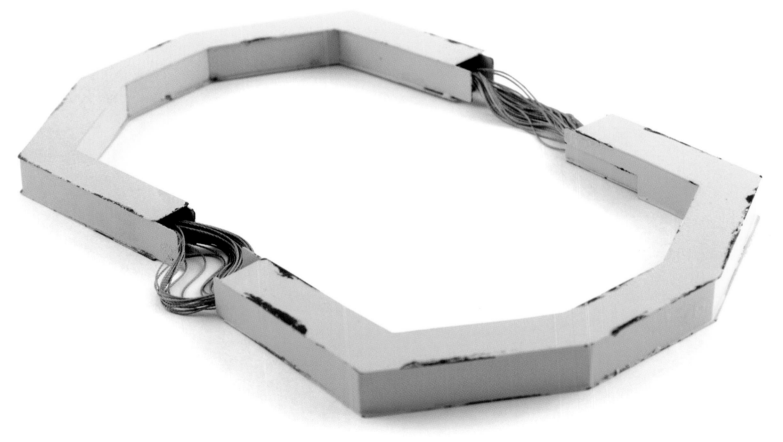

<<   Sara Borgegård Älgå, necklace SILO, 2011, iron, carpet *warp*, lacquer, 510 × 200 × 65 mm

Sara Borgegård Älgå, necklace STRAW, 2011, iron, silk thread, lacquer, 250 × 155 × 50 mm

Sara Borgegård Älgå, necklace BEAM, 2011, iron, carpet warp, 410×140×15 mm

Sara Borgegård Älgå, brooches TWILIGHT, 2011, iron, lacquer, 160 × 35 × 45 mm

BEATRICE BROVIA

Born 1985

EDUCATION
2004–07 B.Sc., Interior Architecture, Politecnico di Milano, Milano, Italy
2007–09 MFA, Ädellab, Jewellery + Corpus, Konstfack University College
of Arts, Crafts and Design, Stockholm, Sweden

Soft and voluminous, Beatrice Brovia's necklaces stimulate associations to live organs. The expressiveness of the works is enhanced by the strong symbolism of fibre and textiles, which brings to the fore the connection these materials have to the body and its clothing and its function as a provider of protection and warmth. There is, however, a transformative process that the artist's materials undergo in her hands, one whose significance she herself has drawn attention to: 'Elusive and ungraspable from the beginning, the soft masses of material are forced into bodily awkward shapes by the manic perseverance of the needlework or by the hardening of an external crust onto sponge-like sculpted forms'. With their loose ends and somewhat improvisational structure, the objects presented to us might appear incidental and imprecise. Yet they reflect a self-conscious, even analytical, approach to making, demonstrating a skilful handling of material properties.   L.J.

Beatrice Brovia, necklace BINDING WORKS II, 2010, cotton thread, binding wire, latex hose, oxidised silver, magnets, 550 × 250 × 90 mm

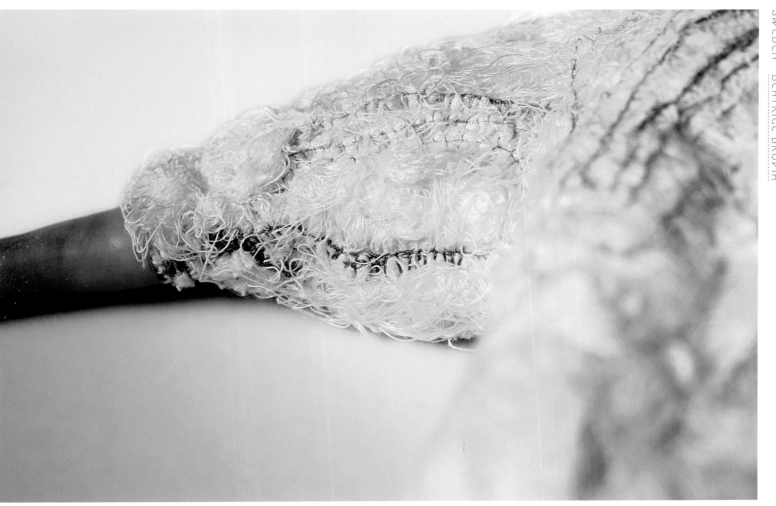

Beatrice Brovia, necklace BINDING WORKS I, 2010, silk fibres, silk threads, latex, oxidised silver, magnets, 400 × 170 × 90 mm

NICOLAS CHENG

Born 1982

EDUCATION
2004–06 BA, Design Academy Eindhoven, the Netherlands
2008–10 MFA, Konstfack University College of Arts, Crafts and Design,
Stockholm, Sweden

PUBLIC COLLECTIONS
The Metropolitan Museum of Art, New York, USA

Born in Hong Kong but trained in the Netherlands and Sweden, Nicolas Cheng is an example of the kind of internationalisation that marks art jewellery in the Nordic countries today. The artists from other parts of the world who seek their way to the North frequently bring with them an ability to adopt a fresh attitude towards the traditions of their new homeland. Nicolas Cheng has described how, in his case, the palpable presence of trees and wood, even in modern urban environments, was one of the things he experienced to be so different in Sweden. The jewellery pieces belonging to his *Wood* series are for the most part constructed from bits and pieces of wood, found in many cases in the surrounding area of his home and studio in Stockholm. The piece included in this exhibition has a part to it that can be flipped up and folded to the side, as though it were a lid of a locket popping open, revealing a small engraving made on the underlying wood. The artist has been inspired here by the texts and symbols he has seen carved into tree bark during his wanderings outdoors – for him, an expression of the way in which the lives of trees and humans gently entwine.   L.J.

<<   BROOCH I from the WOOD series, 2010 (open and closed)

Nicolas Cheng, BROOCH I from the WOOD series, 2010, silver, veneer, rubber, cotton, polyurethane, 120 × 220 × 35 mm

ÅSA ELMSTAM

Born 1978

EDUCATION
2002–06 Ädellab, Jewellery + Corpus, Konstfack University College
for Arts, Crafts and Design, Stockholm, Sweden
2006/07 Sustainable projects, Tokyo Zokei University, Japan

Through the jewellery pieces included in her *Things* series, Åsa Elmstam joins a broader movement within the crafts in depicting, manipulating and playing with objects taken from the domain
of everyday life and the home. Quite frequently, an interest in utility objects as an aesthetic cat-
egory mingles here with a desire to investigate human beings' relationships with their posses-
sions. Åsa Elmstam's necklaces, constructed of miniaturised chairs and other pieces of furniture,
open themselves up for several different interpretations: they can be understood as an expression
of the fatigue we feel from our exposure to an overabundance of things, just as well as they can be
seen as an affectionate glance at our inability to rid ourselves of things we no longer have space or
a use for. These portable arrays of miniature furniture, however, also reflect the widely held
notion of contemporary lifestyles as, in some key sense, nomadic. Rather than a fixed point in our
existence, the home is portrayed here as a set of symbolic representations that can be easily carried around.   L.J.

<<   Åsa Elmstam, earrings THINGS 4, 2010, brass, silver, 50 × 80 × 20 mm

Åsa Elmstam, necklace THINGS 3, 2010, brass, 200 × 200 × 50 mm

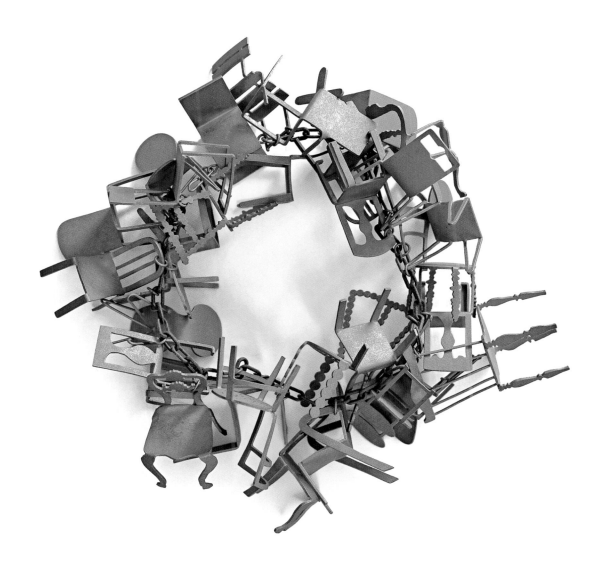

Åsa Elmstam, necklace THINGS 1, 2010, brass, plastic, 200×200×50 mm

DANIELA HEDMAN

Born 1979

EDUCATION
2002/03 Metal, Nyckelvikskolan, Lidingö, Sweden
2003–08 BA and MA, Ädellab, Jewellery + Corpus, Konstfack College
University of Arts, Crafts and Design, Stockholm, Sweden

In her series *GROUND*, Daniela Hedman reflects on the body as a physical object that is tactile and constantly in movement. Her works *TOES* and *FEET* are both part of this series while each retaining its own distinct character. *TOES*, connected together with a strip of leather to form a necklace, can at first glance come across as something primitive and grotesque, much like a prehistoric trophy, and yet it also possesses a palpable air of sensuality. The gentle finish of the wooden toes brings out the beauty of the wood, inviting them to be touched. *FEET*, in contrast, has a more monumental character to it; its pair of life-size soles made from copper plate is meant to be worn as a necklace. The sheer size of the feet and the force that must have gone into their making create an impression of heaviness, but in reality the piece is light to wear thanks to the thinness of the sheet metal used. With all its inbuilt contrasts, *FEET* gives a poetic image of the body as at once heavy, pressing against the ground, and also light, with a spring in the step – always up and about.   L.J.

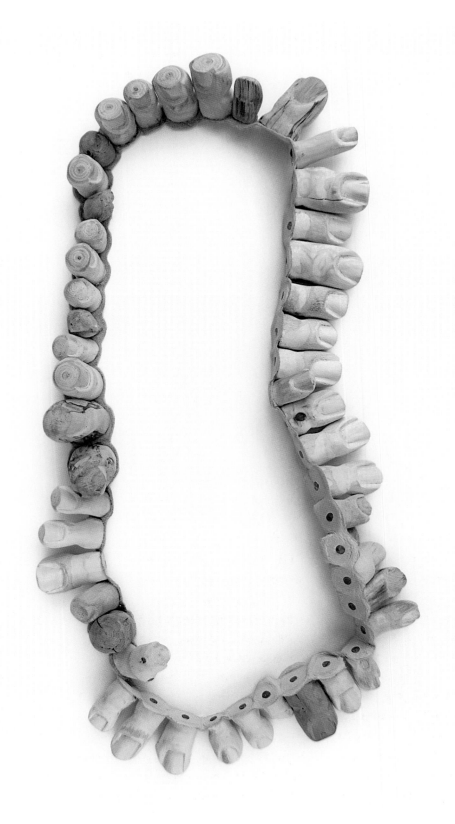

Daniela Hedman, necklace TOES from the GROUND series, 2010, *wood*, leather, copper nails, 400 × 25 × 45 mm

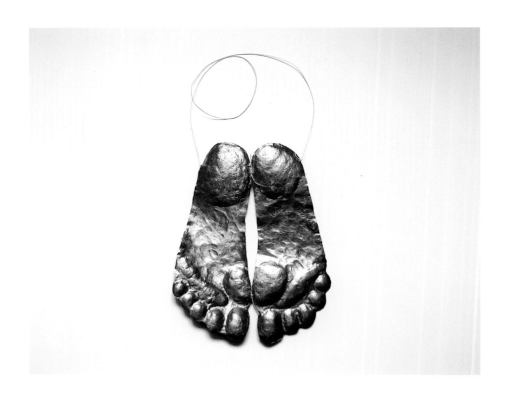

Daniela Hedman, necklace FEET from the GROUND series, 2010, copper, thread, 240 × 100 × 1 mm

HANNA HEDMAN

Born 1980

EDUCATION
2005/06 BFA, Silversmithing and Jewellery, Otago Polytechnic, Dunedin,
New Zealand
2006–08 MFA, Ädellab, Jewellery + Corpus, Konstfack University College
of Arts, Crafts and Design, Stockholm, Sweden

PUBLIC COLLECTIONS
Die Neue Sammlung – The International Design Museum Munich,
Germany
Otago Polytechnic, Dunedin, New Zealand
Nationalmuseum, Stockholm, Sweden
The Röhsska Museum of Fashion, Design and Decorative Arts,
Gothenburg, Sweden

There is often something restless about Hanna Hedman's jewellery pieces. Layers upon layers of metal plate, frequently perforated by holes, create forms that seem to twist and twine as if they wanted to expand and spill out into the room. The dense perforation gives indications of an intense work process at the same time as it gives rise to an exciting play of light and shadow. On closer inspection, one discerns some parts of the pieces to have been made in the image of animals and plants, having, not uncommonly, a marked naturalistic touch to them. In this fashion, the series *While They Await Extinction* presents us with depictions of plant and animal species threatened by, or already driven to, extinction. With reference to this group of works, the artist has commented on how we often have a romantic view of nature and the place of humans within it. Nonetheless, she reminds us, the question is about a conflicting relationship where the impact of man has been a devastating one.   L.J.

<<   Hanna Hedman, necklace SPHENISCUS MAGELLANICUS from the series WHILE THEY AWAIT EXTINCTION, 2011,
silver, oxidised silver, powder-coated copper, paint, 400 × 190 × 70 mm

Hanna Hedman, necklace PERCINA REX from the series WHILE THEY AWAIT EXTINCTION, 2011, oxidised silver, powder-coated copper, paint, 550 × 180 × 80 mm

197

KARIN JOHANSSON

Born 1964

EDUCATION
1989–94 MAF, Art Jewellery, HDK School of Design and Crafts,
University of Gothenburg, Gothenburg, Sweden

PUBLIC COLLECTIONS
The National Museum of Art, Architecture and Design, Oslo, Norway
Nationalmuseum, Stockholm, Sweden
The Röhsska Museum for Fashion, Design and Decorative Arts,
Gothenburg, Sweden

The city as a network of streets, buildings and meeting points provides the starting point for
Karin Johansson's series of works entitled *NEW PLACES: Abstractions of a City*. In it, the artist
adopts the perspective of the flaneur, offering us glimpses from a stroll about town in which individual details that captured her interest – colours, forms, scents and sounds – reappear before our
eyes, heavily stylised and attracting our attention as if they were secretive signs that tell of a
story to be told. The visual language here is familiar from the artist's previous production, yet
with their soft pastel tones and the rarefied look of their reconstructed materials, these vivacious
and witty necklaces also lend a new air to her body of works. Even the relationship between the
piece and its wearer has acquired a new dimension here: as Karin Johansson herself expressed it
when alluding to the architectonic character of these works, their wearers become inhabitants of
the new imaginary places conjured up by the necklaces.   L.J.

Karin Johansson, necklace PROPERTY from the series NEW PLACES: ABSTRACTIONS OF A CITY, 2011, gold, silver, enamel, reconstructed materials, 770 mm

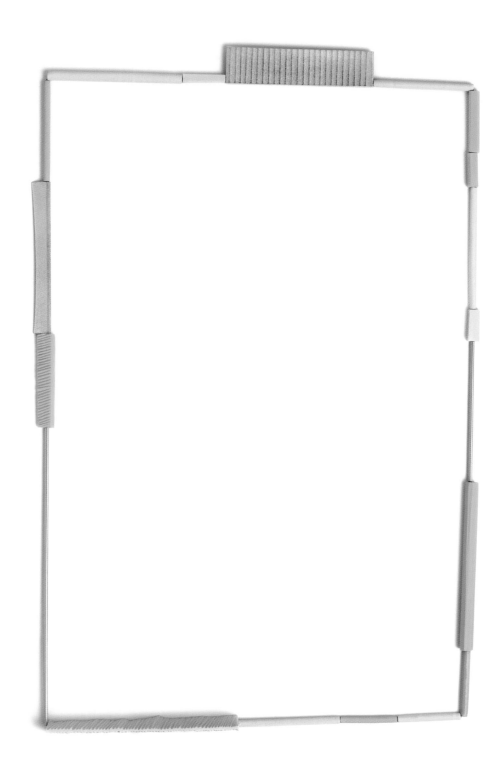

Karin Johansson, necklace EVENING SQUARE from the series NEW PLACES: ABSTRACTIONS OF A CITY, 2012, gold, silver, enamel, reconstructed materials, 950 mm

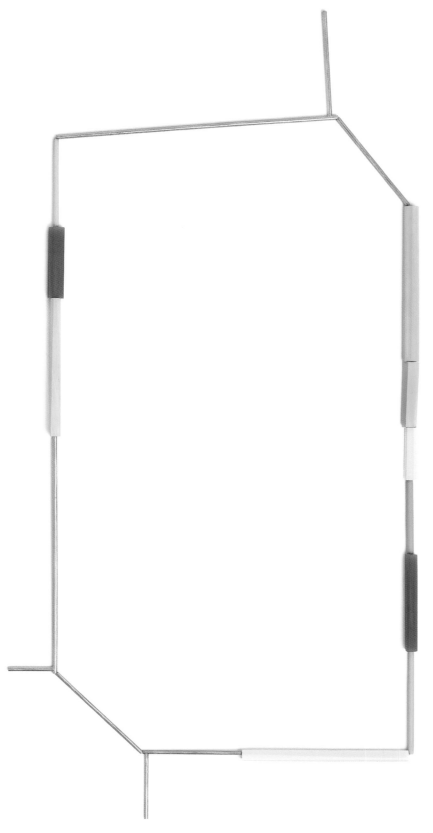

Karin Johansson, necklace BLUE SKY from the series NEW PLACES: ABSTRACTIONS OF A CITY, 2012, gold, silver, enamel, reconstructed materials, 890 mm

JENNY KLEMMING

Born 1981

EDUCATION
2003–05 Metalsmithing, Stenebyskolan, Dals Långed, Sweden
2006–10 BFA and MFA, Art Jewellery, HDK School of Design and Crafts,
University of Gothenburg, Gothenburg, Sweden

Jenny Klemming is one of the several young jewellery artists in Sweden today who use nature as their motif. Twigs and buds of various kinds frequently find their way into her works, as do references to processes such as growth and decomposition. More than any aestheticizing of nature's objects, however, what we are witnessing in this artist's pieces is an expression of her desire to debate the relationship between nature and culture. In a subtle way, her jewellery investigates the vague and often almost accidental character of the boundary rendered between that which is of nature and that which is man-made. Time, change and interpretation become of key importance here. In her artistic approach, Jenny Klemming places emphasis on the kind of long-term perspective that a well-made piece of jewellery always opens up, treasuring the fact that such a piece, when eventually leaving the artist's hands, takes off on a life of its own: 'I like the thought of the jewel's being lost, found, remade, inherited, and worn during its lifetime – that a piece of jewellery has a life span longer than, and separate from, mine.' L.J.

Jenny Klemming, necklace GREENERY, 2011, copper, steel, enamel, c. 1200 mm

203

Jenny Klemming, brooch LANDING, 2011, patinated copper, lepidolite, silver, steel, 55 × 50 × 25 mm

Jenny Klemming, brooch LACED, 2011, copper, steel, silver, lacquer, 95 × 35 × 12 mm

AGNIESZKA KNAP

Born 1966

EDUCATION
1990/91 Metal, Nyckelviksskolan, Lidingö, Sweden
1994–99 MFA, Metal Design, Konstfack University College of Arts,
Crafts and Design, Stockholm, Sweden

PUBLIC COLLECTIONS
Nationalmuseum, Stockholm, Sweden

Agnieszka Knap is one of the rather few Scandinavian jewellery artists specialising in enamelling. While her works indeed often dwell on the seductive side of the technique – showing off their intense colours and shimmering, glossy surfaces – at the same time, they tend towards a dramatic imagery that is anything but comforting. In the artist's *Anatomy of Fear*, a set of four similarly shaped pendants, a red colour field gradually takes centre stage after making its first appearance as merely a small dot on the first piece. Like a viral growth, the redness spreads until, in the last pendant, it comes to dominate completely. As is often found in Agnieszka Knap's previous work, the form and colours here have associations to flowers and leaves, but also, in particular, to the butterfly with its wings extended, or even to the Rorschach ink blot and its bilateral symmetry. This last-mentioned reference to psychology is likely to have special resonance here, given the interest the artist herself has expressed in the spontaneous, personal associations that her jewellery evokes in viewers and wearers.   L.J.

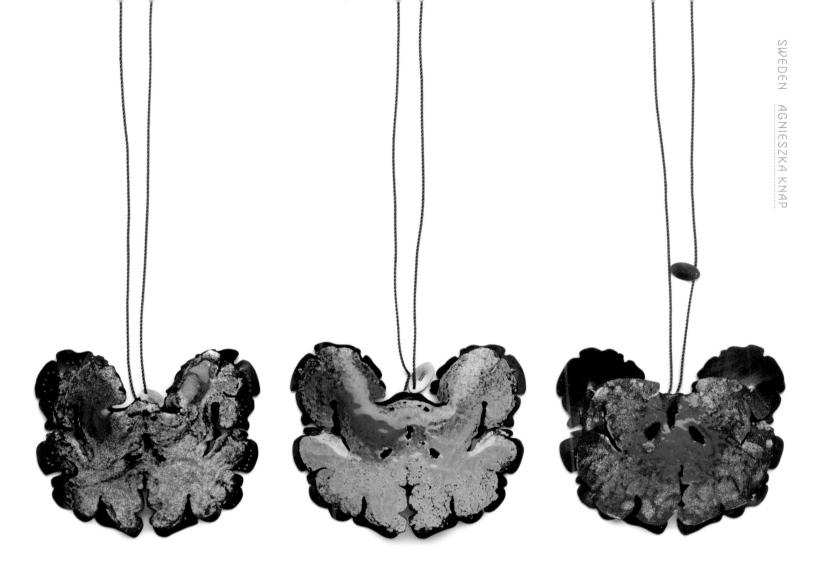

Agnieszka Knap, necklace ANATOMY OF FEAR, 2011, enamel, copper, silver, silk, 80 mm

AGNES LARSSON

Born 1980

EDUCATION
2001/02 Metal, Nyckelviksskolan, Lidingö, Sweden
2002–07 BFA and MFA, Ädellab, Jewellery + Corpus, Konstfack
University College of Arts, Crafts and Design, Stockholm, Sweden

PUBLIC COLLECTIONS
Fondazione Cominelli, Contemporary Jewellery Collection, Brescia, Italy

Grave in tone and dark in hue, Agnes Larsson's *Carbo* necklaces at first sight convey a sense of heaviness and grief. Although it is an element essential to all forms of life, carbon – the main material used in the making of these pieces – is also associated with destruction and evokes the image of a fire's charred remains. The artist's other source material, however, is horsehair, which is traditionally used in the making of ropes, mattresses and bows. Through these uses, the material carries connotations of feelings and phenomena as diverse as strength, comfort and music. In Agnes Larsson's *Carbo* series, the horsehair holds the lumps of carbon together in dramatically charged compositions animated by a tension between a simple overarching design and an inherently fragmented structure. In a few cases, the forms even seem to be teetering on the verge of disintegration. The artist herself has highlighted this duality of her works, poetically suggesting that these lightweight, sometimes shield-like pieces 'with their polished surfaces and deep cracks create a fragile protection against the outside world.' Her work offers living testimony to the fact that in-depth examinations of natural materials have not become obsolete in contemporary crafts. The chosen materials, however, are not always the expected ones, and the focus is on forming paradoxes rather than on uncovering any material essence or truth.   L.J.

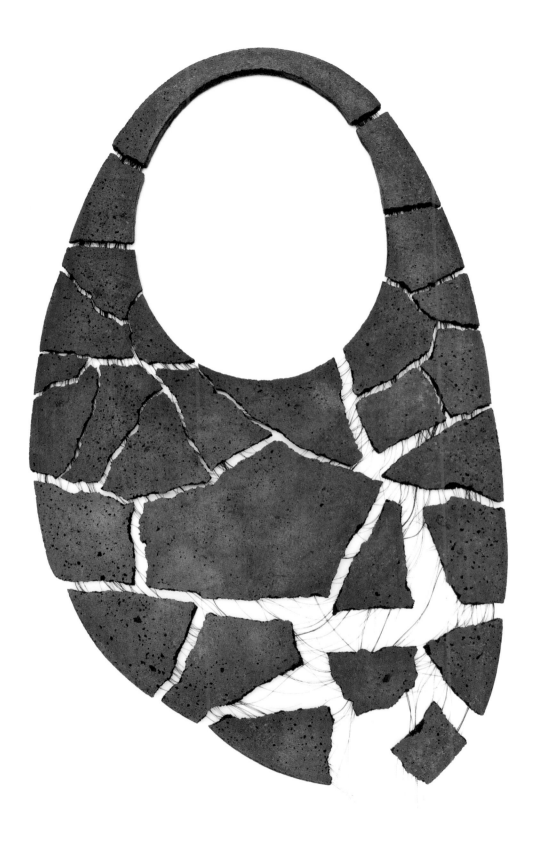

Agnes Larsson, necklace CARBO, 2010, carbon, horsehair, 500 mm

Agnes Larsson, necklace CARBO, 2010, carbon, wire, 430 mm

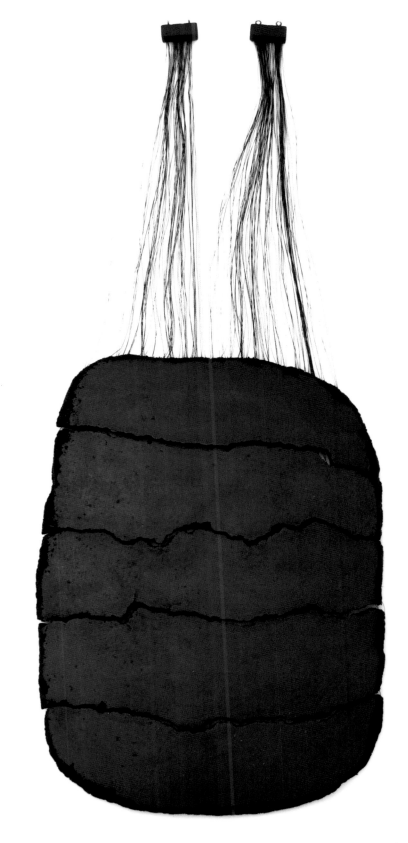

Agnes Larsson, necklace CARBO, 2010, horsehair, iron, 400 mm

KAJSA LINDBERG

Born 1980

EDUCATION
2002–08 MFA, Ädellab, Jewellery + Corpus, Konstfack University College
of Arts, Crafts and Design, Stockholm, Sweden

Jewellery is frequently worn to denote power and social prestige, and portrait art provides us
with endless opportunities to study how important persons in history have used jewellery to stage
their social identity and status. In preparing her series of works entitled *Counterfeiting*, Kajsa
Lindberg started out from the portraits of historical figures that appear on Swedish banknotes.
Among them we find kings and men of science, but also authors like Selma Lagerlöf and even the
opera singer Jenny Lind. What all these portraits have in common is that each of the individuals
in them wears some kind of jewellery. For her work shown here, Kajsa Lindberg copied out the
details of these pieces, enlarged them and printed them on pieces of canvas formed into a necklace. In an ingenious fashion, the project raises questions about money, power and jewellery and
ties them in with reflections on image and imitation, representation and re-representation.   L.J.

<<   Kajsa Lindberg, necklace 20 SEK SELMA LAGERLÖF BLACK from the series COUNTERFEITING, 2011, MDF, acrylic on canvas, screen-print, 280 × 110 × 9 mm

Kajsa Lindberg, necklace 20 SEK SELMA LAGERLÖF from the series COUNTERFEITING, 2011, MDF, acrylic on canvas, screen print, 280 × 110 × 9 mm

213

Kajsa Lindberg, necklace 500 SEK CHRISTOPHER POLHEM from the series COUNTERFEITING, 2011, MDF, acrylic on canvas, screen print, 300×140×7 mm

Kajsa Lindberg, necklace 500 SEK CHRISTOPHER POLHEM BLACK from the series COUNTERFEITING, 2011, MDF, acrylic on canvas, screen print, 300 × 140 × 7 mm

Kajsa Lindberg, necklace 1000 SEK GUSTAV VASA BLACK from the series COUNTERFEITING, 2011, MDF, acrylic on canvas, screen print, 320 × 170 × 9 mm

Kajsa Lindberg, necklace 1000 SEK GUSTAV VASA from the series COUNTERFEITING, 2011, MDF, acrylic on canvas, screen print, 320×170×9 mm

PAULA LINDBLOM

Born 1966

EDUCATION
1998–2003 BFA and MFA, Art Jewellery, HDK School of Design and
Crafts, University of Gothenburg, Gothenburg, Sweden

A common feature of Paula Lindblom's jewellery pieces is the reuse of consumer society's waste products. Objets trouvés discovered at flea markets and discarded plastic containers are combined to form jewellery with a distinct flavour of bricolage, resulting in works whose implicit criticism of our buy-and-toss society is delivered with imaginative and drastic humour. In some of the more recent pieces among these works, we meet animals set in stylised scenery, presented to us also as iterations of clichés about 'the Cold North' that mock our notions of untouched nature as a possible place of refuge. A green plastic bottle that, in its previous life, was perhaps used for toiletries now provides the habitat for a Scandinavian elk in a brooch entitled *The Essence of Nature*. In another work, a lonesome polar bear is seen walking leisurely under a starry sky, but the beauty of this picture is taken away by the title of the piece, which refers to global warming. The stars, too, in actual fact, are just holes in the sky, making one think of what is happening with our Earth's ozone layer.   L.J.

<<   Paula Lindblom, necklace POLAR BEAR – GLOBAL WARMING, 2011, everyday plastic objects/flea market findings, glass beads, glue, c. 30 x c. 60 mm, chain: c. 700 mm

Paula Lindblom, brooch THE ESSENCE OF NATURE, 2012, everyday plastic objects/flea market findings, glass beads, glue, 925 silver, c. 80 x 50 mm

ÅSA LOCKNER

Born 1973

EDUCATION
1993–99 BFA and MFA, Metal Design, Konstfack University College of Arts, Crafts and Design, Stockholm, Sweden

PUBLIC COLLECTIONS
Nationalmuseum, Stockholm, Sweden
The Röhsska Museum for Fashion, Design and Decorative Arts, Gothenburg, Sweden

The necklaces in Åsa Lockner's *Crown Jewels* series can easily appear as collage-like impromptu medleys dominated by components taken from pieces of older costume jewellery. The impression, however, is illusory, as in actual fact the pieces are all made from scratch with nothing in them originating from second-hand sources. The artist purposely plays with conventions and expectations, aiming to create an atmosphere for her works that could be recognised as something familiar from the pieces of the past. As in much of her previous production, there is something of a melancholy tone to them that gently speaks of the passing of time. The jewellery of the past is present as fragments, phantoms and imitation only. Yet, by not using actual material from older objects for her pieces, and by incorporating in them idiosyncratic details like the small piece of growth-ringed wood that attracts the attention in one of the necklaces, the artist avoids falling prey to any obvious sentimentality as such. Instead, the emphasis is on a reflection of how memories and representations of a time gone by are constructed and transformed.   L.J.

<<   Åsa Lockner, necklace CROWN JEWELS VI, 2011, silver, agates, wood, 250 × 200 × 20 mm

Åsa Lockner, necklace CROWN JEWELS VII, 2011, silver, sapphires, agates, moonstone, 220 × 150 × 10 mm

MÄRTA MATTSSON

Born 1982

EDUCATION
2005–08 BA, Art Jewellery, HDK School of Design and Crafts, University
of Gothenburg, Gothenburg, Sweden
2008–10 MA, Goldsmithing, Silversmithing, Metalwork and Jewellery,
Royal College of Art, London, Great Britain

PUBLIC COLLECTIONS
Royal College of Art, London, Great Britain
Hiko Mizuno College of Jewelry, Tokyo, Japan
Nationalmuseum, Stockholm, Sweden

Märta Mattsson's jewellery, in which real insects are often used as a material, emits a scent of
the science collections and curiosity cabinets of a bygone era. Yet, there are also clear connections
to Art Nouveau jewellery and its partiality for motifs like butterflies, dragonflies and spiders.
For the series *Fossils*, as for some of her other groups of works, Märta Mattsson has created pieces
that that captivate us with their sense of a peculiar beauty but can also leave us with a creeping
feeling of unease. We tend to associate insects with danger and anxiety, with invasion, infection
and the spread of diseases. Märta Mattsson herself has called attention to this thin line between
attraction and repulsion that forms a common theme through her works. In so doing, she joins the
ranks of many Nordic jewellery artists whose work dwells upon our relationship to nature and
upon the contradictory feelings of wonder and fear that nature often evokes.   L.J.

<<   Märta Mattsson, brooch CAMOUFLAGE, 2012, cicada, resin, glitter, silver, 90 × 90 mm

Märta Mattsson, necklace FOSSILS, 2012, cicadas, crushed azurite and pyrite, resin, silver, 400 × 700 mm

Märta Mattsson, brooch FOSSILS, 2011, cicadas, crushed pyrite, resin, silver, 150 × 150 mm

LENA OLSON

Born 1969

EDUCATION
1991–96 MFA, Art Jewellery, HDK School of Design and Crafts,
University of Gothenburg, Gothenburg, Sweden

With wood as her primary material, Lena Olson creates jewellery pieces marked by their sculptural simplicity. Their organic forms and the soft finish of their surfaces call forth associations to the human body and its skin. Most obviously this is the case with her rings, in which the direct contact between the jewellery piece and its wearer becomes a signifying element confirming the association between the artefact and the body. On another plane, the inward- and outward-curving shapes of these pieces can also be understood as providing visualisations of the bodily experiences of pressure, tension, movement and rest. Lena Olson's affectionate work with wood has left her with an intimate knowledge of its strengths and possibilities, made evident in the pieces set forth in her series. In the crafts, it has become something of a cliché to describe a maker as someone engaged in a dialogue with her or his material, but in this case the definition rings true, meaningful, and to the point.   L.J.

<<   Lena Olson, ring BRAVE, 2011, pink ebony, 80 × 30 × 25 mm
Lena Olson, ring WIND, 2011, ebony, 70 × 55 × 35 mm

Lena Olson, pendant TAN, 2011, pear wood, 110 × 40 × 35 mm

Lena Olson, pendant BLACK, 2012, ebony, 80 × 50 × 30 mm

LINA PETERSON

Born 1979

EDUCATION
2001–04 BA (Hons), Three Dimensional Crafts, University of Brighton,
Brighton, Great Britain
2004–06 MA, Goldsmithing, Silversmithing, Metalwork and Jewellery,
Royal College of Art, London, Great Britain

PUBLIC COLLECTIONS
Crafts Council Collection, Great Britain
Crafts Council Handling Collection, Great Britain
Royal College of Art, London, Great Britain
The Röhsska Museum for Fashion, Design and Decorative Arts,
Gothenburg, Sweden

There is a common theme that runs through Lina Peterson's jewellery designs and that is curiosity about the world and its things. The artist navigates through the everyday with an alert glance that fixates on aesthetically expressive details picked up from a flux of impressions and experiences. Her works often have an assembled quality to them, displaying audacious combinations of forms, colours and materials of diverse origins. Metals, plastics, wood, textile, mother-of-pearl and cardboard make their appearance in the pieces, with their admixture of natural and artificial materials coming across as a symbolically significant feature within them. In the *Mimic* brooches, it is driftwood and pebbles, found on a beach during a studio residency in Scotland, that provided the artist with her starting point. The objects from nature have been given their counterparts in cast resin and then mounted together with the latter in a manner that highlights how the authentic and the fake become bound up in a mirror view of each other.   L.J.

<<   Lina Peterson, brooch MIMIC II, 2011, pebble, resin, white precious metal, 55 × 60 × 10 mm

Lina Peterson, brooch MIMIC I, 2011, driftwood, resin, white precious metal, 120 × 95 × 30mm

231

ANNIKA PETTERSSON

Born 1981

EDUCATION
2002–04 Metalsmithing, Stenebyskolan, Dals Långed, Sweden
2004–09 BA and MA, Ädellab, Jewellery + Corpus, Konstfack University
College of Arts, Crafts and Design, Stockholm, Sweden

The age-old symbolism of the rose and other flowers is continually being revisited by contemporary jewellery artists. In her group of works entitled *Time to Rend*, Annika Pettersson undermines the romantic notion of the flower by channelling it through a visually expressive, even brutal, style. The wood debris used in the construction of her pieces comes from discarded tree trunks, violently torn and split apart by the artist. Strangely beautiful, these darkly tarnished flowers convey an image of perishability and decay. In a written commentary on her work, Annika Pettersson quotes a passage from Michel Houellebecq's novel *The Map and the Territory*: 'The beauty of flowers is sad because they are fragile and destined for death, like anything on earth, of course, but flowers are particularly fragile, and like animals their corpse is only a grotesque parody of their vital being, and their corpse, like that of an animal, stinks.' L.J.

Annika Pettersson, necklace TIME TO REND 2, 2012, *wood, iron*, 180 × 300 × 80 mm

Annika Pettersson, necklace TIME TO REND 1, 2012, wood, iron, 180×300×80 mm

Annika Pettersson, necklace TIME TO REND 3, 2012, *wood, iron, 270 × 120 × 70 mm*

MARGARETH SANDSTRÖM

Born 1950

EDUCATION

1967–1971 Guldsmedsskolan, Strålsnäs, Sweden

1971–1973 Fachhochschule für Gestaltung, Pforzheim, Germany

PUBLIC COLLECTIONS

Kulturen, Lund, Sweden

Nationalmuseum, Stockholm, Sweden

Östergötlands museum, Linköping, Sweden

The Röhsska Museum for Fashion, Design and Decorative Arts, Gothenburg, Sweden

A concern for detail and an ability, through perforation and various treatments of the exterior, to skilfully variegate the effect of the gold and silver surfaces' encounter with light have long been hallmarks of Margareth Sandström's art jewellery. Organic forms recur frequently in her output, usually through stylised representations of plant parts associated with fertility and reproduction, such as seed capsules, bean pods and maple keys. As a rule, her compositions have a graphic conciseness that accentuates contours rather than their three-dimensional shape. The artist's newer work, introducing rings adorned with highly dimensional, sculpted head shapes, represents in this sense an expansion of artistic means in her repertory. The depiction of human form, however, is in itself nothing new in Margareth Sandström's work; she is a driven practitioner of life drawing and, for a period of time, busied herself making necklaces and brooches with figurative motifs in enamel.   L.J.

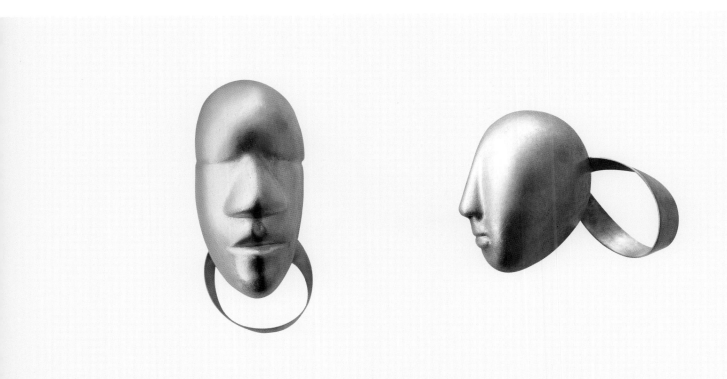

<< Margareth Sandström, ring WEARABLE OBJECT, 2011, silver, 48 × 23 × 41 mm

Margareth Sandström, ring WEARABLE OBJECT, 2011, 18 ct gold, 51 × 50 × 31 mm
Margareth Sandström, ring WEARABLE OBJECT, 2011, silver, 37 × 23 × 45 mm

SANNA SVEDESTEDT

Born 1981

EDUCATION

2004–06 Dômens konstskola, Gothenburg, Sweden

2006–09 BA, Art Jewellery, HDK School of Design and Craft, University of Gothenburg, Gothenburg, Sweden

PUBLIC COLLECTIONS

Fondazione Cominelli, Contemporary Jewellery Collection, Brescia, Italy

Sanna Svedestedt has for many years already worked with leather as a material for her jewellery pieces. In her most recent work, she enlisted for her purposes the *cuir bouilli* technique, in which the leather is first boiled in water and then fashioned into the desired shape and allowed to harden. The treatment makes the leather not just hard but also resistant and durable, which is one of the reasons it has been historically used, among other things, in the making of armoury. For her series *RAW*, Sanna Svedestedt has employed the *cuir bouilli* method to create dark-toned, expressive pieces which, at first glance, can give the impression of having been created in metal. Passing one's hand over them and picking them up, one is then surprised to find the material weighs so little. The works appear typical of the younger generation of Scandinavian jewellery artists, who nourish an active interest in nature and its materials without allowing themselves to have their work follow any beaten paths when it comes to the selection of the motifs and techniques they want to use. The impulses animating Sanna Svedestedt's work derive from both the forest and the city, and the artist herself goes on to name tree bark, rain-washed asphalt and the daring silhouettes of Elsa Schiaparelli's fashion designs as additional sources of inspiration for her series shown here.   L.J.

<< Sanna Svedestedt, RAW RING 3, 2012, cowskin, lacquer, 30 × 120 × 35 mm

Sanna Svedestedt, RAW RING 1, 2012, cowskin, lacquer, 40 × 180 × 40 mm

ANNA UNSGAARD

Born 1962

EDUCATION
1991–97 MFA, Art Jewellery, HDK School of Design and Crafts,
University of Gothenburg, Gothenburg, Sweden

In Anna Unsgaard's jewellery one often observes a tension between contour and volume, with the flat, net-like parts of her pieces playing off against details that have a more pronouncedly sculptural character. Among the artist's recurrent materials are textile thread and plant fibre, and her favoured techniques include crocheting and plaiting. In *Suns on Grass*, five crocheted balls of grass are joined with an equal number of plastic bottle caps to form a necklace. The composition builds largely on the dynamics between different forms that all embody aspects of roundness – the circle, the cylinder and the sphere. The title places the piece in a cosmic context, suggesting an identification of the yellow plastic caps with the sun and, by extension, the grass spheres with Earth. The drastic juxtaposition of the modest and the grand, of the mundane matter-of-factness of throwaway plastics and the vast perspective of the universe, is typical of the artist and befitting of the open, improvisational nature of her work.   L.J.

Anna Unsgaard, necklace SUNS ON GRASS, 2012, grass, plastic, 300 mm

PETER DE WIT

Born 1952

EDUCATION
1971–74 Fachhochschule für Gestaltung, Pforzheim, Germany
1985 Mastership diploma in goldsmithing, Linköping, Sweden

PUBLIC COLLECTIONS (SELECTION)
Designmuseum Danmark, Copenhagen, Denmark
Museum of Decorative Arts, Berlin, Germany
Nationalmuseum, Stockholm, Sweden
The Röhsska Museum for Fashion, Design and Decorative Arts,
Gothenburg, Sweden
The Museum of Fine Arts (The Helen Williams Drutt Collection),
Houston, USA

Peter de Wit is a doyen of Swedish art jewellery, unrivalled in his ability to bring variety to the eternally recurring classical shapes and to rejuvenate them with vitality and dynamics using only a minimum of means. Raised in the Netherlands and educated in Germany in the 1970s, he has served as a major conduit in Sweden for impulses coming from Continental art jewellery and can be counted as one of the early pioneers in the internationalisation of the country's art jewellery scene that only began to take place in earnest in the early 2000s. Kerstin Wickman, who has followed Peter de Wit's work over several decades, has in a recently published essay on his artistry drawn attention to an important tension residing in the formal, otherwise restrained, works typical of this maker's output: 'These are small and intimate works of art. But on closer inspection there is an entire cosmos waiting to be discovered, a universe in which the imagination can lose itself'. In this very sense, as the essayist, too, goes on to conclude, Peter de Wit's jewellery pieces 'bear within them a surprising sense of drama'.   L.J.

<<   Peter de Wit, CUBE IN A CUBE, 2011, 18 ct gold, diamonds 28 stones 1.47ct, 50 × 30 mm

Peter de Wit, ring SPHERE ON SPHERE, 2011, 18 ct gold, 59 × 37 mm
Peter de Wit, ring CUBE WITH RETRACTABLE SHANK, 2011, 18 ct gold, diamonds 18 stones 0,09 ct, 26 × 26 × 21 mm

ANNIKA ÅKERFELT

Born 1971

EDUCATION
1998–2000 Goldsmithing and Design, Lahti Polytechnic, Lahti, Finland
2000–04 BFA and MA, Art Jewellery, HDK School of Design and Crafts, University of Gothenburg, Gothenburg, Sweden

PUBLIC COLLECTIONS
Nationalmuseum, Stockholm, Sweden

Annika Åkerfelt's earliest works often reflected her interest in the body, science and hygiene. Clean, undecorated porcelain shapes were combined with metal and rubber, forming jewellery pieces that suggested associations with prostheses, medical instruments or sanitary goods. In her more recent collections, the artist has opened up the door to a more playful and humorous world, even if her materials have remained more or less the same. Now in also adorning her porcelain objects with decals, she makes room for a visual narrative that offers great possibilities for precision in line and detail. At times, the decal motifs evoke a nostalgic atmosphere of an old-school circus with men in tights and graceful ballerinas. The artist's name, inscribed on the pieces in elegant lettering, is often allowed to function as yet another decorative element of them.   L.J.

<<   Annika Åkerfelt, brooch A ON A BALLOON, 2008, porcelain, transfers for ceramics, silver, steel, 30 × 30 × 10 mm

Annika Åkerfelt, neck piece MEN ON SPHERES, 2008, porcelain, transfers for ceramics, silver, steel, plastic wire, 30 × 30 × 800 mm

AUTHORS' BIOGRAPHIES

LIESBETH DEN BESTEN [L.d.B]

Liesbeth den Besten studied art history and archaeology at the University of Amsterdam. Since 1985 working as an independent writer, curator, advisor for governmental institutions, jury member, exhibition maker and lecturer in the field of crafts and design, especially contemporary jewellery. Teaches at the Jewellery Department, Gerrit Rietveld Academy, Amsterdam. Chairwoman of the Françoise van den Bosch Foundation and member of Think Tank: A European Initiative for the Applied Arts. Publication: *On Jewellery: A Compendium of International Contemporary Art Jewellery* (Stuttgart 2011/reprint 2012).

KNUT ASTRUP BULL [K.A.B.]

Knut Astrup Bull, senior curator at The National Museum of Art, Architecture and Design in Oslo, Norway, has curated numerous exhibitions, including *Hverdagsliv: Everyday Life*, MiST – Nordenfjeldske Kunstindustrimuseum, Trondheim (2007); *Modus Operandi*, Zink Gallery, Lillehammer/MiST – Nordenfjeldske Kunstindustrimuseum, Trondheim (2009/10); *Tendencies – 2010*, F-15 Gallery, Moss (2010); and *Svein Thingnes – Ceramic 1970–2010*, Sogn og Fjordane Art Museum, Førde/MiST - Nordenfjeldske Kunstindustrimuseum, Trondheim (2010/11). Author of *En ny diskurs for kunsthåndverket – En teori om det nye konseptuelle kunsthåndverket* [A New Discourse for Decorative Art – A Theory on Contemporary Conceptual Craft] (Oslo 2007); *Modus operandi – hensiktsmessighetens estetikk* [Modus Operandi – The Aesthetics of Appropriateness] (Trondheim 2009); and *Svein Thingnes – keramikk 1970–2010* [Svein Thingnes – Ceramics 1970–2010] (Sogn og Fjordane 2010).

WIDAR HALÉN [W.H.]

Dr Widar Halén, director of Design and Decorative Arts at The National Museum of Art, Architecture and Design in Oslo, Norway, earned his doctorate at Oxford University with his work 'Christopher Dresser and the Cult of Japan' (1988). He is author of the monograph *Christopher Dresser: A Pioneer of Modern Design* (London 1990; new ed. 1993) and *Norway's Silver Heritage* (Oslo 1997); editor and co-author of *Art Déco, Funkis, Scandinavian Design* (Oslo 1996), *Christopher Dresser and Japan* (Tokyo 2002), and *Scandinavian Design Beyond The Myth: 50 Years of Nordic Design* (Stockholm 2003); and co-author of *The Persistence of Craft* (London 2002), *Grete Prytz Kittelsen: Enamel and Design* (Oslo 2008, New York 2012), and *Norway Says 10* (Oslo 2009). Author of more than one hundred scholarly articles in Norwegian and international art periodicals and organiser of several exhibitions and accompanying catalogues. Member of the boards of The Nordic Forum for Design History, and the Torsten and Wanja Søderberg Prize Committee. Former president of ICOM–ICDAD.

LOVE JÖNSSON [L.J.]

Love Jönsson is a curator at The Röhsska Museum for Fashion, Design and Decorative Arts in Gothenburg, Sweden. His articles, essays and reviews on contemporary crafts have appeared in numerous publications both in Sweden and abroad. From 2005 to 2011, he was a visiting lecturer on the history and theory of crafts at the HDK School of Design and Crafts at the University of Gothenburg, Sweden.

CHARLOTTE MALTE [C.M.]

Charlotte Malte is head of projects and coordinations at Designmuseum Danmark. She has worked in the museum since 2002. Charlotte Malte earned an MA in design history from the University of Copenhagen with her work 'Blåkant Øjets Triumf – et bud på linjerne i Grethe Meyers design' (2009). From 2005 to 2006 she was employed as head of Grønbechs Gård, an exhibition space in Bornholm, specializing in arts and crafts. She has participated in the writing of *De Industrielle Ikoner: design Danmark* (Copenhagen 2004) and has worked as photo editor of *Design – køkkenet* (Copenhagen 2008) and *Design – stolen* (Copenhagen 2009).

PÄIVI RUUTIAINEN [P.R.]

Päivi Ruutiainen, MA, Doctor of Arts (Art and Design) from the University of Lapland, lives in Lahti, Finland. Thesis: 'Is a Phone Booth Jewellery? Contemporary Jewellery in the Field of Art' (Rovaniemi 2012). Lecturer at HUMAK University of Applied Sciences in Kauniainen since 1999 and has written art critiques since 1992, with critiques and articles in Finnish newspapers, magazines and publications. Has curated two contemporary jewellery exhibitions: *Ash and Diamonds* (Helsinki, Stockholm, Lahti, Lapperanta) and *Water and Earth* (Espoo and Reyjkavik).

JUKKA SAVOLAINEN [J.S.]

Jukka Savolainen, director of the Design Museum in Helsinki, Finland, studied art history at St. Andrews University, St Andrews, Scotland, and is currently completing a doctorate in design history at Kingston University, London. He has curated several exhibitions and accompanying catalogues, including *Art Deco 1918–1939* (Helsinki 2005), *Fennofolk – New Nordic Oddity* (Helsinki 2008), *Modern[ism]* (Helsinki 2010) and most recently *Designworld – Designing the New World* (Helsinki 2012).

HARPA THÓRSDÓTTIR [H.T.]

Harpa Þórsdóttir is director of the Museum of Design and Applied Art, Reykjavík, Iceland, and former head of exhibitions at the National Gallery of Iceland. Has curated numerous exhibitions in Iceland on arts, crafts and design. Publications include Ólafur Kvaran (ed.), *Íslensk listasaga, 5. bindi* [Icelandic Art History, vol. 5]; 'Gjörningar, tímatengd verk og myndbandslist' [Performance Art: time-based art and videos] (2011); *Jólaskeiðin, íslensk hönnun og smíði 1946–2008* [The Icelandic Christmas Silver Spoon, from 1946–2008] (Hönnunarsafn Íslands 2008); *Vefur lands og lita, Júlíana Sveinsdóttir*

[Catalogue]; and 'Ofið úr íslenskri ull Júlíana Sveinsdóttir' [Weaving with Icelandic wool, Juliana Sveinsdottir] (Listasafn Íslands 2003).

JORUNN VEITEBERG [J.V.]

Jorunn Veiteberg, PhD in history of art from the University of Bergen, lives and works in Bergen, Norway, and Copenhagen, Denmark. Associate professor at Bergen Academy of Art and Design since 2002 and HDK School of Design and Crafts at the University of Gothenburg since 2012. Publications include *Craft in Transition* (Bergen 2005); *Sigurd Bronger: Laboratorium Mechanum* (Stuttgart 2011); *Thing Tang Trash: Upcycling in Contemporary Ceramics* (Bergen 2011); and *Konrad Mehus: Form Follows Fiction. Jewellery and Objects* (Stuttgart 2012).

IMPRINT

© 2013 ARNOLDSCHE Art Publishers, Stuttgart, The National Museum of Art, Architecture and Design, Oslo, and the authors

All rights reserved. No part of this work may be reproduced or used in any forms or by any means (graphic, electronic or mechanical, including photocopying or information storage and retrieval systems) without written permission from the copyright holders ARNOLDSCHE Art Publishers, Liststraße 9, D–70180 Stuttgart, www.arnoldsche.com, and the National Museum of Art, Architecture and Design, Oslo.

EDITOR
Widar Halén

AUTHORS
Liesbeth den Besten
Knut Astrup Bull
Widar Halén
Love Jönsson
Charlotte Malte
Päivi Ruutiainen
Jukka Savolainen
Harpa Thórsdóttir
Jorunn Veiteberg

PROJECT COORDINATOR
Martina Kaufmann, Art in Motion, Oslo

ARNOLDSCHE PROJECT COORDINATOR
Marion Boschka

ENGLISH TRANSLATIONS
Peter Cripps, Linda Sandoval

ENGLISH TEXT EDITING
Wendy Brouwer, Stuttgart

LAYOUT
Silke Nalbach, nalbach typografik, Mannheim

OFFSET REPRODUCTIONS
Repromayer, Reutlingen

PRINTED BY
Gulde Druck, Tübingen

PAPER
Galaxi Supermat 170 g/sqm

Printed on PEFC certified paper. This certificate stands throughout Europe for long-term sustainable forest management in a multi-stakeholder process.

Bibliographic information published by the Deutsche Nationalbibliothek
The Deutsche Nationalbibliothek lists this publication in the Deutsche Nationalbibliografie; detailed bibliographic data are available in the Internet at www.d-nb.de.

ISBN 978-3-89790-373-9

Made in Germany, 2013

COVER ILLUSTRATION
Lillan Eliassen, necklace EVERY ROAD IS JUST ANOTHER WAY HOME, 2012 (see p.155)

BACKCOVER
Lena Olson, BRAVE, 2011 (p.227)
Liv Blåvarp, SUNDANCE II, 2010 (p.145)
Anna Rikkinen, A DUTCH ENCOUNTER IV, 2011 (p.119)
Kaori Juzu, INTERFERENCE I, 2011 (p.49)
Maarja Niinemägi, WAVE CREST, 2011 (p.74)
Hildur Ýr Jónsdóttir, BEAUTY OR A BEAST, 2012 (p.125)

PHOTOCREDIT
© VG Bild-Kunst, Bonn 2013: Annika Akerfelt, Sigurd Bronger, Linnéa Blakéus Calder, Lillan Elisassen, Aino Favén, Karin Johansson, Agnieszka Knap, Mervi Kurvinen, Åsa Lockner, Konrad Mehus, Lena Olson, Tone Vigeland

Lauri Asanti pp.122/3; Anders Sune Berg p.42; Irina Borsma p.44; Kim Buck pp.10, 39, 40, 41, 43; Linnéa Blakéus Calder p.151; elStudio p.199; Jeppe Gudmundsen p.60; Mats Håkanson pp.220/1; Anne Hansteen Jarre/The National Museum of Art, Architecture and Design, Oslo p.27, 36; Andreas Harvik/The National Museum of Art, Architecture and Design, Oslo p.26; Markus Henttonen pp.115–9; Børre Høstland/The National Museum of Art Architecture and Design, Oslo p.19 (left); Dorte Krogh p.61; Auvo Lukki p.19 (right); Laila Meyrick/velour.no pp.160–3; Lina Peterson pp.230/1; Sanna Svedestedt pp.226–9, 238/9; Truls Teigen/The National Museum of Art, Architecture and Design, Oslo p.20; Tanel Veenre pp.86–9

EXHIBITION VENUES

The National Museum – The Museum of Decorative Arts and Design, Oslo, Norway / Nasjonalmuseet – Kunstindustrimuseet, Oslo, Norge
19.1.–21.4.2013

Designmuseum Danmark, Copenhagen, Denmark / Designmuseum Danmark, København, Danmark
28.6.–15.9.2013

Design Museum, Helsinki, Finland / Designmuseo, Helsinki, Finland
29.11.2013–12.1.2014

Estonian Museum of Applied Art and Design / Eesti Tarbekunsti- ja Disainmuuseum
7.3.–11.5.2014

Röhsska Museum for Fashion, Design and Decorative Arts, Gothenburg, Sweden / Röhsska museet, Göteborg, Sverige
31.5.–21.9.2014

Galerie Handwerk, Munich, Germany / Galerie Handwerk, München, Deutschland
March 2015

THIS BOOK HAS BEEN PRODUCED WITH THE GENEROUS SUPPORT OF

Kulturkontakt Nord
Norden – Kulturkontakt Nord

Nordic Culture Fund
Norden – Nordisk Kulturfond

KULTURRÅDET
Arts Council Norway
Arts Council Norway

DAVID-ANDERSEN
David-Andersen AS

THUNE
Jewelry & Watches
Thune AS

AND THE PARTNER MUSEUMS IN DENMARK, ESTONIA, FINLAND AND SWEDEN

DESIGN MUSEUM DANMARK
Designmuseum Danmark, Copenhagen, Denmark

EESTI TARBEKUNSTI- JA DISAINIMUUSEUM
ESTONIAN MUSEUM OF APPLIED ART AND DESIGN
Estonian Museum of Applied Art and Design, Tallinn, Estonia

DESIGNMUSEO
Design Museum, Helsinki, Finland

Röhsska Museum for Fashion, Design and Decorative Arts, Gothenburg, Sweden

THIS PROJECT IS A COOPERATION BETWEEN

NASJONALMUSEET
The National Museum – The Museum of Decorative Arts and Design, Oslo

KUNSTHØGSKOLEN I OSLO
OSLO NATIONAL ACADEMY OF THE ARTS
Oslo National Academy of the Arts and

NORWEGIAN ASSOCIATION FOR ARTS AND CRAFTS
the Norwegian Association for Arts and Crafts.

REPTILES – Their Latin Names Explained

REPTILES
Their Latin Names Explained
A Guide to Animal Classification

A. F. Gotch

BLANDFORD PRESS
POOLE · NEW YORK · SYDNEY

First published in the UK 1986 by Blandford Press
Link House, West Street, Poole, Dorset BH15 1LL

Copyright © 1986 Blandford Press Ltd

Distributed in the United States by
Sterling Publishing Co, Inc,
2 Park Avenue, New York, NY 10016

Distributed in Australia by
Capricorn Link (Australia) Pty Ltd
PO Box 665, Lane Cove, NSW 2066

British Library Cataloguing in Publication Data

Gotch, A.F.
  Reptiles: their Latin names explained.
  1. Reptiles—Nomenclature
  I. Title
  597.9'0142   QL645
  ISBN 0 7137 1704 1

Typeset by August Filmsetting, Haydock, St. Helens
Printed in Great Britain by Biddles Ltd, Guildford and Kings Lynn

Contents

5

Acknowledgements

The executors of the late A. F. Gotch wish to thank the following people for their help to the author in writing this volume:

Dr E. N. Arnold, British Museum (Natural History)
Professor A. Bellairs
L. R. Conisbee
Dr H. B. Cott
M. J. Gardener
L. G. Kelleway, University College of Swansea, Department of Zoology

and any other person who may have been overlooked inadvertently. Particular thanks are due to S. B. Wills for preparing the manuscript for publication.

1   Generic and Specific Names

The student or amateur naturalist who is interested in the study of systematic zoology is faced with a formidable array of Latin and Greek words, and also with a system of grouping the animals into phyla, classes, orders and families which have little or no meaning to the layman. In this book, my aim is to explain this arrangement and give a meaning to the names by translating them into English; no attempt is made to describe the animals other than the features and associations that explain the reason for the scientific name.

Carl Linnaeus (1707–1778), the famous Swedish botanist, was responsible for the first real attempts to classify and name living organisms, although Aristotle had done some work on a simple form of classification as long ago as 384 BC. In 1761, Linnaeus was granted a patent of nobility, antedated to 1757, and was then styled Carl von Linné, although the name Linnaeus is still used in classification. He gave scientific names to many animals in addition to plants; he named worms and other invertebrates, and fishes, amphibians, reptiles, birds and mammals, and his system of classification and nomenclature is still in use throughout the world. The authoritative tenth edition of his *Systema Naturae* was published in 1758, and this is an all-important date, January 1st of that year being the starting point; all scientific names given before that date are considered invalid.

The Linnaean classification is known as the binominal (or binomial) system, i.e. 'two names'; every plant and animal must be given two names. The first is the generic name (from *genus* which is Latin for 'birth' or 'origin') and a genus

7

comprises a group of closely related animals or plants; the second is the specific name, the name of the actual species, which distinguishes it from any other animal in that group and so from any other animal in the world.

The generic name should be a noun, written with an initial capital, and the specific name should be an adjective, though sometimes it is a noun; it should be written with a small initial letter even if it is a proper name of a place or person, and both names should be in *italics*. To be completely authentic, it should be followed by the name of the zoologist who first gave the animal that name and the date of naming; for example the Toad-headed Agama would be *Phrynocephalus mystaceus* Pallas 1776. The author's name and date should not be in italics; if there has been a change of the generic name, as sometimes happens, the original author's name will be given in parentheses; in written work, underlining can be used to indicate *italics*. This information about the author and date is not always necessary in zoological publications and is not given in this book.

PRIORITY

The saying goes: 'Priority is the basic principle of zoological nomenclature'; the first scientific name given to an animal after January 1st 1758 stands, even though eventually it turns out to be not descriptively accurate. However, by its plenary powers, the International Commission on Zoological Nomenclature can moderate the application of this rule for a special reason, or to preserve long-established names, in order to avoid inconvenience and confusion. A recent ruling has discouraged zoologists from digging out and reviving long forgotten names; they must not displace names that have been accepted for fifty years or more.

HOMONYMS

A new name for an animal is considered invalid if it has been used previously for some other form in the animal kingdom, as this would result in the same name for two different animals; it is known as a homonym. A difference of one letter is sufficient distinction, for example *Apis*, *Apos* and *Apus* are not homonyms. *Platypus* was given as the scientific name for the Duckbill in 1799, but the name had been used for a beetle some years before; it was therefore invalid and a new name had to be given; this was *Ornithorhynchus*.

SYNONYMS

In some cases, alternative names are used and recognised; for example in the primates, an author may use Prosimii and Simiae for the names of the suborders: *pro* (L) before, and *simia* (L) an ape, a monkey; i.e. 'early monkeys' or 'primitive monkeys', and 'modern monkeys'; another author may use Lemuroidea and Anthropoidea: *anthrōpos* (Gr) man, and *-oides* (New L) from *eidos* (Gr) shape, resemblance; i.e. 'lemur-like' and 'man-like'. For the Alligator Snapper, in the family Chelydridae, some authors may use *Macrochelys temminckii* and others *Macroclemys temminckii* (see p. 40). These are known as synonyms and will be shown thus: *Macrochelys temminckii* (= *Macroclemys*). If a generic name has been rejected and considered invalid, but still appears in some publications, it will be shown thus: *Lacerta sicula sanctistephani* (formerly *sancti-stephani*), see p. 106.

TAUTONYMS

It will be seen that, in some cases, the Latin name of an animal has the generic name repeated for the specific name, for example the Loggerhead Turtle *Caretta caretta*. This is known as a tautonym, from *tauton* (Gr) the same and *onoma* (Gr) a name; this has come about because of a change in the generic name; a rule states that the specific name *may not be changed*, even though it results in a tautonym. The ruling has been modified for botanical names and tautonyms are not used.

I would like to quote an extract from an article by Mr Michael Tweedie, which appeared in the magazine *Animals* (now *Wildlife*), and at the same time thank him for permission to do so:

'The wren was among the birds that Linnaeus himself named, and he called it *Motacilla troglodytes*. Under his genus *Motacilla* he included a number of small birds which ornithologists have now split up into several genera, reserving *Motacilla* for the wagtails. In naming the American wren-like birds in the first decade of the 19th century, the French authority Vieillot chose the Linnaean specific name *troglodytes* (troglodyte or cave-dweller, by reference to the form of the nest) as a generic name. Later it was found that the European wren was so closely allied to these that it must go in Vieillot's genus, so it became *Troglodytes troglodytes*.'

The Code (i.e. the rules) of the International Commission on Zoological Nomenclature states that the name of the nominate subspecies must repeat the specific name of the species (see Chapter 2, p. 16). Thus, when subspecies were named, the nominate subspecies of the wren group had to be *Troglodytes troglodytes troglodytes*. The veteran zoologists, who were classical scholars, thoroughly disliked this and there were heated interchanges of correspondence, and they refused to use these 'monstrosities'; but as they passed from the scene the modernists prevailed, the rules were accepted, and so some stability was achieved.

Some authors state that a tautonym indicates the common species in a genus, but this can be misleading; it may, however, in certain cases, indicate the type species. It is true to say that, quite often, the common species, after a change in its generic name, does then have such a name; for example, the Common Skink *Scincus scincus* and the Common Gecko *Gekko gekko*. On the other hand, the names of many common species do not have the tautonymous form; for example, the Common European Viper *Vipera berus* and the Common Chameleon *Chamaele dilepis*.

TYPE SPECIES

The first species to be named in a particular genus is usually, though not always, the type species. Other species in that genus will resemble it more than those in a different genus and they will be distinguished by their specific names; for example *Clemmys guttata* the Spotted Turtle and *Clemmys marmorata* the Pacific Pond Turtle.

ORIGIN OF NAMES

The Latin name of an animal might originate from the naturalist who first discovered it, but it is more likely that it would originate from a zoologist working in a laboratory and studying the anatomy of the animal; the specific name is quite often given in honour of the person who discovered it or some well-known zoologist. The Patagonian Lizard was given the name *Diplolaemus darwinii*, from the Greek *diploē*, a fold, and *laimos*, the throat, an allusion to the folds of skin around the neck; the specific name was given in honour of Charles Darwin, the well-known nineteenth-century English zoologist and author of *The Origin of Species*.

USE OF LATIN AND GREEK

The advantages of using Latin and Classical Greek are obvious; if Linnaeus had used the Swedish language his system would not have been accepted internationally and, in any case, other countries would not have understood it. In those days, Latin was the international language of European scholars and Linnaeus wrote most of his scientific work in Latin to make it more widely read and understood. Even today there are classical scholars throughout the world who are familiar with Latin and Classical Greek and who understand the meaning of the words. It is true they would find some of the words wrongly construed and incorrectly spelt, and even hybridised, combining a mixture of Latin and Greek to form one word; anathema to the purist. Sometimes they are obscure native words which are known as 'barbarisms', and even a 'coined' invention, with no proper meaning and not explained by the zoologist when he described the animal and gave the name. By international agreement, once these names appear in print and are accepted by the International Commission on Zoological Nomenclature, any mistakes must remain.

However the 1961–1963 revised Code permits correction of spelling, for example the name *Alligator mississippiensis*, the American Alligator, has been misspelt as *mississipiensis* since the name was given in 1802, but now it can be corrected. The Code also now forbids the use of hyphens and diacritic marks such as the apostrophe, the diaeresis and the umlaut: so *Hyperoödon* becomes simply *Hyperoodon* and *mülleri* becomes *muelleri*. The Comma Butterfly *Polygonia c-album*, meaning 'many-angled with a white c' has the honour of being allowed to use the hyphen; one of the very few exceptions. The name refers to a white letter 'c'which is plainly marked on the under surface of each wing.

The classical significance of the names is not of first importance, but some knowledge of Latin and Greek is a help in remembering the names and will often tell you something about the animal; for instance *Hydrosaurus amboinensis* must surely mean a lizard that lives in or near water, and probably comes from a place called Amboin; so, for the specific name, a Greek or Latin dictionary will not help, but an atlas could give the answer: it inhabits Amboina (=Ambon Island) in the Moluccas, and is known as a Water Lizard. The real importance of the names is that they are international fixed labels, identifying a particular species for zoologists throughout the world.

In many cases the names are derived from Greek words, but they are 'Latinised', that is to say they are put in a Latin form and so are referred to as 'Latin names'; it is the popular term but rather disparaged by zoologists who prefer to call them 'scientific names'; purists even suggest that the correct term is 'Linnaean names'.

PECULIAR NAMES

Sometimes the names are just invented; when Boddaert, in 1783, named the Kookaburra, or Laughing Jackass as it is sometimes called, he was so hard put to it in deciding on a generic name that would distinguish it from other kingfishers, that he used the word *Dacelo*; the generic name of the Common Kingfisher is *Alcedo* which is Latin for a kingfisher; *Dacelo* is simply an anagram of *Alcedo*.

Many other peculiar names have been given apart from anagrams, for instance *Ia io* for a bat, named by Oldfield Thomas; the shortest name ever given to a mammal. Ia was a young woman of classical times and Thomas says: 'Like many women of those times a bat is essentially flighty'; *io* is a Latin exclamation of joy, like hurrah! He obviously had a sense of humour. An inveterate 'coiner' of names, he also invented *Zyzomys* for an Australian mouse but never gave an explanation; perhaps he wanted to make sure that it would appear last in any index! Dr P. Boddaert (1730–1796) was a Danish zoologist; Oldfield Thomas was an English zoologist and was at one time curator of mammals at the British Museum (Natural History), in London.

LOCAL AND PERSONAL NAMES

Many zoologist have used the names of little-known localities such as Amboina, mentioned above, which can make interpretation difficult, and there are references to ancient Greek mythology which may have no special significance (see notes under *Eryx jaculus* on p. 128). Very often a naturalist or collector who discovered the animal is honoured by using his or her name; Derjugin's Lizard *Lacerta derjugini* was named in honour of Dr K. M. Derjugin (1878–1938) of the Leningrad State University. Commemorative names usually have -*i*, -*ii*, or -*iana* added to the name to form the genitive if the person is a man, and -*ae*, or -*iae* if a woman; in rare cases, two people are honoured, for example a zoologist and his wife, so the genitive plural *-orum* will be used. Note that, in such cases, the specific name is written with a small initial letter in accordance with the rules of nomenclature, although it is a personal name.

MISLEADING NAMES

Some animals have been given a name that is misleading when translated; this may have come about because they were named when knowledge of them was incomplete; here are some examples: *anguis* (L) a snake, was used for the Slow-worm, which is not a snake but a legless lizard; *galē* (Gr) a weasel or marten-cat, used for a Wallaby, which is a marsupial; and *kapros* (Gr) a wild boar, used for the Hutiacouga, which is a rodent.

2 Separating the Animals into Groups

A division or group is known as a taxon, plural taxa, from the Greek word *taxis*, an arrangement, though the term is not often used for groups higher than classes. The divisions are named as shown in the following list, the main divisions in the left-hand column:

KINGDOM
Subkingdom
PHYLUM
Subphylum
Superclass
CLASS
Subclass
Superorder
ORDER
Suborder
Superfamily
FAMILY
Subfamily
Genus
Subgenus
Species
Subspecies (or *Race*)

These categories do not all have to be used in the classification of any particular group or species; each division or subdivision is given its own name as will be seen in Chapter 6 onwards. For example, the very big snake family Colubridae, which includes the Grass Snakes, the Smooth Snake, the Milk Snake, the Rat

15

Snakes, and many others, has been divided into subfamilies, one of these being Natricinae, the Grass Snakes or Water Snakes; and this subfamily has been divided into several subspecies.

A subspecies will have a subspecific name, for example the Adriatic Ruin Lizard *Lacerta sicula adriatica*; this is known as trinominal (or trinomial), i.e. three names. It is a subspecies of the Ruin Lizard *Lacerta sicula*. A rule made by the International Commission on Zoological Nomenclature states that the subspecific name of the species on which a group is founded must be the same, i.e. it must *repeat* the specific name. Thus in this case it becomes *Lacerta sicula sicula*; therefore it is easily distinguished and is known as the nominate subspecies. A subspecies is always basically the same as the species, but there is some slight difference; it usually has a different geographical distribution and develops different characteristics and colour patterns.

In deciding to which particular taxon an animal belongs, the zoologist must study its anatomy; during the early days of classification not enough attention was paid to this aspect and many animals were placed in the wrong taxon simply because of their outward appearance. These mistakes have gradually been corrected over the years and animals have been moved into a different genus, which accounts for the tautonymic names (see p. 9). However, there is always likely to be a difference of opinion among the scientists concerned in this work; during a discussion on the classification of mammals, Baron Cuvier, the famous French zoologist, is reputed to have said:

'Show me your teeth and I will tell you what you are'.

Apart from the anatomical structure some notice is taken of the habits of an animal: where does it live, what does it eat? As already mentioned it is no use looking at an animal and deciding from its appearance to which group it belongs; for instance, consider the lizard known in Great Britain as the Slow-worm; the uninitiated, on seeing this animal, would cry:

'Look, a snake'! Further, many would probably get a stick and beat the poor thing to death, though a more harmless and docile little creature it would be difficult to find; this could be one of the reasons for the decrease in numbers of the Slow-worm in the British Isles.

What then makes this creature a lizard and not a snake, even though it has no legs? For one thing, it has eyelids and snakes do not have eyelids, although lizards do; and for another thing, if caught by the tail, the Slow-worm, like the lizard can break it off. This is known as autotomy, from *auto-* (Gr) self, and *tomē* (Gr) a cutting off; there is a muscular mechanism in the tail which breaks it off and then actuates to prevent loss of blood; the tail then grows again. This leaves the surprised predator with only the broken-off tail, while the Slow-worm makes good its escape. Indeed the Latin name, *Anguis fragilis*, suggests this, though it also shows that Linnaeus, who named it, thought it was a snake; *anguis* (L) a snake, *fragilis* (L) brittle – the 'brittle snake'. One can imagine his surprise if he grabbed it by the tail and was left with it wriggling in his hand; there is no doubt that the dismembered piece does wriggle, as I have seen it myself, and this adds to the general surprise and confusion and gives more time for the main body to escape.

3 The Phyla

The main divisions of the Animal Kingdom are the phyla (singular, phylum) from *phulon* (Gr) a stock, race, or kind. There is not complete agreement among taxonomists as to the number of phyla, as some have separated a group and classified it as a subphylum, and it can take many years before international agreement is reached. As a result a number of different systems have become more or less established and generally recognised and, although they are basically the same, there are certain differences which can be confusing; for example one well-known system is based on 22 phyla and another on 27 phyla.

In any particular phylum, there will be assembled all the animals having a common basic plan. Let us take as an example the phylum Chordata. The distinctive character of this phylum is the notochord; *nōton* (Gr) the back, and *khordē* (Gr) gut, string, giving rise to *chordata* (New L) meaning 'provided with a back-string'. This is a cord running along the back made of a special tough elastic tissue and present in all animals in this phylum. In the humblest members of the group, such as the lancelets, small marine creatures about 5 cm (2 in) long, the notochord is retained throughout life. In the higher forms, the true vertebrates, it is present in the embryo, but is replaced more or less completely by the stronger and yet flexible spinal column of jointed vertebrae. However, as all the animals in the phylum Chordata do not develop a spinal column, and there are other differences, the group is divided into four subphyla, the subphylum Vertebrata being one of these.

The system used in this book comprises 27 phyla, one of which, Echinodermata, has two subphyla, and another, Chordata, four subphyla. Considering that Chordata includes such diverse animals as the acorn worms, the mice, the birds, the whales and man, it is no wonder that subphyla are needed. Even so, the one subphylum Vertebrata contains all the animals best known to us: birds, fishes and reptiles; amphibians such as the frogs and newts; and mammals such as dogs, horses, antelopes, lions, whales and human beings.

I do not advise anyone attempting to learn, like a parrot, the Latin and Greek names that now follow; in the course of study they will become familiar without any special effort and, in any case, the brain need not be packed full of words and facts; the great thing is to known how and where to look them up in appropriate books. The sequence of the animals listed is not fixed; it begins with what the compiler considers to be the most primitive forms of life and ends with the most advanced. The number of species given for each phylum is approximate; taxonomists do not always agree about the number of species in a particular group and it can never be finally settled as new species may be discovered at any time and some species may become extinct.

The phyla are as listed below; they are known as 'invertebrates', i.e. having no backbone, with the exception of the last subphylum, the Vertebrates:

PROTOZOA   30,000 species. Amoebae, mycetozoans, etc.
prōtos (Gr) first; *zōon* (Gr) an animal, a living thing.
amoibē (Gr) a change, an alteration. The amoeba, a tiny single-celled animal, continually changes its shape.
mukēs (Gr), genitive *mukētos,* a fungus; any knobbed body shaped like a fungus.

PORIFERA (or PARAZOA, SPONGIDA)   4,500 species. Sponges.
poros (Gr) a way through, a passage; *fero* (L) I bear, I carry.

COELENTERATA (or CNIDARIA)   9,000 species. Jellyfish, corals, etc.
koilos (Gr) hollow; *enteron* (Gr) bowel, intestine.

CTENOPHORA   80 species. Comb jellies, sea gooseberries.
kteis (Gr) genitive *ktenos*, a comb; *phora* (Gr) carrying, bearing; a reference to the rows of ciliary combs which beat and propel them through the water.

MESOZOA   7 species. Minute worms, parasites in the kidneys of squids and octopuses.
mesos (Gr) middle; *zōon* (Gr) an animal, a living thing.

PLATYHELMINTHES   9,000 species. Flatworms, liver flukes, bilharzia, etc.
platus (Gr) flat; *helmins* (Gr) genitive *helminthos*, a worm.

NEMERTEA   570 species. Ribbon worms, bootlace worms.
nēma (Gr) genitive *nēmatos*, a thread.

NEMATODA (or NEMATA)   10,500 species. Roundworms, vinegar eelworms, etc.
nēma (Gr) genitive *nēmatos*, a thread; *-oda* (New L) from *eidos* (Gr) form, like.

ROTIFERA (or ROTATORIA)   1,200 species. Wheel animalcules, the smallest many-celled animals about 1 mm (less than$\frac{1}{16}$ in) long, mostly living in fresh water.
rota (L) a wheel; *fero* (L) I bear, I carry; they do not, of course, carry a wheel, but the first ones discovered and examined under a microscope showed tiny hairs round the mouth; these wave in a circular motion that gives the impression of a turning wheel.

GASTROTRICHA   100 species. Gastrotrichs, tiny transparent creatures less than 0.5 mm ($\frac{1}{50}$ in) long, mostly living in fresh water.
gaster (Gr) the belly, stomach; *thrix* (Gr) genitive *trikhos*, hair; they have hairs on their underparts.

KINORHYNCHA (or ECHINODERA, ECHINO-DERIDA) 30 species. Kinorhynchs, marine animals about 1 mm (less than$\frac{1}{16}$ in) long.
kineō (Gr) I move; *rhunkhos* (Gr) a snout, beak; they pull themselves along by a kind of snout.

PRIAPULIDA 6 species. Priapulids, wormlike marine animals 7.6 cm (about 3 in) long, living on muddy bottoms and sometimes at a great depth. Priapos was the god of gardens and vineyards and Priapus, in Roman mythology, meant a representation or symbol of the male generative organ, or phallus. The name priapulida probably refers to the shape of the animal, which is not unlike the human penis. *-ida* (New L) from *idea* (Gr) species, sort.

NEMATOMORPHA (or GORDIACEA) 80 species. Horsehair worms, not usually marine, and very variable in length from 10 cm (4 in) upwards, and from 0.3 to 3 mm ($\frac{1}{80} - \frac{1}{8}$ in) in diameter.
nēma (Gr) genitive *nēmatos*, thread; *morphē* (Gr) form, shape. Sometimes found in horse drinking troughs, hence the English name.

ACANTHOCEPHALA 400 species. Spiny-headed worms; parasites in the intestines of vertebrates.
akantha (Gr) a thorn, prickle; *kephalē* (Gr) the head.

ENTOPROCTA (or ENDOPROCTA, CALYSSOZOA, KAMPTOZOA, POLYZOA–ENDOPROCTA, POLYZOA ENTOPROCTA) 60 species. Entoprocts; a flower-like body on a stalk less than 6 mm ($\frac{1}{4}$ in) high. The anus opens within a circlet of tentacles, hence the name.
entos (Gr) within; *prōktos* (Gr) anus, hinder parts.

CHAETOGNATHA 30 species. Arrow worms; common in sea water near the shore or in the depths, from 2 to 10 cm ($\frac{3}{4}$ to 4 in) in length.
khaitē (Gr) hair, mane; *gnathos* (Gr) jaw; there are short bristles surrounding the mouth.

POGONOPHORA (or BRACHIATA)   22 species. Beard worms; a deep sea animal about 3 mm ($\frac{1}{10}$ in) in diameter and up to 33 cm (13 in) long. They have no digestive system and how they obtain nourishment is still a cause of further research. *pōgōn* (Gr) a beard; *phora* (Gr) carrying.

PHORONIDA (or PHORONIDEA)   15 species. Phoronids; small marine animals that range from 2 to 30 cm (1 to 12 in) in length. They build themselves a tube in which to live, and catch their food by means of tentacles projecting from the end of the tube. The reason for their name is obscure, but is thought to originate from Phoronis, surname of Io, the daugher of Inachus; there is a stange legend which involves her wandering all over the earth.

BRYOZOA (or POLYZOA, POLYZOA ECTOPROCTA, ECTOPROCTA)   6,000 species. Moss animals; tiny animals, about 0.4 mm ($\frac{1}{64}$ in) long, which live in sea water and fresh water. You might find them attached to the bottom of your boat when you pull it ashore, although you may well mistake them for mossy plants.
bruo (Gr) I swell, sprout, giving rise to bryon, lichen or tree moss; *zōon* (Gr) an animal.

BRACHIOPODA   260 species. Lamp shells; the brachiopod shell is shaped somewhat like the oil lamps used by the Greeks and Romans in ancient times.
brakhus (Gr) short; *pous* (Gr) genitive *podos*, a foot; they do not have feet, but this refers to a short stalk by which they attach themselves to some support.

SIPUNCULA (or SIPUNCULOIDEA)   250 species. Peanut worms; marine animals about 20 to 40 cm (8 to 18 in) long and 12 mm ($\frac{1}{2}$ in) in diameter. They can change their shape, and sometimes take the shape of a peanut. A peculiar feature is a pump-like action with one part of the body sliding up and down inside the posterior cylindrical part, thus collecting nourishment.

siphōn (Gr) a sucker, as of a pump; *-culus* (L) suffix meaning small; 'a little pump'.

ECHIURA (or ECHIUROIDEA, ECHIURIDA) 60 species. Curious sausage-shaped marine animals, up to about 30 cm (12 in) long, and having a proboscis which, in some species, may be 1 m (3 ft) long. This is used for gathering food. *ekhis* (Gr) an adder, serpent; *oura* (Gr) the tail; the 'serpent' part is more a nose than a tail.

MOLLUSCA 50,000 species. Oysters, octopuses, slugs, snails, squids, etc.
mollusca (L), neuter plural of *molluscus*, soft.

ANNELIDA (or ANNULATA) 6,000 species. Leeches, earthworms, ragworms, etc.
anellus (L) a little ring; *-ida* (New L), from *idea* (Gr) species, sort; the rings that mark the body of an earthworm or a ragworm give this phylum its name.

ARTHROPODA About 815,000 species, including the insects which number about 800,000 species, possibly many more. Crustaceans, spiders, insects, etc.
arthron (Gr) a joint; *pous* (Gr) genitive *podos*, a foot; in this case it is taken to mean leg, as the arthropods have jointed legs. Some also have a hard external skeleton; *crusta* (L) a shell, crust.

ECHINODERMATA 5,500 species. Echinoderms, which are given two subphyla.
ekhinos (Gr) a hedgehog; *derma* (Gr) the skin; a reference to the sea urchin's body which is equipped with movable spikes.

Subphylum Pelmatozoa   Sea lilies, feather stars.
pelma (Gr) genitive *pelmatos*, the sole of the foot, can mean a stalk; *zōon* (Gr) an animal. The sea lily has a flower-like body supported on a stalk, the feather star begins life on a stalk but later breaks away and is free to swim about.

Subphylum Eleutherozoa   Sea urchins, sea cucumbers, starfishes, etc.
eleutheros (Gr) free, not bound as on a stalk; *zōon* (Gr) an animal.

CHORDATA   about 44,750 species. Divided into four subphyla, each possessing a notochord.
nōtos (Gr) the back; *khordē* (Gr) gut, string; *chordata* (New L) having a notochord or backstring; the notochord, or 'backstring', is a rodlike structure made of tough elastic tissue which is present in all early embryos in the phylum Chordata.

Subphylum Hemichordata (or Stomochordata, Branchiotremata)   90 species. The acorn worms and their kin.
hēmi (Gr) prefix meaning half; suggesting halfway between primitive chordates and the next stage; the notochord is found only in the proboscis.

Subphylum Urochordata (or Tunicata)   1,600 species. Sea squirts, salps, etc.
oura (Gr) the tail; *khordē* (Gr) gut, string; the notochord extends into the tail.

Subphylum Cephalochordata (or Acrania, Leptocardii)   13 species. Lancelets, small marine animals about 5 cm (2 in) long and pointed at both ends.
lancea (L) a small spear; *kephalē* (Gr) the head; *khordē* (Gr) gut, string, the notochord extends into the head.

Subphylum Vertebrata   About 43,000 species. The vertebrates: fishes, amphibians, reptiles, birds, and mammals, including man.
vertebra (L) a joint, especially a joint of the back, derived from *verto* (L) I turn. With the exception of certain fishes, such as the cartilage fishes, during development from the embryo the notochord is replaced by the bony spinal column.

4 The Vertebrates*

In the subphylum Vertebrata there is a great variety of animals and so they are divided into groups, or taxa, called classes. There are certain recognised sequences for compiling lists of animals but they are arbitrary and different authors adopt different plans. It is not possible to make a linear series that is scientifically correct from the point of view of evolution because animals have not descended one from another in a long line. The classes are listed below.

MARSIPOBRANCHII (or **AGNATHA**) Lampreys and hagfishes.

SELACHII (or **CHONDROPTERYGII, CHONDR-ICHTHYES, ELASMOBRANCHII**) Sharks, dogfishes, rays, i.e. cartilage fishes.

BRADYODONTI Rabbit fishes.

PISCES (or **OSTEICHTHYES**) Bony fishes.

AMPHIBIA Frogs, toads, newts, and their kin.

REPTILIA Tortoises, turtles, lizards, snakes, crocodiles and the Tuatara.

AVES Birds.

*Including the lampreys and cartilage fishes

MAMMALIA   Dogs, cats, horses, whales and their kin, including Man.

The reptiles are divided into 4 taxa called orders, with 5 suborders, and these are again divided into 82 families and subfamilies; the family names have the ending *-idae*, and the subfamilies *-inae*; the complete list can be seen in Chapter 6. The names are formed by adding the suffix to the stem of the name of the type-genus, for example the family name of the crocodiles is formed from the generic name *Crocodylus* and so becomes Crocodylidae. The type-genus is that genus whose structure and characteristics are most representative of the group as a whole, although in some cases it may have been selected because it is the largest, best-known, or earliest-described genus.

To bring us up to date so far, let us work through an example, the skinks. We will list the divisions, starting with the phylum and going through to the species:

Phylum	**CHORDATA**
Subphylum	**VERTEBRATA**
Class	**REPTILIA**
Order	**SQUAMATA**
Suborder	**SAURIA**
Family	**SCINCIDAE**
Subfamily	**SCINCINAE**
Genus	
and species	*Scincus conirostris* Eastern Skink
	S. muscatensis Arabian Skink
	S. philbyi Philby's Arabian Skink
	Ophiomorus brevipes Short-footed Sand Skink
	O. persicus Persian Snake Skink
	(others)

It is considered sufficient, where the genus is the same as the one mentioned immediately before, simply to put the initial capital letter, as will be seen in the list above. The English interpretation of all the foregoing Latin names will be found in the section dealing with the skinks (see p. 86).

Now let us look at another example, a well-known snake subspecies, the Burmese Python *Python molurus bivittatus*, with translations into English of each stage of its classification:

Phylum   CHORDATA

khordē (Gr) gut, string; giving rise to *chordata* (New L) having a notochord or backstring; *nōtos* (Gr) the back. The notochord is made of a special tough elastic tissue, and is present in the embryo of all animals in this phylum.

Subphylum   VERTEBRATA

vertebra (L) a joint, specially a joint of the back, derived from *verto* (L) I turn; *vertebrata* (New L) having a jointed back. In this subphylum the notochord develops into the spinal column.

Class   REPTILIA
repto (L) I crawl; *reptile* (L) a crawling animal, a reptile.

Order   SQUAMATA
squama (L) scale.

Suborder   SERPENTES
serpens (L) genitive *serpentis*, a serpent.

Family   BOIDAE
boa (L) a kind of snake; *-idae* (New L) suffix added to generic names to indicate the name of a family.

Subfamily   PYTHONINAE

puthōn (Gr) the serpent slain by Apollo, thence surnamed the Pythian.

Genus   *Python*

Species   *molurus*   *moluros* (Gr) a kind of serpent.

Subspecies   *molurus bivittatus*   *bi-* (L) prefix meaning two; *vitta* (L) a ribbon, a band; *-atus* (L) suffix meaning provided with; *bivittatus* is known as the subspecific name, so this snake is the Two-banded or Burmese Python *Python molurus bivittatus*.

5 Reptiles in General – The Class Reptilia

The reptiles, which have descended from the amphibians and which are the ancestors of the birds and mammals, are classed as Reptilia. They number about 5,400 species and are one of the three groups of cold-blooded vertebrates, the other two being the fishes (Pisces) and the amphibians (Amphibia); with the two warm-blooded vertebrate groups, the birds (Aves) and the mammals (Mammalia), they constitute the subphylum Vertebrata (see Chapter 4). The four orders of the Reptilia are given below, the Squamata being divided into two suborders:

Order	**CHELONIA**	
	Turtles, tortoises and terrapins	220 species
Order	**CROCODYLIA**	
	Crocodiles, alligators and gavials	21 species
Order	**RHYNCHOCEPHALIA**	
	The Tuatara	1 species
Order	**SQUAMATA**	
Suborder	**SAURIA** Lizards	2,800 species
Suborder	**SERPENTES** Snakes	2,200 species

Nowadays zoologists prefer not to use the term 'cold-blooded' when referring to fish, reptiles and amphibians, because the temperature of the blood varies with the surroundings; the condition is known as poikilothermic, from the Greek *poikilos*, variable, and *thermē*, heat. In some cases the blood can become so hot in the sun that a lizard, for instance, must seek the shade or it would perish. It is now known that the body temperature of some 'cold-blooded' animals, for instance

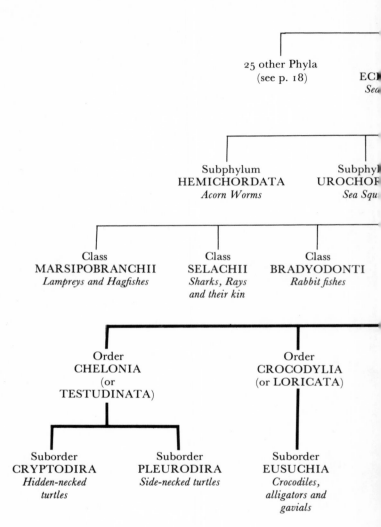

25 other Phyla
(see p. 18)   EC
                                     Sea

Subphylum   Subphy
HEMICHORDATA   UROCHOR
Acorn Worms   *Sea Squ*

Class   Class   Class
MARSIPOBRANCHII   SELACHII   BRADYODONTI
Lampreys and Hagfishes   *Sharks, Rays*   *Rabbit fishes*
                       and their kin

Order   Order
CHELONIA   CROCODYLIA
(or   (or LORICATA)
TESTUDINATA)

Suborder   Suborder   Suborder
CRYPTODIRA   PLEURODIRA   EUSUCHIA
Hidden-necked   *Side-necked turtles*   *Crocodiles,*
turtles   *alligators and*
                                            gavials

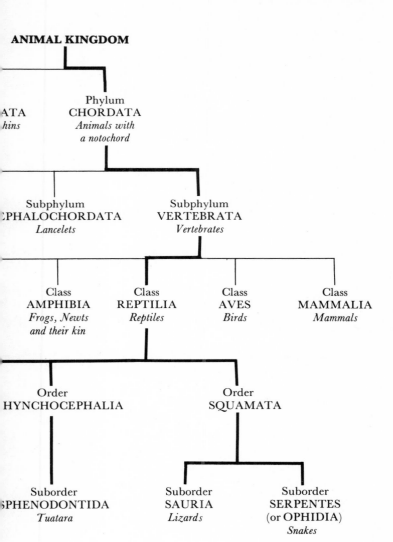

ANIMAL KINGDOM

ATA
hins

Phylum
CHORDATA
*Animals with
a notochord*

Subphylum
:PHALOCHORDATA
Lancelets

Subphylum
VERTEBRATA
Vertebrates

Class
AMPHIBIA
*Frogs, Newts
and their kin*

Class
REPTILIA
Reptiles

Class
AVES
Birds

Class
MAMMALIA
Mammals

Order
HYNCHOCEPHALIA

Order
SQUAMATA

Suborder
;PHENODONTIDA
Tuatara

Suborder
SAURIA
Lizards

Suborder
SERPENTES
(or OPHIDIA)
Snakes

certain snakes, may at times be higher than the temperature of the surroundings.

The 'warm-blooded' condition in birds and mammals is known as homeothermic (or homoiothermic) from the Greek *homoios*, like or similar; i.e. the temperature of the blood remains about the same under all conditions and is automatically controlled by the animal's nervous system. It is higher in birds than mammals, about 41°C (106°F). The reptiles are almost entirely dependent on the temperature of the surroundings to regulate the temperature of the blood, so there are two areas where they will never be found: the Arctic and the Antarctic. There is one small lizard, *Lacerta vivipara*, that ventures north as far as the Arctic Circle, but no reptiles live in the Antarctic. In many cases, they depend on some heat from the sun; their movements are slow and they are not interested in food until the body becomes warm, and then they are usually very active and agile, particularly the lizards. Most reptiles are at their best at a temperature between 25°C (77°F) and 38°C (100°F), although surprisingly the Tuatara prefers a temperature of only about 12°C (53°F). Reptiles are most abundant in hot tropical areas and gradually decrease in number towards the northern and southern parts of the world; in temperate climates they usually hibernate in winter.

The teeth are modified to suit a particular diet and, in the case of some snakes, to accommodate the poison fangs, and in all snakes for swallowing their prey whole. In most lizards, the teeth are fixed to the side of the jaw bone. These are known as pleurodont, from *pleura* (Gr) the side, and *odous* (Gr), genitive *odontos*, a tooth; some lizards, for example the agamids, have the teeth fixed to the top of the jaw bone and are known as acrodont, from *akros* (Gr), at the top.

Venomous snakes are known as 'front-fanged' and 'rear-fanged', depending on whether the poison fangs are situated at the front part of the mouth or at the rear; the scientific names are Proteroglypha and Opisthoglypha, from *proteros* (Gr) first, in space or time, and *gluphē* (Gr) anything carved, can mean a whole cut; and *opisthe* (Gr) after, behind. This refers to the grooves on the fangs that conduct the poison to the wound. Snakes with fangs that are actually hollow, like a hypodermic needle, are termed Solenoglypha from *sōlēn* (Gr) a pipe or channel, and the non-venomous snakes Aglypha, from the Greek prefix *a* meaning not, or there is not.

The rear-fanged Opisthoglypha, are not usually dangerous to Man; as the fangs are at the back of the mouth they are not easily brought into action on a large animal; an exception to this is the Boomslang *Dispholidus typus*, which is known to have caused several fatalities, including the tragic death of the well-known American herpetologist Karl Schmidt.

In most reptiles, the sense of smell is augmented by an anatomical structure known as Jacobson's Organ, which consists of two pits in the roof of the mouth lined with a sensitive membrane similar to that of the nose. It is well developed in snakes and most lizards, and is present in tortoises and turtles and the Tuatara, but is only vestigial in crocodiles. To make use of this organ, the tongue picks up tiny particles from the air, almost as though tasting the air; the tongue is then withdrawn into the mouth and the tips of the tongue are inserted into the organ where the sensitive membrane records the smell. It is very noticeable in snakes, who constantly flick the tongue in and out, which means they are smelling the air, the ground, or their prey, and it is probably used in courtship. Monitor lizards also have this habit, which suggests that Jacobson's Organ is particularly important in their case.

6 Reptile Orders, Suborders, Families and Subfamilies

Order	**CHELONIA** (or **TESTUDINATA**) Turtles, tortoises and terrapins
Suborder	**CRYPTODIRA** Hidden-necked Turtles
Families	**DERMATEMYDIDAE** River Turtle
	CHELYDRIDAE Snapping Turtles
	KINOSTERNIDAE Musk Turtles
	PLATYSTERNIDAE Big-headed Turtle
	EMYDIDAE Pond Turtles, Terrapins
	TESTUDINIDAE True Tortoises
	CHELONIIDAE Marine Turtles
	DERMOCHELYIDAE Leatherback Turtle
	CARETTOCHELYIDAE Papuan Turtle
	TRIONYCHIDAE Soft-shelled Turtles
Subfamilies	**CYCLANORBINAE** Soft-shelled Turtles
	TRIONYCHINAE Soft-shelled Turtles
Suborder	**PLEURODIRA** Side-necked Turtles
Families	**PELOMEDUSIDAE** Side-necked Turtles
	CHELIDAE Snake-necked Turtles
Order	**CROCODYLIA** (or **LORICATA**) Crocodiles and their kin
Suborder	**EUSUCHIA**

Families	**ALLIGATORIDAE** Alligators
	CROCODYLIDAE Crocodiles
	GAVIALIDAE Gavial or Gharial

Order	**RHYNCHOCEPHALIA** The Tuatara
Suborder	**SPHENODONTIDA** The Tuatara
Family	**SPHENODONTIDAE** The Tuatara

Order	**SQUAMATA** Lizards and Snakes
Suborder	**SAURIA** (or **LACERTILIA**) Lizards
Families	**GEKKONIDAE** Geckos
	PYGOPODIDAE Scaly-footed Lizards
	DIBAMIDAE Two-legged Lizards
	IGUANIDAE Iguanas
Subfamilies	**SCELOPORINAE** Spiny Lizards and their kin
	TROPIDURINAE Keel-tailed Lizards and their kin
	IGUANINAE Iguanas
	BASILISCINAE Basilisks
	ANOLINAE Anoles, Long-legged Lizards

Families	**AGAMIDAE** Agamas and their kin
	CHAMAELEONIDAE Chameleons
	SCINCIDAE Skinks
Subfamilies	**TILIQUINAE** Blue-tongued Skinks and their kin
	SCINCINAE Skinks
	LYGOSOMINAE Slender Skinks and their kin

Families	**FEYLINIIDAE** Feylin's Lizards
	ANELYTROPSIDAE Mexican Blind Lizard
	CORDYLIDAE Girdle-tailed Lizards
Subfamilies	**CORDYLINAE** Girdle-tailed Lizards
	GERRHOSAURINAE Plated Lizards and their kin

Families   **XANTUSIIDAE**   Night Lizards
TEIIDAE   Teiids, Racerunners, and their kin
LACERTIDAE   True Lizards or Typical Lizards
ANGUIDAE   Lateral Fold Lizards
Subfamilies   **DIPLOGLOSSINAE**   Folded-tongue Lizards and their kin
GERRHONOTINAE   Alligator Lizards
ANGUINAE   Slow-worms

Families   **ANNIELLIDAE**   Legless Lizards
XENOSAURIDAE   Crocodile Lizards and their kin
HELODERMATIDAE   Beaded Lizards
VARANIDAE   Monitors
LANTHANOTIDAE   Earless Monitor
BIPEDIDAE   Two-legged Worm Lizards
AMPHISBAENIDAE   Ringed or Worm Lizards
TROGONOPHIDAE   Sharp-tailed Worm Lizards

Suborder   **SERPENTES** (or **OPHIDIA**)

Families   **TYPHLOPIDAE**   Blind Snakes
LEPTOTYPHLOPIDAE   Slender Blind Snakes
ANILIIDAE   Pipe Snakes
UROPELTIDAE   Shield-tailed Snakes
XENOPELTIDAE   Sunbeam Snake
ACROCHORDIDAE   Wart Snakes
BOIDAE   Boas and Pythons
Subfamilies   **LOXOCEMINAE**   Mexican Python
PYTHONINAE   Pythons
BOINAE   Boas
BOLYERIINAE   Round Island Boas

Family	**COLUBRIDAE** Typical Snakes
Subfamilies	**XENODERMINAE** Xenodermin Snakes
	SIBYNOPHINAE Spear Snakes
	XENODONTINAE Hog-nosed Snakes and their kin
	NATRICINAE Water Snakes
	COLUBRINAE Typical Snakes
	CALAMARINAE Reed Snakes
	LYCODONTINAE Wolf Snakes
	DIPSADINAE Thirst Snakes
	DASYPELTINAE Egg-eating Snakes
	HOMALOPSINAE Rear-fanged Water Snakes
	BOIGINAE Boigine Snakes
Families	**ELAPIDAE** Cobras
	HYDROPHIIDAE Sea Snakes
Subfamilies	**LATICAUDINAE** Sea Kraits
	HYDROPHIINAE Sea Snakes
Families	**VIPERIDAE** Vipers
	CROTALIDAE Pit Vipers and Rattlesnakes

7 Turtles, Tortoises and Terrapins
CHELONIA (or TESTUDINATA)

Galapagos Giant Tortoise
Testudo elephantopus

Turtles, tortoises, and terrapins, with about 220 species, all belong to the order Chelonia, the main differences being anatomical; while some live on the land, others live mainly in water, either sea water or fresh water. They are the oldest type of living reptiles, older than the ancient fossil dinosaurs and other reptiles that are now extinct. The layman may tend to think that frogs, newts and their kin are reptiles, but they cannot be so classified; they are fundamentally different creatures, starting life in water and breathing by means of gills, as for example tadpoles. Even when their gills disappear and they venture onto the land, breathing by means of their lungs, for many species the skin plays an important part in breathing and must never be allowed to dry out; they are classified in the order Amphibia.

The Chelonia can be divided into two suborders, the Cryptodira and the Pleurodira; *kruptos* (Gr) secret, hidden; *deirē* (Gr) neck, throat; the neck, when withdrawn, is bent in a vertical plane and the head and neck are then not visible and thus protected; *pleura* (Gr) a rib, can mean the side; the neck is bent sideways when withdrawn and is not completely hidden.

In the USA, those living on land are called tortoises and we

38

tend to follow this ruling in Great Britain, although the European Pond Tortoise *Emys orbicularis* lives partly in water and partly on land; turtles live in water although some spend part of their time on land. The word terrapin is derived from an American-Indian word *terrapene* a small turtle, and some American herpetologists consider the name terrapin should only be used for the Diamondback Terrapin *Malaclemys terrapin*. In Great Britain, we tend to think of terrapins as the small fresh water turtles kept as pets and often seen in pet shops in small aquaria. Exchange of books on natural history between English-speaking countries seems to have added to the confusion of the names and the Latin names do not help as some turtles have a Latin name (though actually a Greek word) that translates as a tortoise, e.g. the Spotted Turtle *Clemmys guttata*, where *klemmus* (Gr) means a tortoise.

The order is divided into 12 families and 2 subfamilies which now follow under their various headings.

Order CHELONIA

khelōnē (Gr) a tortoise.

Suborder CRYPTODIRA

kruptos (Gr) secret, hidden; *deirē* (Gr) neck, throat, the neck, when withdrawn, is bent in a vertical plane; the head and neck are then not visible and are thus protected.

Family DERMATEMYDIDAE 1 species

derma (Gr) genitive *dermatos* skin, leather; *emus* (Gr) genitive *emudos* a freshwater turtle.

American River Turtle *Dermatemys mawii*
Dermatemys see Family Dermatemydidae above. Occupying a family on its own because the anatomical features do not show that it belongs to any of the larger groups; the Latin name is

strange, as the shell is bony rather than leathery. It is quite a large turtle, growing to a length of about 40 cm (16 in). Inhabiting large rivers and ranging from Mexico to Guatemala.

Family   CHELYDRIDAE   2 species

kheludros (Gr) an amphibious serpent, a kind of tortoise.

Snapping Turtle   *Chelydra serpentis*
The translation of *kheludros* given above is as given in Liddell and Scott's *Greek-English Lexicon; serpens* (L) genitive *serpentis* a serpent; the name does not seem suitable, although it has a vicious bite and will even attack human beings. It is widespread in North America.

Alligator Snapper   *Macrochelys temminckii* (= *Macroclemys*)
makros (Gr) long, large; *khelus* (Gr) a tortoise; Professor C. J. Temminck (1778–1858) was a Dutch zoologist and at one time Director of the Natural History Museum at Leiden in the Netherlands. This is one of the largest freshwater turtles known and may weigh up to 90 kg (200 lb), and grow to a length of 75 cm (29 in); it lives in rivers in the southern USA, particularly the Mississippi Basin.

Family   KINOSTERNIDAE   9 species, possibly more

kineō (Gr) I move; *sternon* (Gr) the breast, chest; the central part of the plastron, i.e. the lower part of the shell, the chest, is integral with the upper part, the carapace; however two parts of the plastron, a forward part and a rear part, are hinged to it and can move up and down, so enclosing the head and legs when necessary.

Common Musk Turtle   *Sternotherus odoratus*
sternon (Gr) the breast, chest; *therus* is derived from *thairos* (Gr) the hinge of a door; the plastron is hinged (see Family Kinosternidae above); *odor* (L) a smell;   -*atus* (L) suffix mean-

ing provided with; it has a strong musky smell and is sometimes known as the 'stinkpot'! Inhabiting a large area of north-eastern USA, from Maine and southern Ontario, southwest to the Gulf States and Mexico.

Keel-backed Musk Turtle *S. carinatus*
carina (L) a keel; *atus* (L) provided with; a reference to the ridge along the central line of the back. Inhabiting the central southern area of the USA bordering on the Gulf of Mexico.

Mud Turtle *Kinosternon subrubrum*
Kinosternon see Family Kinosternidae, p. 40; *sub-* (L) under, almost; *rubrum* (L) red; a reference to the brown shell. Inhabiting the eastern area of the USA.

Family PLATYSTERNIDAE 1 species
platus (Gr) flat; *sternon* (Gr) the chest.

Big-headed Turtle *Platysternon megacephalus*
Platysternon see Family Platysternidae above; *megas* (Gr) wide, big; *kephalē* (Gr) the head; 'a flat-chested big-head'! A more correct interpretation would be 'big-headed flat-chest', as in strict nomenclature the generic name is a noun and the specific name is an adjective. A most peculiar animal, unlike any other turtle, so has to be classified on its own in its special family; the head is so big and wide that, at its base, it appears to be almost as wide as the body; it cannot be completely withdrawn into the shell and is heavily armoured; even more extraordinary, with its sharp claws, it climbs well and is reported to have been seen up trees! It inhabits southern Burma, ranging south to Vietnam, east along a coastal belt of southern China, and the Philippines.

Family EMYDIDAE 76 species
emus (Gr) genitive *emudos* a freshwater turtle.

Blanding's Turtle   *Emys blandingii*
Emys see Family Emydidae above. Named after William
Blanding, a nineteenth-century American herpetologist. It
inhabits the area of the Great Lakes of North America.

European Pond Tortoise   *E. orbicularis*
orbis (L) a circle; *orbiculus* a little circle or disc; *-aris* (L)
pertaining to; a small tortoise (sometimes called a Swamp
Turtle) with a length up to 25 cm (9½ in); it is 'at home' in
water or on the land. Inhabiting Europe, but not the northern
parts, and a small area in North Africa.

Painted Turtle   *Chrysemys picta picta*
khrusos (Gr) gold; *emus* (Gr) a freshwater turtle; a reference to
the unmarked golden-yellow plastron; *pictor* (L) a painter; a
reference to the brightly coloured markings on the carapace,
head, and legs. Inhabiting the Atlantic coastal area of the
USA; this is the nominate subspecies (see pp. 10 and 16).

(No recognised English name)   *C. p. belli*
The subspecies inhabit distinctive areas and will not necessarily
all be known as Painted Turtles; they are likely to have local
names. Dr J. G. Bell (1812–1889) was an American physician
and taxidermist; he accompanied Audubon on his Missouri
River expedition in 1843; J. J. L. Audubon (1785–1851) was
the famous American ornithologist and artist. This turtle
inhabits the eastern side of the Rockies and ranges south to
northern Mexico.

(No recognised English name)   *C. p. marginata*
margo (L) genitive *marginis* edge, border; *-atus* (L) provided
with; the carapace has bright red markings round the edge.
Ranging from the Alleghenies to the Great Lakes, North
America. This turtle and the two above are subspecies (see pp.
10 and 16).

Diamondback Terrapin   *Malaclemys terrapin*
malakos (Gr) soft, gentle; *klemmus* (Gr) a tortoise; *terrapene*
(American-Indian) a small turtle. This is a good example of the

confusion of names in the order Chelonia: here we have the English word terrapin, coined from the American-Indian *terrapene*, which translates as a small turtle, and the Greek word *klemmus* which means a tortoise. If any animal can be called a terrapin this is it; indeed some American herpetologists say that this is the one and only terrapin. 'Diamondback' is a reference to the shape of the plates of the carapace; it has a wide distribution along the Atlantic coast of the USA from Massachusetts, south to Florida, west to Texas and south to northern Central America.

Eastern Box Turtle   *Terrapene carolina*
terrapene see Diamondback Terrapin above. Named from Carolina, it is not confined to that part of the USA. The name Box Turtle refers to the two hinged lobes of the plastron (see Family Kinosternidae, p. 40) which can be closed to form an almost airtight box. It inhabits a large area of the USA from the east coast ranging west as far as Texas.

Spotted Turtle   *Clemmys guttata*
klemmus (Gr) a tortoise; *gutta* (L) a drop, a spot; *-atus* (L) provided with; a reference to the yellow and orange spots on the shell. Inhabiting the eastern part of the USA and the area of the Great Lakes.

Pacific Pond Turtle   *C. marmorata*
marmor (L) marble; *-atus* (L) provided with; having the appearance of marble. It is becoming rare as it has been extensively hunted and sold in markets for the decorative carapace. Inhabiting the border of the Pacific Ocean from Vancouver south to the border of Mexico.

Muhlenberg's Turtle   *C. muhlenbergii*
Named after G. H. E. Muhlenberg (1753–1815), an American botanist, in whose honour a plant genus was also named. This little turtle, only about 10 cm (4 in) long, spends a lot of its time on land in swampy areas, eating plant food; it is sometimes known as the Bog Turtle. Inhabiting New Jersey and surrounding areas on the eastern part of the USA.

Black Pond Turtle   *Geoclemys hamiltonii*
gē (Gr) the earth; *klemmus* (GR) a tortoise; the only species in this genus, and probably more often seen on land than in the water. Sir Ian Hamilton (1853–1947), was an officer in the British Army who served in India and other places in the Far East. Inhabiting a broad belt of country from north-western India across to the River Ganges, where it is most common in the Lower Ganges area.

(No recognised English name)   *Geoemyda spinosa*
gē (Gr) the earth; *emus* (Gr) genitive *emudos*, a freshwater turtle; the turtles in this genus are mainly terrestrial; *spina* (L) a prickle, or spine of certain animals; *-osus* (L) full of, augmented; an allusion to the peculiar spines which arise from the plates of the carapace. Inhabiting the Malay Peninsula, Sumatra and Borneo.

(No recognised English name)   *G. pulcherrima*
pulcher (L) beautiful; *pulcherrima* very beautiful; 'A very beautifully coloured turtle' (Grzimek). Inhabiting southern California, Mexico and the northern part of Central America.

Family   TESTUDINIDAE   35 species

testudo (L) genitive *testudinis* a tortoise; members of this family are essentially land tortoises, visiting the water only for drinking and bathing. Their feet are shaped for walking, quite different from the paddle-shaped feet of the turtles.

West African Hinge-backed Tortoise   *Kinixys erosa*
kineō (Gr) I move; *ixus* (Gr) the back, the waist; an allusion to the rear part of the carapace, which is hinged and can move up and down; *erosus* (L) gnawed off, eaten into; an allusion to the anterior plates of the plastron which have a 'scooped-out' shape. Inhabiting a wide belt of country in central Africa from Senegal to Lake Victoria.

Spider Tortoise   *Pyxis arachnoides*
puxis (Gr) a box made from box-wood, also any box; a reference

to the carapace and plastron forming a box; *arakhnēs* (Gr) a spider; *-oides* (New L) from *eidos* (Gr) form, like; it is not the shape of a spider; this is an allusion to the furrows on the carapace which have a radiating pattern that looks something like a spider's web. It is found only in Madagascar and inhabits a small area on the western side.

Galapagos Giant Tortoise   *Testudo elephantopus*
testudo see Family Testudinidae, p. 44; *elephas* (Gr) genitive *elephantos* an elephant; *pous* (Gr) the foot; 'elephant-footed'. This enormous tortoise can grow to a length of 1.1 m (3 ft 6 in), and live to a great age; it is difficult to establish authentic figures because they can certainly live for well over 100 years, so no man is ever likely to observe one individual from birth to death; even small tortoises can live to a great age. Inhabiting the Galapagos Islands.

Starred Tortoise   *T. elegans*
elegans (L) neat, elegant; a reference to the very decorative carapace with yellowish stars on a brown background. Owing to the great heat at mid-day in its habitat, it hides in shady places at this time; even in captivity in a temperate climate it is determined to have its 'siesta' and crawls to a secluded place for some pleasant inactivity! Inhabiting the southern part of the Malay Peninsula, Sumatra, Java and Borneo.

Indian Ocean Giant Tortoise   *T. gigantea*
gigas (Gr) genitive *gigantos* a giant; another huge tortoise living in quite a different place, in fact the other side of the world. It may grow to a length of 1.2 m (nearly 4 ft), slightly larger even than *elephantopus* (see above) and also living to a great age. It inhabits the Seychelles and other islands in the Indian Ocean.

Common European Tortoise   *T. greaca*
greacus (L) of Greece; the specific name is misleading as it inhabits quite large areas of southern Europe and northern Africa, ranging east to the Caspian Sea. This species is often to be seen for sale in pet shops.

Mediterranean Tortoise   *T. hermanni*
Professor J. Hermann (1738–1800) was a Professor of Natural History in Strasburg. This tortoise, and *T. greaca*, above, are very similar in habits and appearance, the difference being that *greaca* has spurs on the thighs and *hermanni* has similar spurs on the tail. Both species are sold as pets and can usually be found in pet shops; if you have one, close examination will tell you its species. It inhabits Greece, southern Italy, Corsica, Sardinia and southern France.

Leopard Tortoise   *T. pardalis*
pardus (L) a leopard; *-alis* (L) relating to, similar to; an allusion to the brightly coloured, almost orange carapace, covered with dark spots. This is quite a large tortoise and can grow to a length of about 65 cm (just over 2 ft); in the hot summer period it usually aestivates. Widespread in Africa south of the Sahara.

African Spurred Tortoise   *T. sulcata*
sulcus (L) a furrow; *-atus* (L) provided with; the name is a reference to the concentric furrows on the carapace. The English name is an allusion to the horny spines on the legs; usually slightly bigger than *pardalis* (above); it inhabits a large area of the central part of Africa.

Desert Gopher Tortoise   *Gopherus agassizi*
The name gopher is used for various burrowing animals and is said to derive from *gaufre* (Fr) a honeycomb, on account of the many holes made by these animals; this is a burrowing tortoise. It is named in honour of Professor J. L. R. Agassiz (1807–1873), a Swiss zoologist and famous as a teacher of zoology; he founded the Zoological Museum at Harvard University. It inhabits the plains and deserts of southern USA and northern Mexico; to escape the terrible heat of these areas during the day, it digs long tunnels and only appears in the cool of the evening and night to look for food, probably mostly cacti as these contain moisture.

Texas Tortoise   *G. berlandieri*
J. L. Berlandier (1805–1851), was a Belgian botanist who was

employed by the Mexican government from 1827 to 1834; he was first collecting in Texas in 1827 and a genus of plants was named in his honour. Inhabiting southern USA and Texas.

Mexican Tortoise   *G. flavomarginatus*

flavus (L) yellow, golden; *margo* (L) genitive *marginis* a border, an edge; a reference to the yellow border of the carapace. This tortoise is now very rare and may even be extinct; it lives in southern USA and Mexico.

Family   CHELONIIDAE   5 species

khelōnē (Gr) a tortoise. This family consists of true marine turtles, built for swimming with powerful flippers in front; they only come ashore to lay their eggs.

Green Turtle   *Chelonia mydas*

Chelonia see Family Cheloniidae above. This is the edible turtle, which has been used as food for centuries and the one from which turtle soup is made, although some other species are eaten. One hears accounts of how they are turned on their backs in the hold of a ship so that they cannot move about or escape, and remain alive and therefore fresh. There is possibly a second reason for this procedure: when out of water the enormous weight of the shell restricts the breathing, so if not turned on their backs they would eventually die from suffocation. Inhabiting tropical seas, but becoming rare on account of being hunted for food, and now in danger of extinction.

Hawksbill   *Eretmochelys imbricata*

eretmos (Gr) an oak; *khelus* (Gr) a tortoise; a reference to the paddle-shaped flippers; *imbrex* (L) genitive *imbricis* a hollow tile; *-atus* (L) provided with. Imbricate means overlapping like the tiles on a roof; when young, the scales of the Hawksbill are noticeably overlapping, but become less so as it grows older. The hooked shape of the mouth gives rise to the English name. This is the turtle used for 'tortoise-shell', the translucent plates of the carapace are very decorative; here is another instance of the confusing names in this order; a turtle is used to make tortoise-shell; Inhabiting tropical seas and in danger of extinction.

Loggerhead *Caretta caretta*
caretta is a name coined from *carey* (Sp) meaning tortoise-shell. Turtles in the family Cheloniidae have big heads, too big to be drawn back into the shell, and the Loggerhead's head is even bigger than the other heads in this family. They have a wide distribution, ranging both north and south of the tropical seas.

Ridley *Lepidochelys olivacea*
lepidus (L) elegant, neat; *chelys* (L) a tortoise; from *khelus* (Gr) a tortoise; pure Latin would be *testudo; oliva* (L) an olive; *-aceus* (L) similar to, like; 'olive-coloured'. This is the smallest sea turtle, less than 1 m (about 3 ft), and lives in the gulf of Mexico and other tropical seas. It is named after H. N. Ridley FRS who was in Brazil and also on the island of Fernando de Noronha in 1887.

Family DERMOCHELYIDAE 1 species
derma (Gr) skin, leather; *khelus* (Gr) a tortoise; an allusion to the smooth skin which lacks any external shell, but has small bony plates embedded in the skin. There are several species of turtles which for purposes of classification have been put in a family on their own; this is because their general habits and behaviour, and particularly their anatomical structure, do not indicate that they belong to any of the larger groups.

Leatherback Turtle *Dermochelys coriacea*
Dermochelys see Family Dermochelyidae above; *corium* (L) leather; *-aceus* (L) similar to, like. This turtle can grow to an enormous size, even bigger than the giant tortoises of the genus *Testudo;* a weight of 1 tonne has been suggested, but this is probably an exaggeration. It inhabits tropical seas, though it has been known to range as far north as the coast of England and Maine in the USA.

Family CARETTOCHELYIDAE   1 species

caretta is a name coined from *carey* (Sp) meaning tortoise-shell; *khelus* (Gr) a tortoise.

Papuan Turtle   *Carettochelys insculpta*
Carettochelys see Family Carettochelyidae above; *insculptus* (L) carved; the plates are pitted, which gives the appearance of being carved; it is sometimes known as the Pitted-shell Turtle. Inhabiting south-eastern New Guinea.

Family TRIONYCHIDAE   25 species, possibly more.

tria (Gr) three; *onux* (Gr) genitive *onukhos* a claw; see also Subfamily Trionychinae below. The carapace and the plastron are covered by a tough tissue of skin, hence the name 'soft-shelled'; they are freshwater turtles. For purposes of classification the family can be divided into two subfamilies; the reader should be reminded, as first mentioned in Chapter 4, that the suffix *-idae* denotes a family and *-inae* a subfamily.

Subfamily CYCLANORBINAE   6 species

kuklas (Gr) encircling; *orbis* (L) anything of a circular shape, a disk.

Indian Flap-shelled Turtle   *Lissemys punctata*
lissos (Gr) smooth; *emus* (Gr) a freshwater turtle; *punctum* (L) a puncture; *-atus* (L) provided with; spotted as with punctures; a reference to the yellow spots on the carapace and head. This turtle has two flaps on the plastron that close over the back legs when they are withdrawn. Inhabiting India, Sri Lanka and Burma.

Senegal Soft-shelled Turtle   *Cyclanorbis senegalensis*
Cyclanorbis see Subfamily Cyclanorbinae above; a reference to the flat and almost circular shell; *-ensis* (L) belonging to, usually a place; 'of Senegal'. It ranges along a broad belt of country in Africa from Senegal to the Nile.

Subfamily   TRIONYCHINAE   19 species, possibly more

tria (Gr) three; *onux* (Gr) genitive *onukhos* a claw; they have five toes, but only three claws; the fourth and fifth toes are clawless and webbed to form paddles.

Long-headed Soft-shelled Turtle   *Chitra indica*
chitra is from *chitraka* (Sanskrit) having a speckled body; a reference to the spotted carapace; cf. cheetah, from its spotted coat; *indicus* (L) Indian. It has an unusually long and narrow head and neck. Inhabiting northern India, the Burma-Vietnam area and Malaysia.

Malayan Soft-shelled Mud Turtle   *Pelochelys bibroni*
pelos (or *pellos*) (Gr) dark-coloured, dusky; *khelus* (Gr) a tortoise. Inhabiting Malaysia.

Euphrates Soft-shelled Turtle   *Trionyx euphraticus*
Trionyx see Subfamily Trionychinae above; *-icus* (L) belonging to. Inhabiting Asian Turkey, Syria, Israel, Iraq and the River Euphrates to the Persian Gulf.

Spiny Soft-shelled Turtle   *T. spiniferus*
spina (L) a thorn, a spine; *fero* (L) I bear; an allusion to the spiny tubercles on the front of the shell. Inhabiting the St Lawrence and Mississippi Rivers in North America.

African Soft-shelled Turtle   *T. triunguis*
tri (L) three; *unguis* (L) a claw, a hoof; here we have the name first in Greek and then in Latin: 'a three-clawed three-claw'. Inhabiting a large area of central Africa from the Red Sea to the west coast.

Suborder   PLEURODIRA

pleura (Gr) side; *deira* (Gr) neck, throat; the head and neck, when withdrawn, are bent sideways and part of the neck remains visible.

Family PELOMEDUSIDAE 10 species

pelos (or *pellos*) (Gr) dark coloured, dusky; Medusa was one of the three Gorgons, winged females with their heads covered in snakes instead of hair. In 1758, Linnaeus used several names from classical mythology for the names of certain species and it is probable that they were given without thought of any physical significance. Other zoologists, such as Lacépède, have followed his example; the genus *Pelomedusa*, from which the family takes its name, is the only one in the family and was named by Lacépède in 1788.

African Water-tortoise or Turtle   *Pelomedusa subrufa*
Pelomedusa see Family Pelomedusidae above; *sub-* (L) under, somewhat; *rufus* (L) red, ruddy; it is brownish rather than red. This turtle, although mainly aquatic, spends a certain amount of time roaming about on land looking for food, both plants and animals. When water holes dry up in the hot season, it buries itself in the mud at the bottom and sleeps; an example of aestivation, a 'summer hibernation'. The word is derived from *aestas* (L) summer, and *aestivo* (L) I spend the summer. Sometimes known as the Helmeted Terrapin, so now we have an animal that has, by various authors, been called a tortoise, a turtle and a terrapin, but there is no need to allow these English names to confuse you; simply remember that turtles and terrapins are essentially swimming animals and tortoises are walking animals; this rule has very few exceptions, when certain species are 'at home' in water and on land. As already mentioned, even the Latin names, when the Latin or Greek words are translated, can be confusing; the essential thing to remember is that these names, whether 'right or wrong', are *fixed labels*, internationally recognised throughout the world, and apply to only *one particular species*. *P. subrufa* is widespread in Africa south of the Sahara, including the western part of Madagascar, but not the very southern part of the mainland.

Adanson's Mud Turtle   *Pelusios adansonii*
pelusios is a coined name derived from *pēlos* (Gr) earth, mud; an

allusion to its habit of aestivating in a mud wallow (see African Water-tortoise above). Named after N. Adanson (1727–1806) a well-known French naturalist. 'His explorations in Senegal and collections and descriptions of its plants and animals were noteworthy' (E. C. Jaeger). Inhabiting Senegal and a wide belt of country stretching east as far as Uganda.

Madagascar Turtle   *Podocnemis madagascariensis*
pous (Gr) genitive *podos*, the foot; *knēmis* (Gr) legging, a greave, armour between knee and ankle; an allusion to the enlarged scales at the back of each leg; *-ensis* (L) suffix meaning belonging to, usually a place. Surprisingly, although not known on the mainland of Africa it inhabits quite a large area on the western side of Madagascar.

Family   CHELIDAE   23 species

khelus (Gr) a tortoise. The turtles in this family are known as Snake-necked Turtles; they are in the suborder Pleurodira; they bend the neck sideways to conceal the head under the front edge of the carapace, but the neck still remains visible.

Matamata   *Chelys fimbriatus*
Chelys see Family Chelidae above; *fimbriatus* (L) fringed; a reference to the fleshy fringes of skin on the head and neck. Matamata is a Portuguese name derived from the Tupi language of a people of South America, especially those living in the Amazon Basin in Brazil. This turtle is largely crepuscular and nocturnal and inhabits a large area of northern South America, including the Amazon Basin.

Otter Turtle   *Hydromedusa tectifera*
hudōr (Gr) water; when used as a prefix, *hudrō-;* Medusa was one of the three Gorgons (see Family Pelomedusidae, p. 00); *tectum* (L) a roof, a covering; *fero*(L) I bear, carry; a reference to the carapace. It inhabits the Argentine and Paraguay area of South America.

Brazilian Turtle   *Phrynops rufipes*
phrunos (Gr) a species of toad; *ops* (Gr) the eye, face, can also

mean appearance; 'toad-like'; an allusion to the broad head, a deeply split mouth and almost no neck; *rufus* (L) red; *pes* (L) the foot; the legs and throat are a brownish red. Inhabiting a large area of Brazil based on the upper Amazon Basin.

Colombian Turtle   *Batrachemys dahli*
batrakhos (Gr) a frog; *emus* (Gr) a freshwater turtle; 'frog-like turtle'. Professor K. Dahl (1871–1951) was a Norwegian zoologist. Some herpetologists may consider that this species, only recently discovered, and named in 1958, should be in the genus *Phrynops* (above), together with other species in *Batrachemys*. Apart from the frog-like head there are other anatomical features that suggest this move. It is found only in a small area in Colombia, South America.

(No recognised English name)   *Platemys platycephala*
platus (Gr) wide, flat; *emus* (Gr) a freshwater turtle; the carapace and head are unusually flat; *kephalē* (Gr) the head. It inhabits the northern half of the Amazon Basin and ranges west as far as the Andes.

Australian Snake-necked Turtle   *Chelodina longicollis*
khelus (Gr) a tortoise; *dina* is derived from *deinos* (Gr) terrible; 'a terrible tortoise'; quite apart from the confusion of 'turtle' and 'tortoise', this is a misleading name as they are not usually vicious; 'These creatures are quite inoffensive and are not known to bite, however roughly handled' (Schmidt & Inger). It is quite a small turtle, only about 13 cm (5 in) long; *longus* (L) long; *collum* (L) the neck. Inhabiting a large area in the southeastern part of Australia.

Krefft's Turtle   *Emydura krefftii*
emus (Gr) genitive *emudos* a freshwater turtle; *oura* (Gr) the tail; J. L. G. Krefft (1830–1881) was an Australian zoologist at the Natural History Museum in Sydney. This turtle inhabits a large area in north-eastern Australia, ranging from the Joseph Bonaparte Gulf to the Mackenzie River in Queensland.

8 Alligators, Crocodiles and the Gavial
CROCODYLIA (OR LORICATA)

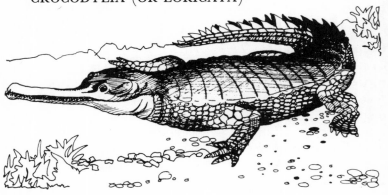

Gavial
Gavialis gangeticus

These large reptiles all belong to the order Crocodylia, with only 21 known species. Many people want to know how one can tell the difference between a crocodile and an alligator; the two are, in fact, very similar. As a general rule the alligators are smaller, but this cannot be taken as a safe guide; the American Alligator has been known to grow to a length of 6 m (over 19 ft), which is about the same as a big crocodile, though the normal length of any species in the order Crocodylia probably does not exceed 5 m (16 ft). The most obvious difference is in the teeth; put in simple terms, in the crocodile the enlarged fourth tooth of the lower jaw can be seen when the jaws are closed; in the alligators this tooth is covered by the upper jaw.

Crocodiles spend much of their time floating at the surface and, though almost completely submerged, their anatomical structure allows them to continue to breathe. The ears, eyes and nostrils are the highest points on the head and project just above the surface, but a curious feature is that they have no lips covering the jaw bone, so the mouth when closed is not completely watertight. There is, however, a valve to close the throat and the air passages from the nostrils open behind this valve. The nostrils can also be closed by valves and the eyes have upper and lower lids and a nictitating membrane.

The only remaining species of gavial lives in India, mostly in the Ganges, the Indus and the Brahmaputra Rivers. It is sometimes known as a gharial and the two names have probably come about through a misspelling and there is some disagreement as to which is correct. In India, the name gharial is used but, as the family is recognised by scientists throughout the world as Gavialidae, it seems reasonable to use the name gavial. Although classified in the order Crocodylia it is not as closely related to the crocodiles and alligators as these two families are to each other. The food of the gavial consists almost entirely of fish and it has a long slender snout, quite different in appearance to that of the crocodiles; this enables it to catch fish by a sideways 'swipe' of the head and jaws.

The newly hatched crocodile, like the cobra, is an aggressive little creature. While helping Dr Hugh Cott with his research into crocodiles on the Nile in Uganda, we found that handling them required considerable caution to avoid a bite; this would not be serious, but with their sharp little teeth they could quickly draw blood, and if they did not attack us they attacked each other! The population of the Nile Crocodile is becoming much reduced through poaching, for the value of the skin, and if they become extinct it would be a sad blow for conservation, and for the Kabalega Falls National Park (formerly Murchison Falls). We did our best to assist their preservation by digging out crocodile nests that we knew were ready for hatching and, after taking measurements of the newly hatched young crocodiles, and other statistics, we put them in the river. In the normal course of events many must be lost through predators like the Nile Monitors, who dig up the nests and eat the eggs, or other predators who seize the youngsters on their way to the water.

Some crocodiles are known to guard the spot where the eggs are buried, and even take some care of the young after hatching, which is unusual behaviour for a reptile; with great delicacy, the mother crocodile will pick up the young in her huge jaws and carry them to the water, which keeps them safe during this perilous journey. It is estimated that only about

10% of baby turtles reach the water before being seized by predators, as they receive no parental care after the eggs are laid and buried.

Order   CROCODYLIA (or LORICATA)

crocodilus (L) a crocodile.

Suborder   EUSUCHIA

eu- (Gr) prefix meaning well, nicely, sometimes used to mean typical; *soukhos* (Gr) the name for the crocodile in one part of Egypt.

Family   ALLIGATORIDAE   7 species

alligator is derived from *el* (Sp) the, and *lagarto* (Sp) a lizard.

American Alligator   *Alligator mississippiensis*
Alligator see Family Alligatoridae above; *-ensis* (L) suffix meaning belonging to; inhabiting the River Mississippi and other rivers in the south-eastern part of the USA. The scientific name was originally misspelt as *mississipiensis* and the Code (Rules) of the International Commission on Zoological Nomenclature did not allow misspelling to be corrected when a name had appeared in print and become established, but this ruling has been modified recently and corrections of spelling are permitted.

Chinese Alligator   *A. sinensis*
sinae (Late L) Chinese; *-ensis* (L) suffix meaning belong to. This alligator was not known in the western world until late in the nineteenth century; it inhabits the lower reaches of the Yangtze River.

Spectacled Caiman *Caiman crocodilus*
caiman (Sp) an alligator; *crocodilus* (L) a crocodile; it inhabits
Central America ranging south to the central part of South
America, particularly the valleys of the Orinoco and Amazon
Rivers. The English name refers to a ridge of bone on the
forehead connecting the eyes like the bridge of a pair of
spectacles.

Broad-nosed Caiman *C. latirostris*
latus (L) wide, broad; *rostrum* (L) genitive *rostris* the snout.
Inhabiting eastern Brazil.

Black Caiman *Melanosuchus niger*
melas (Gr) genitive *melanos* black; *soukhos* (Gr) the name for the
crocodile in one part of Egypt; *niger* (L) black. Inhabiting the
valleys of the Orinoco and the Amazon Rivers and ranging
north to the Guiana region.

Dwarf Crocodile *Palaeosuchus palpebrosus*
palaios (Gr) ancient; *soukhos* see Black Caiman above; the
crocodiles and their kin are the sole survivors of the ancient
reptiles like the dinosaurs; *palpebra* (L) the eyelid; *-osus* (L)
suffix meaning full of; a reference to the prominent bony scales
above the eyes. This small crocodile is only about 1.5 m (4 ft 10
in) in length. Inhabiting northern and central South America.

Smooth-fronted Dwarf Crocodile *P. trigonatus*
trigōnos (Gr) three-cornered; *-atus* (L) suffix meaning provided
with; a reference to the shape of the head. Inhabiting north and
central South America, particularly the Amazon Basin. The
name 'smooth-fronted' refers to the absence of the bony ridge
on the forehead connecting the eyes, as in the Spectacled
Caiman.

Family CROCODYLIDAE 15 species
krokodeilus (Gr) a kind of lizard = *crocodilus* (L) a crocodile.

American Crocodile   *Crocodylus acutus*
Crocodylus see Family Crocodylidae above; *acutus* (L) sharp,
pointed; a reference to the snout which tapers more to a point
than that of other crocodiles. It has a wide distribution from
Florida to Central America, north-western South America and
the West Indies.

Slender-snouted Crocodile   *C. cataphractus*
kataphraktos (Gr) clad in armour, decked in. Inhabiting the
Congo River valley.

Morelet's Crocodile   *C. moreletii*
Named after P. M. A. Morelet (1809–1892), the French
naturalist and explorer who discovered this crocodile in
Mexico in 1850; then followed a long period during which no
more were seen, and zoologists were in some doubt as to
whether this was a genuine new species or had now become
extinct; however, several more were discovered and collected in
1923 near Belize. It inhabits south-eastern Mexico and Central
America as far east as Guatemala.

Nile Crocodile   *C. niloticus*
-icus (L) suffix meaning belonging to; one of the big crocodiles
and becoming scarce now in Africa due to poaching for the
value of the skin; however, many can still be seen on the Nile
below the Kabalega Falls (formerly Murchison Falls); it also
inhabits Madagascar.

New Guinean Crocodile   *C. novaeguineae*
Distinguished by a rather narrow snout, it inhabits New
Guinea and neighbouring islands of Indonesia, such as Sula,
and some of the Philippine Islands.

Mugger   *C. palustris*
palustris (L) marshy, swampy; it inhabits India and Sri Lanka
and is particularly well known in the River Ganges. The
English name is from *magar* (Hindi) a water monster.

Salt-water Crocodile   *C. porosus*
porosis (Gr) a callosity; *-osus* (L) suffix meaning full of; a

reference to the double row of scaly humps on the upper surface of the snout. This is probably the largest crocodile known, with a length of about 7 m (23 ft), considerably longer than the Nile Crocodile which has always tended to have its length exaggerated by African explorers. This crocodile, being able to swim in the open sea, has a very wide distribution in south-east Asia, ranging from southern India, through the Philippines, the Moluccas and New Guinea, to the New Hebrides and south to northern Australia.

African Dwarf Crocodile   *Osteolaemus tetraspis*
osteon (Gr) a bone; *laimos* (Gr) the throat; a reference to the bony shields on the throat and belly; *tetra* (Gr) four; *aspis* (Gr) a shield; it has four large horny plates arranged in a square on the nape of the neck, known as 'nuchal shields'. This is one of the smallest crocodiles with a length of about 1.9 m (5 ft 10 in); it inhabits the tropical part of central and western Africa.

False Gavial   *Tomistoma schlegelii*
tomos (Gr) cutting, sharp; *stoma* (Gr) the mouth; it has a long narrow snout with many sharp teeth and thus *resembles* a true gavial, but in fact it is closely related to the crocodiles and so became known as the False Gavial; Professor H. Schlegel (1804–1884) was a Dutch zoologist and Director of Leiden Museum from 1858 until his death in 1884. It inhabits the Malayan Peninsula, Sumatra and Borneo.

Family   GAVIALIDAE   only 1 species
gavial is derived from *ghariyāl* (Hindi) a name for the crocodile.

Indian Gavial or Gharial   *Gavialis gangeticus*
Gavialis see Family Gavialidae above; *-alis* (L) suffix meaning pertaining to; *icus* (L) suffix meaning belonging to; in addition to the Ganges it also inhabits the Mahanadi and Brahmaputra Rivers. It is largely aquatic, the legs being weak and little used and the tail large and powerful and used in swimming; the long narrow snout enables it to make a sideways 'swipe' for catching fish, its main diet.

9 The Tuatara RHYNCHOCEPHALIA

Tuatara
Sphenodon punctatus

This strange reptile, although in outward appearance a lizard, has to be classified in an order and family of its own for it is not a lizard. It has been called 'a living fossil', being the only survivor of a very ancient order of reptiles, the Rhynchocephalia; it roamed the earth, along with the ancient turtles, even before the rise of the dinosaurs. There appears to have been no real change or modification in its anatomy for about 200 million years and it possesses a number of peculiar features. The structure of the skull is most unusual; it has abdominal ribs; it has no copulatory organ, so fertilization has to be achieved by the male pressing its cloaca to that of the female; it cannot tolerate much heat and, although most reptiles are active with a body temperature of between 25°C and 38°C (77°F and 100°F), the Tuatara prefers a temperature of about 12°C (54°F); the arrangement of the teeth is unlike that of any other animal.

Order RHYNCHOCEPHALIA

rhunkhos (Gr) the beak, snout; *kephalē* (Gr) the head; the front part of the skull is elongated into a snout and sometimes the animal is known as a 'beak-head'.

Suborder   SPHENODONTIDA

sphen (Gr) a wedge; *odous* (Gr) genitive *odontos* a fang, tooth; *-ida* (New L) suffix used for zoological group names; a reference to the two wedged-shaped teeth situated in front of the maxillary bone; the teeth as a whole have a very unusual formation.

Family   SPHENODONTIDAE   1 species

Tuatara   *Sphenodon punctatus*
Sphenodon see Suborder Sphenodontida above; *punctum* (L) a hole, a prick; *punctatus* (L) spotted as with punctures; the young Tuatara has light spots on the throat, body, and legs, especially noticeable after shedding the skin, but these spots gradually fade with age. Originally inhabiting New Zealand, it is no longer found on the two main islands, but inhabits a number of small islands, mostly off the northern coast of North Island. The English name Tuatara arises from the native name for the animal and refers to the spiny crest along its back; *tua* (Maori) the back; *tara* (Maori) a spine.

10 Lizards SQUAMATA: SAURIA

Jackson's Chameleon
Chameleo jacksonii

The lizards, of the order Squamata, suborder Sauria, with a total of about 3,000 species, come in a great variety of shapes and sizes; a number of species have no legs and thus have the appearance of a snake. They range in size from the tiny Caribbean Gecko *Sphaerodactylus elegans*, about 4 cm (1½ in) long, to the huge Komodo Dragon *Varanus komodoensis* at 3 m (almost 10 ft). They have a world-wide distribution, although mostly in the warm regions; no reptiles inhabit the Arctic or Antarctic areas.

As already mentioned in Chapter 2, there are a number of anatomical features, some easily seen or demonstrated, that prove the creatures to be lizards although they may look like snakes: they have eyelids (except the geckos) and most have the ability to break off their tail (autotomy) as a means of escape, which then grows again. If lizards are kept in captivity, and the smaller species make most interesting, active and quite intelligent pets, they soon become tame; I do not advise an experiment to see whether the tail breaks off! Although the tail will grow again, it will not be so long and decorative as originally.

I was interested to see, on one occasion, an experienced

herpetologist pick up a lizard by its tail when he was catching some for me to take home; he said they seem to know when they are in danger and, if you hold the tail lightly, they will not shed it. I have seen two male lizards fighting over territory and one shed its tail, which continued to wriggle vigorously and arch about; this might serve to distract the attention of a predator so that the lizard has time to escape. In captivity, lizards should, if possible, be kept in an outdoor vivarium (which I prefer to call a 'herpetarium' although this is not a recognised word), where they have plenty of room to run about and where they can get as much sun as they need; this is essential if they are going to remain in good health. However, there must be rocks and plants under which they can hide to escape the heat of the mid-day sun if necessary, or the blood may become too hot and this would be fatal (see Chapter 5 about blood-heat control in reptiles).

Order SQUAMATA

squama (L) a scale.

Suborder SAURIA lizards

saura (Gr) genitive *sauros* a lizard.

Family GEKKONIDAE about 550 species

gekoq is a Malayan word; the name gecko, or tokay, is derived from the sound made by the Asian species; their ability to make little chirps and croaks is unique among lizards. Furthermore, they are able to crawl up very smooth surfaces and even hang upside down on ceilings. It is now established that this is not done by means of suction pads on the feet but by pads furnished with thousands of minute hooks, too small to be seen with the naked eye, which cling to the tiny irregularities of any surface, even glass.

Common House Gecko *Hemidactylus mabouia*
hemi (Gr) half; *daktulos* (Gr) a finger or toe; a reference to the
clinging pads on the under surface of the toes being divided into
two halves, separated longitudinally along the centre line; they
are sometimes known as 'half-toes'. *mabuya* (New L) from an
American-Spanish word for a type of lizard. Inhabiting Central America and northern South America and Africa south of
the Sahara, including Madagascar.

Turkish Gecko *H. turcicus*
-icus (L) suffix meaning belonging to; it inhabits the eastern
Mediterranian coast, the Red Sea area and other parts of the
Near East.

European Leaf-fingered Gecko *Phyllodactylus europaeus*
phullon (Gr) a leaf; *daktulos* (Gr) a finger or toe; an allusion to
the broad leaf-like clinging pads; *europaeus* (L) of Europe.
Inhabiting Corsica, Sardinia and neighbouring islands.

Naked-toed Gecko *Gymnodactylus pulchellus*
gumnos (Gr) naked; *daktulos* (Gr) a finger or toe; an allusion to
the toes which do not have the clinging pads; *pulcher* (L)
beautiful; *-ellus* (L) diminutive suffix: 'a little beauty'. Inhabiting the southern part of eastern Europe and ranging east to
northern Arabia and Iran.

Dwarf Gecko *Lygodactylus capensis*
lugos (Gr) a pliant twig, a willow twig, i.e. flexible; *daktulos* (Gr)
a finger or toe; an allusion to the curling movement of the toes
which enables the clinging pads to grip and release; *-ensis* (L)
belonging to; named from Cape Province, it inhabits the
western part of Africa. Although named Dwarf Gecko, it is not
the smallest gecko and is about 8 cm (3 in) long.

Spotted Gecko *Pachydactylus maculatus*
pakhus (Gr) thick, fat; *daktulos* (Gr) a finger or toe; a reference to
the tips of the toes being expanded like clubs; *macula* (L) a spot,
or mark; *-atus* (L) provided with; it has dark spots on a

brownish background. Inhabiting the eastern part of South Africa.

Fan-footed or House Gecko   *Ptyodactylus hasselquistii*
ptuon (Gr) a winnowing shovel or fan; *daktulos* (Gr) a finger or toe; an allusion to the clinging pads which are wide and expanded like fans. F. Hasselquist (1722–1752) was a Swedish naturalist living in Palestine from 1747 to 1752, where doubtless he died from one of the diseases of the East for which no cure was known in those days. This gecko ranges from Algeria across the northern part of Africa to Iraq and Iran, where it often makes its home in houses.

Lizard-toed Gecko   *Saurodactylus fasciata*
saura (Gr) a lizard; *daktulos* (Gr) a finger or toe; as the English name suggests, it has lizard-like toes without the usual clinging pads, and so will not be seen on smooth walls or ceilings of houses; it is a ground dweller; *fascia* (L) a band or girdle; *-atus* (L) provided with; a reference to the dark marking on the back. Inhabiting Algeria and Morocco.

Day Gecko   *Phelsuma quadriocellata*
Named by Gray in 1831 after a Mr Phelsum, but herpetological records do not give any details about this naturalist; *quadruus* (L) fourfold; *ocellus* (L) a little eye; *-atus* (L) suffix meaning provided with; 'having four little eyes'; this is an allusion to four black spots outlined with blue on the sides of the body, one behind each fore leg and one just in front of each hind leg. Dr J. E. Gray FRS (1800–1875) was a zoologist at the British Museum (Natural History) in London from 1840 to 1874. This gecko is often seen out hunting during the daytime; it inhabits central and southern Madagascar.

Leaf-tailed Gecko   *Uroplatus fimbriatus*
oura (Gr) the tail; *platus* (Gr) flat, wide; a reference to the peculiar tail which from a normal base spreads out flat and wide, 'leaf-tailed'; *fimbriatus* (L) fringed; the sides of the body and legs have a scaly flange or fringe which is pressed down

when the animal is at rest, thus reducing any shadow and making it very inconspicuous. Inhabiting Madagascar.

Tokay or Common Gecko   *Gekko gekko*
gekko the name is onomatopoeic (see Family Gekkonidae, p. 63); the whole family Gekkonidae takes its name from this genus, although many species do not make the peculiar croaking noises. The double name, i.e. using the generic name again as the specific name, is known as a tautonym; for an explanation of this strange feature of nomenclature see TAUTONYMS, p. 9. This gecko is widespread and frequently seen in south-east Asia, including India, the Burma-Vietnam area, Malaysia, Indonesia and the Philippines. Visitors to this part of the world are likely to be surprised and startled in the middle of the night by a loud bark, apparently coming from immediately overhead! It is indeed overhead and made by this gecko crawling about on the ceiling hunting for insects.

Emerald Gecko   *G. smaragdinus*
smaragdos (Gr) a precious stone; *-inus* (L) like, belonging to; according to Liddell and Scott's *Greek–English Lexicon*: 'A precious stone of a light green colour; probably not the same as our emerald, but a semi-transparent stone like the *aqua marina*'; a reference to the colour of this gecko. Inhabiting the Philippines.

Kuhl's Gecko   *Ptychozoon kuhli*
ptux (Gr) genitive *ptukhos* a fold, a layer; *zōon* (Gr) a living being, an animal; a reference to the fold of skin which extends along the sides of the head, body, thighs, and tail; this can be stretched out and may assist the gecko when jumping or falling, like a glider; it may also assist in camouflage (see *Uroplatus fimbriatus*, p. 65). Dr Heinrich Kuhl (1796–1821), a German naturalist, was in the Dutch East Indies (now known as Indonesia) in 1820 and 1821; a family of fishes, Kuhliidae, is also named after him. Inhabiting south-east Asia including Indonesia.

Panther Gecko   *Eublepharis macularius*
eu- (Gr) prefix meaning well, nicely; sometimes used to mean typical; *blepharon* (Gr) the eyelid; 'well-made eyelid'; 'typical eyelid'; most geckos have eyelids that are fused and transparent, forming a permanent covering over the eye; this gecko has movable eyelids; *macula* (L) a spot, a mark; *-arius* (L) suffix meaning pertaining to; a reference to the black spots on the head, body and tail, and this also gives it the English name. In fact the name panther is frequently used for the unspotted type of leopard, but a panther and a leopard are the same animal. Inhabiting Afghanistan, Pakistan and western India.

Caribbean Gecko   *Sphaerodactylus elegans*
sphaira (Gr) a ball, a sphere; *daktulos* (Gr) a finger or toe; a reference to the round clinging pads on the toes; *elegans* (L) neat, elegant; possibly the smallest living reptile, it measures only 4 cm ($1\frac{1}{2}$ in) total length, although the Nossi Bé Dwarf Chameleon has been recorded as measuring 3.2 cm ($\frac{1}{4}$ in). This gecko inhabits The Antilles.

Kidney-tailed Gecko   *Nephrurus laevis*
nephros (Gr) the kidneys; *oura* (Gr) the tail; the peculiar tail is not only bulbous but has a small knob at the end and is really not much like a kidney; the function of the knob is not known; *laevis* (L) = *levis* (L) light (in weight); can also mean quick, nimble. Inhabiting desert areas in the western part of Australia.

Fat-tailed Gecko   *Oedura marmorata*
oidos (Gr) a swelling; *oura* (Gr) the tail; the tail is probably used as a store of fat when food is scarce; *marmor* (L) marble; *-atus* (L) provided with; 'marbled'; a reference to the colour pattern of white marking on a brown background. One of the larger geckos with a length up to 18 cm (7 in). Inhabiting Australia.

Horned Gecko   *Phyllurus cornutus*
phullon (Gr) a leaf; *oura* (Gr) the tail; a very unusual tail that is sometimes an almost flat rectangular shape spreading out immediately behind the narrow base; *cornu* (L) the horn of an

animal; *cornutus* (L) horned; it has two small horns, one on each side of the head. Inhabiting the north-eastern part of Australia.

Family   PYGOPODIDAE   13 species
pugē (Gr) the rump, buttocks; *pous* (Gr) genitive *podos* the foot; 'rump-footed'; this small family of lizards has no fore legs and the hind legs consist only of small scaly flaps at the rear end of the body, at about the level of the cloaca. Peculiar creatures, they have been given various English names: Scaly-footed Lizards, Flap-footed Lizards and Snake Lizards. They are said to behave like snakes as part of a defensive behaviour, but two things 'give the show away': they have small external ear openings and small flaps instead of hind legs; they are also able to shed their tails but this attribute cannot be demonstrated without damaging the small harmless creature. For anatomical reasons, they appear to be closely related to the geckos.

Common Scaly-foot   *Pygopus lepidopodus*
Pygopus see Family Pygopodidae above; *lepis* (Gr) a scale; *lepidōtos* (Gr) covered with scales; *pous* (Gr) genitive *podos* a foot. This is one of the largest species and may be 65 cm (26 in) long; it is widespread in Australia except the most eastern part.

Western Scaly-foot   *P. nigriceps*
niger (L) black; *ceps* (New L) from *caput* (L) the head; a reference to the black marking round the neck. Inhabiting western Australia.

(No recognised English name)   *Aprasia pulchella*
aprasia (Gr) is a word meaning 'no sale', which seems a very odd name for a genus of lizards; it appears that, when Gray gave this name to the genus in 1839, in his description of the animal he gave no indication of the derivation of the name; *pulcher* (L) beautiful; *-ellus* (L) a diminutive suffix: 'a little beauty'. It inhabits western Australia. Dr J. E. Gray FRS (1800–1875) was an English zoologist and at one time keeper at the British Museum (Natural History) in London.

Family   DIBAMIDAE   3 species

dibamos (Gr) on two legs; the females have no legs and the males have hind legs that are only vestigial, consisting of fin-like flaps.

(No recognised English name)   *Dibamus novaeguineae*
Dibamus see Family Dibamidae above; *novaeguineae* (New L) New Guinea. This strange creature is blind and wormlike and yet, like a lizard, it can shed its tail to escape from predators if necessary. It inhabits New Guinea and the Sumatra, Java, Flores group of islands.

Family   IGUANIDAE   about 650 species

iguana is derived from *iwana*, meaning a lizard; it is Spanish-Arawak, the language of a people of the West Indies. For purposes of classification, the Iguanidae can be divided into five subfamilies; the reader should be reminded, as first mentioned in Chapter 4, that the suffix *-idae* denotes a family and *-inae* a subfamily.

Subfamily   SCELOPORINAE

skelos (Gr) the leg; *poros* (Gr) a passage through the skin; a reference to the large femoral pores.

Western Fence Lizard   *Sceloporus occidentalis*
Sceloporus see Subfamily Sceloporinae above; *occidentalis* (L) western. Like most lizards it has a habit of basking in the sun and is often seen on the top of fence posts; it inhabits large areas of western and southern North America, ranging south into Central America.

Tree Lizard   *Urosaurus ornatus*
oura (Gr) the tail; *saura* (Gr) a lizard; an allusion to the typical lizard tail; *ornatus* (L) ornament, decoration; it has dark spots and bars on a grey-brown background, which is good camouflage; it is very difficult to see if it remains still on a tree trunk or branch; the male is decorated with blue or green spots

on the belly. Inhabiting southern California, Arizona and northern Mexico.

Banded Rock Lizard *Petrosaurus mearnsi*

petra (Gr) a rock; *saura* (Gr) a lizard; the usual habitat is amongst rocks where it basks in the sun and can easily hide from predators; Dr E. A. Mearns (1856–1916) was a Lieutenant Colonel in the US Medical Corps in Mexico from 1892 to 1894; he was a keen naturalist and student of wildlife and at least two birds have been named in his honour. The English name of this lizard refers to a black band across the neck; it inhabits a restricted area from southern California to northern Mexico.

Greater Earless Lizard *Holbrookia texana*

Girard named this lizard in 1851 in honour of Dr J. E. Holbrook (1794–1871), a well-known herpetologist and the author of a number of books on American reptiles. (It is unusual for a naturalist to be commemorated by having his name used for a genus in zoology, being more common in botany, for example the well-known Butterfly Bush *Buddleia davidii* named after Adam Buddle, the English botanist.) The English name is misleading as it is only about 8 cm (3 in) long; furthermore it has ears but there are no visible external ear openings; it inhabits the south-western part of the USA. Charles Girard (1822–1895) was another well-known American herpetologist; a subspecies of the Striped Whipsnake *Coluber taeniatus girardi* was named in his honour.

Zebra-tailed Lizard *Callisaurus draconoides*

kallos (Gr) beauty; *kalli-* (Gr) is used as a prefix to denote beauty; *saura* (Gr) a lizard; probably not more attractive than other lizards in this family except for the tail which is decorated with black bands; *drakōn* (Gr) a dragon; *-oides* (New L) from *eidos* (Gr) apparent shape, resemblance. Inhabiting south-western USA.

Texas Horned Lizard *Phrynosoma cornutum*

phrunos (Gr) a species of toad; *sōma* (Gr) the body; sometimes

known as the Horned Toad, it has a toad-like body; *cornu* (L)
the horn of animals; *cornutus* (L) horned; a reference to the spiky
horns on the rear part of the head. A most peculiar lizard in
appearance and yet quite common in Texas where it can
sometimes be seen even in towns and gardens, and other parts
of the western USA and Mexico. They have an extraordinary
defensive weapon when angry or frightened which consists of
squirting blood from the eyes! It is not known how this can be
of any use for protection or attack.

Flat-tailed Horned Toad   *P. macalli*
G. A. McCall (1802–1868) was a Brigadier General in the US
Army; the name was given by Cope in recognition of his keen
interest in wildlife and his extensive collections for the Smith-
sonian Institution. It is also known as the Flat-tailed Horned
Lizard and the Latin name has been given as *P. m'calli*, but the
apostrophe is forbidden in modern usage (see Chapter 1 under
USE OF LATIN AND GREEK). E. D. Cope (1840–1897) was a well-
known American zoologist and at one time was the editor of
The American Naturalist. This Horned Lizard inhabits the
western part of the USA and Mexico.

Collared Lizard   *Crotaphytus collaris collaris*
krotōn (Gr) a louse, a tick; *phuton* (Gr) a creature, an animal; an
allusion to the insectivorous diet; *collum* (L) the neck; *collaris* (L)
pertaining to the neck, a collar; a reference to two black bands
across the back of the neck; it inhabits the country bordering
the Mississippi River. This is the nominate subspecies (see
Chapter 2).

Bailey's Collared Lizard   *C. c. baileyi*
This subspecies was named after V. O. Bailey (1864–1942), at
one time chief field naturalist with the US Biological Survey
and author of several books on the wildlife of America.
Inhabiting an area to the west of that occupied by *C. c. collaris*
above.

Subfamily   TROPIDURINAE

tropis (Gr) genitive *tropios* which later became *tropidos* a ship's keel; *oura* (Gr) the tail; a reference to a ridge along the upper surface of the tail.

(No recognised English name)   *Tropidurus torquatus*
Tropidurus see Subfamily Tropidurinae above; *torquatus* (L) wearing a collar; a reference to the fold of skin around the neck. Inhabiting the Amazon area.

(No recognised English name)   *Strobilurus torquatus*
strobilos (Gr) anything twisted, that turns round; can mean a fir cone; *oura* (Gr) the tail; the tail is unusually round and very spiny, giving the appearance of a fir cone; *torquatus* (L) wearing a collar; see *Tropidurus torquatus* above. Inhabiting a small area in the eastern part of Brazil, south of the Amazon.

Spiny-tailed Iguanid   *Uracentron azureum*
oura (Gr) the tail; *kentron* (Gr) a spike; *azureus* (New L) blue, derived from *azul* (Sp) blue; in life this lizard is a rather bright green, but specimens preserved in museums change to a more bluish colour. Inhabiting the Amazon Basin area in Brazil.

(No recognised English name)   *Plica umbra*
plico (L) I fold; the skin at the side of the neck is folded and can be distended when the lizard is threatened or angry; *umbra* (L) a shade, can mean a shady place; a reference to its habitat, as it seems to prefer shady places in the rain forest rather than bright sunlight. Most lizards require some heat from the sun before they become active and feel the need for food, but this lizard and some related species can feed at lower temperatures. Inhabiting the rain forests of the lower Amazon Basin.

Santiago Smooth-throated Lizard   *Liolaemus altissimus*
leios (Gr) smooth; *laimos* (Gr) the throat; *altus* (L) high; *altissimus* (L) very high; the habitat of this lizard is unusually high, just below the snow line, but it is still able to find insects at that height. Inhabiting the mountains to the east of Santiago.

Magellan Smooth-throated Lizard   *L. magellanicus*
The Magellan Straits separate Tierra del Fuego from the
mainland at the southern end of South America; this lizard
inhabits Tierra del Fuego and it is safe to assume that no lizard
lives nearer to the South Pole.

Narrow-tailed Lizard   *Stenocercus crassicaudatus*
stenos (Gr) narrow; *kerkos* (Gr) the tail; *crassus* (L) thick, heavy;
caudatus (L) having a tail; this apparently contradictory name
was caused by a change of the generic name: originally named
Scelotrema crassicaudatum, for anatomical reasons it was transfer-
red to the genus *Stenocercus;* by observing the Rules (now known
as the Code) of Zoological Nomenclature, the contradiction
could not be avoided by changing the specific name as this is
forbidden (see p. 9). Most *Stenocercus* species do have a narrow
tail but that of *S. crassicaudatus* is robust and rather spiny.
Inhabiting Ecuador and Peru.

Weapon-tailed Lizard   *Hoplocercus spinosus*
hoplon (Gr) a tool, a weapon, usually a weapon of war; *kerkos*
(Gr) the tail; *spina* (L) a prickle or spine of animals; *-osus* (L)
suffix meaning full of; the tail is short and heavy and the scales
are very spiny. Inhabiting southern Brazil.

Subfamily   IGUANINAE

iguana is derived from *iwana*, meaning a lizard; it is Spanish-
Arawak, the language of a people of the West Indies.

West Indian Iguana   *Iguana delicatissima*
Iguana see Subfamily Iguaninae above; *delicatus* (L) giving
pleasure, delicate; *delicatissimus* (L) very delicate; a reference to
the tail which easily breaks off if seized by a predator, a
characteristic known as autotomy. Inhabiting the islands of the
West Indies.

Common Iguana   *I. iguana*
iguana see Subfamily Iguaninae above: This is a big lizard, with
a high crest, and is quite an impressive creature; it can grow to

a length of 2.2 m (about 7ft 6 in). It is widespread and inhabits Central America, the islands of the West Indies and the northern half of South America. For an explanation of the name *Iguana iguana* see TAUTONYMS, p. 9.

Rhinoceros Iguana   *Cyclura cornuta*

kuklos (Gr) round, circular; *oura* (Gr) the tail; an allusion to the tail which is circular in form, quite heavy and powerful, and can inflict considerable damage with a 'side-swipe' action; it is a fairly large lizard with an overall length of about 70 cm (2 ft 3 in); *cornu* (L) the horn of animals; *cornutus* (L) horned; it has horns on the nose like a rhinoceros. Inhabiting Haiti.

Marine Iguana   *Amblyrhynchus cristatus*

amblus (Gr) blunt; *rhunkhos* (Gr) the snout, beak; *crista* (L) a tuft or crest, usually used for the crest on the head of animals; *cristatus* (L) crested; it has an unusually short blunt nose and a spiky crest on the top of the head and extending along the back. This lizard is a good swimmer, with a tail that is flattened like the blade of an oar, in contrast to the rounded tail of *Cyclura*, and the legs are not used for swimming; it is herbivorous and searches in the sea for seaweed and algae. Inhabiting the Galapagos Islands.

Land Iguana   *Conolophus subcristatus*

kōnos (Gr) a cone, or peak of a helmet; *lophos* (Gr) a crest; *sub-* (L) a prefix meaning under, or somewhat; *crista* (L) a tuft or crest, usually used for the crest on the head of animals; *cristatus* (L) crested; it has a small raised cone on the head and the crest along the back is smaller than that of *Amblyrhynchus*. This iguana inhabits the Galapagos Islands, and Darwin studied its habits while he was making a special study of the finches of these islands, which are sometimes known as 'Darwin's Finches'. C. R. Darwin FRS (1809–1882) was the zoologist who became famous for his work on the theory of evolution by natural selection; today there are some zoologists who tend to disagree with his theory.

Fijian Iguana *Brachylophus fasciatus*
brachus (Gr) short; *lophos* (Gr) a crest; a reference to the short spines that form the crest along the back, much smaller than those of other iguanas; *fascia* (L) a band or girdle; *fasciatus* (L) banded; it has broad dark bands round the green body and tail. Inhabiting the Fiji and Tonga Islands in the South Pacific, it is rare and now considered to be an endangered species.

Desert Iguana *Dipsosaurus dorsalis*
dipsa (Gr) thist; *saura* (Gr) a lizard; 'a thirsty lizard'; as it lives in desert areas, Baird and Girard, who named this iguana in 1852, evidently thought that drinking water would be a problem for it; eating plants, probably cacti which contain water, would help to solve this problem; it also eats insects. Records show that this remarkable lizard can survive in temperatures of over 40°C (about 100°F) which would certainly kill most reptiles, as already mentioned in Chapter 5. Professor S. F. Baird (1823–1887) was a very well-known and hard-working American ornithologist; several birds have been named after him. C. Girard (1822–1895) was an American herpetologist; a subspecies of snake is named in his honour. This iguana inhabits the desert areas of south-western USA.

Chuckwalla *Sauromalus ater*
saura (Gr) a lizard; *omalos* (Gr) level, flat; a reference to the broad flat body; *ater* (L) black; in the male, the head, neck, legs and front part of the body are dark or black, and the rear part is reddish grey with a yellow tail. The name chuckwalla is derived from a Mexican-Spanish name, *chacahuala*; it inhabits the desert areas of the south-western USA.

Subfamily   BASILISCINAE
basiliskos (Gr) a little king, a chieftain.

Common Basilisk *Basiliscus basiliscus*
Basiliscus see Subfamily Basiliscinae above. Known as a basilisk, it takes its name from the mythical creature which was portrayed with a crown-like crest on the head and whose

glance could kill, as could its fiery breath; a strange name for a
harmless lizard but it has a casque on the head which no doubt
was the reason that Linnaeus, in 1758, gave it this name.

Helmeted Lizard *Corytophanes cristatus*
korus (Gr) genitive *koruthos* a helmet; *phainō* (Gr) I show; *crista*
(L) usually a tuft on the head of animals; *cristatus* (L) crested; it
has a bony casque or helmet on the head and a crest of skin on
the neck; the size of these can be increased to form a display
when the animal is angry or threatened. It inhabits Honduras
in Central America and ranges south to the north-western part
of Colombia, South America.

Subfamily ANOLINAE

anoli (West Indian) a lizard.

Long-legged Lizard *Polychrus marmoratus*
polukhroos (Gr) many-coloured; a reference to its ability to
change colour; *marmor* (L) marble; *marmoratus* (L) marbled; the
brown back with pale markings gives an impression of marble.
The unusually long hind legs enable it to leap rather like a frog
and so to jump from branch to branch of a tree; sometimes
known as the Bush Lizard, it is widespread in tropical South
America.

Brazilian Tree Lizard *Enyalius catenatus*
enualios (Gr) warlike, ferocious; a reference to its behaviour
when meeting other male lizards; normally a dark brown
colour, when angry it changes to green; *catena* (L) a chain; can
mean a chain of gold or silver worn by women as an ornament;
-atus (L) provided with; an allusion to the 'chains' of white
spots running in various directions across the back. Inhabiting
south-eastern Brazil.

Patagonian Lizard *Diplolaemus darwinii*
diploē (Gr) a fold, doubling; *laimos* (Gr) the throat, gullet; an
allusion to the folds of skin round the neck; named after Charles
R. Darwin (1809–1882), the English zoologist and author of

the theory of organic evolution. Patagonia is the name given to the southern part of Argentina; this lizard was discovered there by Darwin.

(No recognised English name)   *Anisolepis iheringii*
anisos (Gr) unequal, uneven; *lepis* (Gr) a scale; a reference to the type of scales on the body, some large and some small. Professor H. von Ihering (1850–1930) was Director of the Museum in São Paulo, Brazil from 1893 to 1916. This lizard inhabits Brazil.

Keel-toed Lizard   *Tropidodactylus onca*
tropis (Gr) genitive *tropios* which later became *tropidos* a keel; *daktulos* (Gr) a finger or toe; a reference to the lack of adhesive pads on the toes; *onkos* (Gr) (= *ogkos*) mass, bulk; can mean a tumour; a reference to the unusually large dewlap on the throat of the male. Inhabiting a belt of country along the north-eastern coast of South America from Venezuela to Guinea.

False Chameleon   *Chamaeliolis chamaeleontides*
khamaileon (Gr) a chameleon; *Chamaeliolis* is a name coined by Duméril in 1837 when this lizard was discovered and named; *chamaeleontides* has the suffix -*ides* (L) a relationship; the 't' is evidently inserted for the sake of euphony. It is not a chameleon, but similar in appearance; its slow deliberate movements, quite unlike a normal lizard, the prehensile tail and the fact that it lives in trees all add to the illusion. It inhabits Cuba. Professor A. M. C. Duméril (1774–1860) was a well-known French herpetologist and author.

Carolina or Green Anole   *Anolis carolinensis*
anoli (West Indian) a lizard; -*ensis* (L) suffix meaning belonging to; it is not confined to Carolina and inhabits other south-eastern states of the USA. Like other anoles, it can change colour and is sometimes known as the American Chameleon, but it is not a chameleon; due to anatomical reasons, the change of colour is much slower in the anoles than it is in the chameleons; in the former, the change is controlled by chemical changes in the blood and in the latter by the nerves in the skin.

Knight Anole   *A. equestris*
equestris (L) relating to horsemen; can mean relating to the knights; a reference to the head, which is casque-like and bears some resemblance to an armoured helmet. Anoles are widespread in Central America, the Greater and Lesser Antilles and the northern half of South America.

Leaf-nosed Anole   *A. phyllorhinus*
phullon (Gr) a leaf; *rhis* (Gr) genitive *rhinos* the nose; it has a peculiar flat formation of scaly tissue that extends beyond the nose but the function of this is not known. Inhabiting Brazil.

Sagré's Anole   *A. sagrei*
R. de la Sagré (1801–1871) was a Cuban historian and at one time Director of the Botanical Gardens in Havana; this anole was named in his honour by Duméril in 1837. It inhabits Cuba.

Family   AGAMIDAE   about 300 species

agama (New L) derived from the Dutch-Guianan language.

Common Agama   *Agama agama*
Agama see Family Agamidae above. The repetition of the generic name for the specific name is caused by a change of the generic name when some revision of the classification took place; it does not necessarily mean that it will be known as the 'common species'. (For further information see TAUTONYMS, p. 9) This lizard has a brightly coloured head and neck and, to a limited extent, can change colour; it is widespread in the central area of Africa and can frequently be seen sunning itself on walls and houses in populated areas.

Asian Agama   *A. agilis*
agilis (L) agile, busy; an unusual agama with eyes that are independently movable, like those of a chameleon. The range is from Arabia to Pakistan.

Black-necked Agama   *A. atricollis*
ater (L) black; *collum* (L) the neck; quite a big lizard with a

length up to 30 cm (12 in). It inhabits southern and eastern Africa.

Nigerian Agama   *A. benuensis*
-*ensis* (L) suffix meaning belonging to; it takes the name from the River Benue in Nigeria. A brightly coloured lizard with white and green spots and dark stripes. It inhabits Nigeria and Cameroon.

African Spiny-tailed Lizard   *Uromastyx acanthinurus*
oura (Gr) the tail; *mastix* (Gr) a whip; *akantha* (Gr) a thorn, a prickle; *oura* (Gr) the tail; 'a thorny-tailed whip-tail'; it has a short heavy tail which it lashes vigorously from side to side as a means of defence. Inhabiting desert areas in the northern part of Africa.

Egyptian Spiny-tailed Lizard   *U. aegypticus*
-*icus* (L) suffix meaning belonging to; one of the largest lizards in this family it can grow to a length of 75 cm (29½ in). Named from Egypt, it ranges across northern Africa from Algeria to north-western Arabia.

Toad-headed Agama   *Phrynocephalus mystaceus*
phrunos (Gr) a species of toad; *kephalē* (Gr) the head; *mustax* (Gr) genitive *mustakos* a moustache; it has a strange-looking head which somewhat resembles that of a toad; 'moustache' refers to folds of skin with spiky scales on either side of the mouth which can be distended during a threat display and which appear to increase the size of the gaping mouth. Inhabiting south-eastern Russia and ranging to central Asia.

Moloch   *Moloch horridus*
Moloch was the tribal god of the Ammonites, who demanded the human sacrifice of children by fire; *horridus* (L) rough, bristly; it can also mean frightful, horrible. In spite of its name, the Moloch is a harmless inoffensive lizard, but grotesque in appearance, its body being covered with large spikes. The name was given by Gray in 1841; he was well known for inventing many apparently meaningless scientific names for

animals or, as a friend of mine put it, 'an inveterate coiner'! Doubtless the formidable appearance of this lizard suggested the name. Ants are its chief food and it inhabits the deserts of central Australia. Dr J. E. Gray FRS (1800–1875) was Keeper of Zoology at the British Museum (Natural History) from 1840 to 1874.

Bearded Lizard   *Amphibolurus barbatus*
amphibolos (Gr) thrown round, attacked on both sides; *oura* (Gr) the tail; the reason for this name is obscure and not explained in the herpetological records in the British Museum (Natural History); *barbatus* (L) bearded; the beard consists of a fold of skin beneath the chin equipped with sharp spines which can be expanded as a threat display. Widespread in Australia except the north.

(No recognised English name)   *Diporiphora bilineata*
di- (Gr) prefix meaning two; *poros* (Gr) a passage through the skin, pores; *phora* (Gr) a carrying, a bearing; an allusion to the two small pores in the scales just forward of the anus; *bilineatus* (L) having two lines; a reference to the two white lines along the body. Inhabiting the northern part of Australia and New Guinea.

Frilled Lizard   *Chlamydosaurus kingi*
khlamus (Gr) genitive *khlamudos*, a short cloak, or mantle; *saura* (Gr) a lizard; an allusion to the cloak-like frill of skin round the shoulders which can be spread out as a gesture of defiance and is also used in courtship display; named after Rear Admiral Philip P. King FRS (1791–1856), the author of books on Australia. After serving on *HMS Mermaid* and *HMS Adventure* he settled in Sydney. Inhabiting New Guinea and northern Australia.

Water Lizard   *Hydrosaurus amboinensis*
hudor (Gr) water; as a prefix it becomes *hudro-; saura* (Gr) a lizard; it takes the specific name from Amboina (= Ambon Island) in the Moluccas, Indonesia, but it is known throughout

that area, including Celebes (now known as Sulawesi), the Moluccas and New Guinea. A big lizard with a length up to 110 cm (40 in); the tail is flattened in a vertical plane and the toes have lobes of skin, all aids to swimming. The local name is soa-soa.

Angle-headed Lizard *Gonocephalus godeffroyi*
gōnia (Gr) an angle, a corner; *kephalē* (Gr) the head; the name is descriptive, as the angle of the snout, seen from the side, appears more obtuse than in other lizards, so that the whole head is seen to be almost an equilateral triangle; J. C. Godeffroy (1813–1885) established the Godeffroy Museum in Hamburg and organised many journeys by naturalists to the South Pacific to collect specimens. Inhabiting north-eastern Australia, New Guinea and many islands in that area ranging to the Solomon Islands.

(No recognised English name) *Acanthosaura lepidogaster*
akantha (Gr) a thorn, a prickle; *saura* (Gr) a lizard; *lepis* (Gr) genitive *lepidos*, a scale; *gaster* (Gr) the belly; it has a row of spines along the neck and a spine on each side of the head behind the eyes; 'a scaly-bellied thorn-lizard'. Inhabiting southern China and the northern part of Thailand and Vietnam.

Lyre-headed Lizard *Lyriocephalus scutatus*
lura (Gr) a lyre; *kephalē* (Gr) the head; it has some peculiar scale formations and marks on the head but to liken it to a lyre requires some imagination; *scutum* (L) a shield; *scutatus* (L) armed with a shield; a reference to a hump on the snout covered with smooth scales; the function is not known. It inhabits Sri Lanka (formerly Ceylon).

Indian Bloodsucker *Calotes versicolor*
kalotēs (Gr) (= *kallos*) beauty; a rare word formed by Chrysippus; *versicolor* (L) changing colour, of various colours; an

allusion to its ability to change colour, which it does very quickly; this means that the change is made by nerves in the skin, like the chameleons, and not by a change in the blood hormones, like the anoles. It is sometimes, incorrectly, called a chameleon. The name 'bloodsucker' does not mean literally what it says, but refers to the scarlet colour of the head and neck, and this is particularly bright and spectacular when the mood is aggressive or during courtship display. Inhabiting Iran and ranging east and south through India to southern China and Malaysia. Chrysippus (*c.* 280–207 BC) was a Greek Stoic born at Soli, Cilicia, and later studied at the Academy in Athens.

Bornean Bloodsucker   *C. cristatellus*
crista (L) a crest; usually means a tuft on the head of animals; *cristatus* (L) having a crest; *-ellus* (L) diminutive suffix: having a little crest; it has a small crest of scales from the rear of the head extending a short distance along the back. Named from Borneo, it also inhabits the southern Thailand to Vietnam area and the Philippines.

Ceylon Deaf Agama   *Cophotis ceylanica* (= *ceylonica*)
kōphos (Gr) blunt, obtuse, dumb, deaf; *ous* (Gr) genitive *ōtos* the ear; it is not deaf, but has no exposed tympanum such as is found in most lizards; *-icus* (L) suffix meaning belonging to; Ceylon is now known as Sri Lanka. This agama is unusual as it has a prehensile tail.

Horned Agama   *Ceratophora stoddarti*
keras (Gr) genitive *keratos* the horn of an animal; *phora* (Gr) a bearing, carrying; it has a peculiar small horn on the tip of the nose. The specific name is given in honour of Colonel Stoddart, of the Royal Staff college, who collected this lizard for Gray in 1831. It inhabits Sri Lanka (Ceylon).

(No recognised English name)   *Ptyctolaemus gularis*
ptux (Gr) genitive *ptukhos* a fold, layer; *ptuktos* (Gr) folded; *laimos* (Gr) the throat, gullet; *gularis* (L) pertaining to the throat; an

allusion to the folds of skin round the neck and throat. Inhabiting Assam, Asia.

Butterfly or Smooth-scaled Lizard   *Leiolepis belliana*
leios (Gr) smooth; *lepis* (Gr) a scale, particularly the scales of a lizard; Thomas Bell (1792–1880) was a naturalist who helped Dr Gray with his work. The name butterfly is an allusion to the brilliant colouring which includes shades of orange, black, brown, green and yellow, and may have an irridescent sheen. Inhabiting the Thailand-Kampuchea area, Malaysia and Sumatra.

Flying Dragon   *Draco volans*
draco (L) genitive *draconis* from *drakōn* (Gr) a dragon; *volo* (L) I fly; *volans* (L) flying; it cannot fly in a true sense, but has membranes of skin on the sides of the body which it can distend and is thus able to make quite long gliding flights of about 50 m (55 yds). The lizards in this genus are the only ones that have this ability. Inhabiting Malaysia, the Philippines and Indonesia.

Black-bearded Dragon   *D. melanopogon*
melas (Gr) genitive *melanos* black; *pōgōn* (Gr) the beard; a reference to the black dewlap which, when distended, could be likened to a beard. Inhabiting Sumatra and Borneo.

Family   CHAMAELEONIDAE   about 80 species (probably more)

The Liddell and Scott *Greek-English Lexicon* gives the complete word *khamai-leōn*, and simply translates it as the chameleon, but the name is derived from two Greek words: *khamai* (Gr) on the ground, near the ground, or dwarf; *leōn* (Gr) a lion, hence 'a lion near the ground', a little lion; a peculiar name as the chameleon can hardly be said to resemble a lion!

The chameleon is well known for its ability to change colour, although a number of other lizards can also do this. Equally remarkable are the eyes, which swivel independently of each other, and the tongue which can be shot out with incredible speed to trap an insect; it can be extended to a length equal to that of the head and body together. Although chameleons normally move with slow, deliberate steps, they can scuttle away quite fast on the ground if frightened. The peculiar hesitant movement typical of chameleons, when they seem to sway to and fro several times with each step, is considered to be an imitation of a leaf swaying in the wind, to deceive predators, and also to deceive their prey as they move up for the fatal strike with the tongue.

The colour change can be effected by light or by an emotional state, and can be quite fast (see *Anolis carolinensis*, p. 77); it does not necessarily match the background. I once watched two chameleons meet on a picture rail in a house in Uganda and neither would give way; they both turned black with rage! On another occasion, I brought one into my camp, sitting on my hand and clutching my fingers with its little feet; my African servants fled in terror, as they think that if touched by a chameleon you become sterile.

African Chameleon   *Chamaeleo africanus*
Chamaeleo see Family Chamaeleonidae above. This is one of the big chameleons, measuring up to a length of 37 cm (about $14\frac{1}{2}$ in). It inhabits the northern part of Africa south of the Sahara, ranging from the west coast across to Ethiopia and Somalia.

Two-lined Chameleon   *C. bitaeniatus*
bis (L) two, double; *taenia* (L) a band, a ribbon; *-atus* (L) suffix meaning provided with; it means striped and refers to two light stripes on a dark background along the sides of the body. Inhabiting a large area on the eastern side of Africa including Uganda, Kenya, Tanzania and the northern part of Mozambique.

Short-horned Chameleon   *C. brevicornis*
brevis (L) short; *cornu* (L) the horn of animals; the 80 (or more) species of chameleons display a variety of horns, some being flexible and hardly worthy of the name; this species has a very

short single horn in the male, but absent in the female. Inhabiting Madagascar.

European or Mediterranean Chameleon   *C. chamaeleon chamaeleon*

Although the name suggests that it lives in Europe, southern Spain and Crete are probably the only places in Europe where it can be found; apart from this it inhabits the borders of the southern Mediterranean from Israel ranging west to Morocco. It is the nominate subspecies.

Zeylan Chameleon   *C. c. zeylanicus*
This subspecies of *Chamaeleo chamaeleon* inhabits India and Sri Lanka and is probably the only chameleon to be found in that part of Asia.

Common Chameleon   *C. dilepis*
dis (Gr) twice, or two; *lepis* (Gr) a scale, particularly the scales of a lizard; a reference to two lobes at the back part of the head which are erected when it meets another chameleon; this might be accompanied by a change of colour. Inhabiting the southern part of Africa from the area of the equator ranging south.

Fork-horned or Fork-nosed Chameleon   *C. furcifer*
furca (L) a fork; *fero* (L) I bear, carry; the name 'fork-nosed' is misleading as it is the horn on the nose that is forked and this gives it a peculiar appearance. Inhabiting Madagascar.

Jackson's Chameleon   *C. jacksonii*
Sir F. J. Jackson (1860–1929) was a naturalist and author and was Governor of Uganda from 1911 to 1917. This chameleon has three horns, one on the snout and two slightly further back on the head; it inhabits Kenya, Uganda and Tanzania. I have seen these chameleons, and other species, on many occasions in Kenya and Uganda without especially looking for them; they are quite happy to live more or less permanently on the rose trees and bushes in private gardens.

(No recognised English name)   *C. lateralis*
latus (L) genitive *lateris* the side, flank; *-alis* (L) suffix meaning relating to; the body is normally a dull green with a light stripe along the flank but, as an example of how chameleons defy being described accurately by colour, this species, when angry, shows a network of various colours including blue and yellow. It is widespread in Madagascar but seems to prefer the highlands in the central area.

Dwarf Chameleon   *C. pumilus*
pumilus (L) a dwarf, a pigmy; a very small chameleon with a length of only about 14 cm ($5\frac{1}{2}$ in). Inhabiting a small area round the southern coast of South Africa.

Nossi Bé Dwarf Chameleon   *Brookesia minima*
The genus *Brookesia* was given by Gray in 1827; he decided on this name when examining the private museum of a Mr Joshua Brookes and gave it in recognition of his services to zoology; further information about Mr Brookes is not recorded; *minimus* (L) smallest; only one other species of chameleon is known to be so small, with a length of 3.2 cm ($1\frac{1}{4}$ in). Found only on Nossi Bé, a small island off the north-west coast of Madagascar.

Armoured Chameleon   *B. perarmata*
per- (L) prefix meaning well, very; *armatus* (L) armed; a reference to the double row of thorn-like spines along the back. Inhabiting the western part of Madagascar.

Flat-headed Chameleon   *B. platyceps*
platus (Gr) flat or wide; *ceps* (New L) from *caput* (L) the head; it has a flat top to the head. Inhabiting Malawi, East Africa.

Family   SCINCIDAE   about 700 species
scincus (L) a kind of lizard. The skinks are one of the largest families of lizards and almost worldwide in distribution in the tropical and warm areas, although most are found in Africa, southern Asia and Australasia. Many species look just like ordinary lizards, for example the pretty little Five-lined Skink

Mabuya quinquetaeniata, while others have degenerate legs or none at all, for example the South African Plain Skink *Scelotes inornatus*. Many species are good burrowers and spend much of their time underground.

Subfamily TILIQUINAE

Tiliqua is an obscure name given by Gray in 1825; herpetological records at the British Museum (Natural History) do not give any explanation.

(No recognised English name) *Tiliqua nigrolutea*
Tiliqua see Subfamily Tiliquinae above; *niger* (L) black; *luteus* (L) saffron yellow; it has a blackish pattern on the back merging into shades of dark to light brown. Inhabiting the southern part of Australia and Tasmania.

Stump-tailed Skink *T. rugosa*
ruga (L) a wrinkle; *-osus* (L) suffix meaning full of, prone to; wrinkled; a reference to the plates on the head and back which are thick and rough. The tail is very short and fat, so much so that it looks very like the animal's head and, to a casual observer, gives the impression of a two-headed lizard. Inhabiting western and south- western Australia.

Blue-tongued Skink *T. scincoides scincoides*
scincus (L) a kind of lizard; *-oides* (New L) from *eidos* (Gr) apparent shape, form. Inhabiting Western Australia. This is the nominate subspecies; two other subspecies are given below.

Giant Blue-tongued Skink *T. s. gigas*
gigas (L) a giant; one of the largest skinks with a length of about 50 cm (19½ in). Inhabiting New Guinea, the Moluccas and other islands in that area.

Intermediate Blue-tongued Skink *T. s. intermedia*
intermedius (L) between; another large skink coming between *gigas* and *scincoides* in length. Inhabiting the northern part of Western Australia.

Subfamily SCINCINAE

scincus (L) a kind of lizard.

Eastern Skink   *Scincus conirostris*
Scincus see Subfamily Scincinae above; *conus* (L) a cone; *rostrum* (L) the beak, snout; a reference to the shape of the nose which is adapted for burrowing through the sand. Inhabiting Iran.

Arabian Skink   *S. muscatensis*
-ensis (L) suffix meaning belonging to, usually a place; named from Muscat, it inhabits Arabian desert areas.

Philby's Arabian Skink   *S. philbyi*
H. St John Bridger Philby (1885–1960) was an explorer, author and orientalist and became a friend of Ibn Sa'ud. He crossed the 'Empty Quarter' (Rub al' Khalé) in southern Arabia in 1932. This skink inhabits the southern part of Arabia.

Common Skink   *S. scincus*
For explanation of the generic name being repeated for the specific, see TAUTONYMS, p. oo. Inhabiting desert areas ranging across northern Africa from Senegal to Egypt and Israel.

Short-footed Sand Skink   *Ophiomorus brevipes*
ophis (Gr) a snake; *moros* (= *phobos*) (Gr) fear, fright; some of the skinks in this genus have no visible legs and their method of moving is very snake-like; *brevis* (L) short; *pes* (L) the foot. This skink inhabits desert or sandy areas of southern Iran where it can easily bury itself.

Persian Snake Skink   *O. persicus*
-icus (L) suffix meaning belonging to; Persia is now known as Iran; it inhabits western Iran. This species has no legs and has the appearance of a snake.

Speckled Snake Skink   *O. punctatissimus*
punctum (L) a hole, a puncture; *punctatus* (New L) spotted as with punctures; *-issimus* (L) suffix meaning very, much; it has a

pale body covered with very small spots and, having no legs, looks very much like a snake. Inhabiting Greece and Turkey.

Three-toed Sand Skink   *O. tridactylus*
trias (Gr) the number three; *daktulos* (Gr) a finger, can mean a toe; although a true skink such as *Scinctus scinctus* has five toes and normal legs, a gradual degeneration has brought about a reduction in the number of toes and the length of the legs in many species; this species has already been reduced to three toes on each foot. Inhabiting West Pakistan, Afghanistan and the adjoining part of eastern Iran.

Algerian Skink   *Eumeces algeriensis*
eu- (Gr) a prefix meaning well, nicely; sometimes used to mean the typical or most advanced animals in a group; *mēkos* (Gr) length, stature; a large skink, it can be 42 cm ($16\frac{1}{2}$ in) in total length, with a long tail and five toes on each foot, in fact a typical lizard. Furthermore, lizards in this genus are among the very few reptiles that show any care for the young after the eggs have hatched, guarding them and licking them clean, and indeed will guard the eggs and turn them regularly before hatching like the birds. Considering that the birds evolved from the more advanced lizards this is not so surprising. *-ensis* (L) belonging to, usually a place; taking its name from Algeria, it is also found in Morocco and Tunisia.

American Five-lined Skink   *E. fasciatus*
fascia (L) a band, girdle; *fasciatus*, banded; a misleading name as the lizard has five stripes or lines along the body and not bands. Inhabiting the eastern part of North America.

Broad-headed Skink   *E. laticeps*
latus (L) broad, wide; *ceps* (New L) from *caput* (L) the head. Sometimes known as the Greater Five-lined Skink, it inhabits North America.

(No recognised English name)   *Sphenops sepsoides*
sphen (Gr) a wedge; *ops* (Gr) eye, face; can mean appearance; a reference to the wedge-shaped snout used for burrowing

through the sand; *seps* (Gr) a serpent, the bite of which causes putrefaction; can also mean a type of lizard; *oides* (New L) from *eidos* (Gr) apparent shape, form. Inhabiting Egypt and Israel.

Cylindrical Skink   *Chalcides chalcides*
khalkis (Gr) genitive *khalkidos* a lizard with copper-coloured stripes on the back; this species is a bronze colour with several dark lines along the back; the body is more cylindrical than typical lizards and is snake-like in appearance. When in a hurry, the legs are not used and it adopts a snake-like movement. Inhabiting eastern Mediterraean countries.

Eyed Cylindrical Skink   *C. ocellatus*
ocellus (L) a little eye; *-atus* (L) suffix meaning provided with; it has a thick cylindrical body and tail, and is marked with small black spots and streaks of white. Inhabiting Sudan, Somalia, the Mediterranean area of northern Africa and ranging east to southern Asia.

Green Cylindrical Skink   *C. viridanus*
viridis (L) green, can mean all shades of green; *-anus* (L) belonging to; it is similar to other skinks in this genus but with an olive green back. Inhabiting western Canary Islands.

Subfamily   LYGOSOMINAE

lugos (Gr) a pliant twig, especially a twig for wickerwork; *soma* (Gr) the body; the subfamily name is taken from the genus *Lygosoma*, a skink with a long slender body.

Indian Keeled Skink   *Mabuya carinata*
mabuya (New L) from American-Spanish, a lizard; the name originates from the Brazilian species; *carina* (L) a keel; *-atus* (L) a suffix meaning provided with; a reference to the form of the toes. The Mabuya Skinks are widespread, being found in southern Asia, Africa and the Americas, but are not known in New Guinea and Australia. This skink inhabits Sri Lanka (formerly Ceylon).

Eastern Smooth Skink   *M. laevis*
laevis is from *levis* (L) smooth. Inhabiting the small islands in
south-eastern Asia.

Common Mabuya   *M. mabuya*
A brown skink widespread in Mexico and ranging south
through Central America to Brazil and Bolivia.

African Five-lined Skink   *M. quinquetaeniata*
quinque (L) five; *taenia* (L) a band, a ribbon; -*atus* (L) suffix
meaning provided with; the five lines are not bands but stripes
running lengthways. On one occasion in Uganda, Dr Cott and
I were resting near the Nile just below the Kabalega Falls
(formerly Murchison Falls) drinking our flask of tea (laced with
limejuice from limes picked from a nearby tree!), when one of
these pretty little lizards scampered across the rocks at our feet;
they are widespread in northern Africa and down the Nile
valley.

(No recognised English name   *Sphenomorphus florensis*
sphen (Gr) a wedge; *morphē* (Gr) form, shape; a reference to the
short wedge-shaped head; -*ensis* (L) suffix meaning belonging
to, usually a place; inhabiting Flores Island, Indonesia.

Indian Skink   *S. indicus*
-*icus* (L) suffix meaning belonging to. Inhabiting the lower
slopes of the Himalayas in India and Tibet.

Slender Skink   *Lygosoma novaeguineae*
lugos (Gr) a pliant twig, specially a twig for wickerwork; *soma*
(Gr) the body; a reference to the long slender body. Inhabiting
New Guinea.

Kashmir Smooth Skink   *Leiolopisma ladacensis*
leios (Gr) smooth, soft; *lopos* (Gr) shell, bark; *lopisma* (Gr) a rare
word used by Eustathius in 1160 AD with the same meaning;
Ladakh is a district in Kashmir, India; -*ensis* (L) suffix meaning
belonging to, usually a place. This skink has been found in the
mountains of Kashmir at a height of over 4,500 m (15,000 ft).
Eustathius (died *c.* 1193) was a Greek scholar who studied the

ancient classic authors; the unusual word *lopisma* was first published seven centuries later in 1863.

Himalayan Smooth Skink   *L. himalayana*
-anus (L) suffix meaning belonging to. In this species, the male can be distinguished by the bright red marking on the sides of the body during the mating season; it can be found living at an altitude of over 3,500 m (about 12,000 ft) in the Himalayas.

The Emo   *Emoia cyanura*
Gray named this species The Emo in 1845, but does not give an explanation; it seems likely that the name refers to a person, or the people, of one of the remote islands where it lives; *kuaneos* (Gr) blue; *oura* (Gr) the tail; there are about 40 species in this genus. Dr J. E. Gray FRS (1800–1875) was a zoologist at the British Museum (Natural History) from 1840 to 1874. These lizards are widespread in the Indo-Pacific island region.

Black-sided Emo   *E. atrocostata*
ater (L) black; *costa* (L) a rib; can mean the side; *atus* (L) provided with; 'having black sides'. Inhabiting the coasts of islands near Singapore, it has been seen swimming and hunting for prey in the sea.

Keeled Skink   *Tropidophorus sinicus*
tropis (Gr) genitive *tropios* which later became *tropidos* a ship's keel; *phora* (Gr) a carrying, bearing; a reference to the pronounced keels on the scales which probably assist them when swimming; they are one of the few skinks which are good swimmers. *sinae* (New L) a people of south-east Asia, usually taken to mean the Chinese; *-icus* (L) suffix meaning belonging to; this can be interpreted in the wider sense of south-east Asia as the skinks in this genus are also found in the Malay Peninsula, Borneo, Celebes (now known as Sulawesi) and the Philippines.

Lidless Skink   *Ablepharus pannonicus*
a- (Gr) prefix meaning not, or there is not; *blepharon* (Gr) an eyelid; an allusion to the eyelids which are fixed permanently

shut and transparent; -*icus* (L) suffix meaning belong to; named from Pannonia, an ancient country not shown on modern maps; it is an area now known as Yugoslavia and included neighbouring countries such as Hungary. One of the very few skinks found in Europe it inhabits Hungary and Romania.

Wahlberg's Skink   *Panaspis wahlbergi*
pan (Gr) all; *aspis* (Gr) a viper, an asp; the eyelids are permanently shut, as in *Ablepharus* above, and for this reason the lizards in this genus are sometimes known as 'snake-eyes'; J. A. Wahlberg (1810–1856) was a Swedish naturalist who was in Africa from 1839 to 1845. This skink inhabits Kenya and ranges south through Tanzania.

Two-legged Skink   *Scelotes bipes*
skelos (Gr) the leg; -*tes* (Gr) suffix meaning pertaining to; *bis* (L) two, double; *pes* (L) the foot; the skinks in this genus show a complete range of reduced legs and toes, from *Scelotes bojeri*, which has quite normal legs and the usual five toes, to *S. inornatus* which has no legs at all. This skink, *bipes*, as the name tells us, has only two legs, the hind legs, and only two toes on each leg. Inhabiting Madagascar.

Bojer's Skink   *S. bojeri*
Wenzel Bojer (1800–1856) was a Czechoslovakian naturalist from Prague; he collected in Madagascar and Zanzibar and was Curator of the Mauritius Natural History Museum. This skink has four perfectly good legs with five toes on each foot; it inhabits Mauritius.

Plain Skink   *S. inornatus*
It is not surprising that this skink has acquired the name 'plain'; it has no legs at all; the Latin name has the same meaning: *ornatus* (L) ornament, decoration; *inornatus* (L) plain. It inhabits South Africa.

Black-sided Skink   *S. melanopleura*
melas (Gr) genitive *melanos* black; *pleura* (Gr) a rib; usually plural, the ribs or sides of a man or any other animal. This

skink has five toes but the legs are much reduced and very short; it inhabits Madagascar.

Dart Skink   *Acontias plumbeus*
akōn (Gr) a javelin, a dart; *akontias* (Gr) a quick-darting serpent; it is not, of course, a serpent but is a limbless lizard, so it may well have been mistaken for a snake when the name was given; *plumbeus* (L) lead-coloured. Inhabiting Africa and Madagascar.

(No recognised English name)   *Sepsina angolensis*
sēps (Gr) a putrefying sore; a snake whose bite causes putrefaction; a kind of lizard; *-inus* (L) suffix meaning like; it has a snake-like body and very small legs and in ancient times it was thought to have a poisonous bite; *-ensis* (L) suffix meaning belonging to; it inhabits the Angolan area.

Family   FEYLINIIDAE   4 species

Feylinia appears to be named after a naturalist or collector named Feylin, but research in the Department of Zoology at the British Museum (Natural History) gives no explanation of the name.

Curror's Skink   *Feylinia currori*
Feylinia see Family Feyliniidae above. Little is known about J. Curror, an officer in the Royal Navy, except that he supplied the information that enabled Gray to describe the animal. It is limbless and lives underground in tropical Africa. Dr J. E. Gray FRS (1800–1875) was a zoologist at the British Museum (Natural History) from 1840 to 1874.

Family   ANELYTROPSIDAE   1 species

anelytros (Gr) without sheath, or covering; *opsis* (Gr) aspect, appearance; or *ops* (Gr) the eye; Cope describes this lizard as having the epidermis absolutely continuous over the eye, the eye being scarcely visible through the single ocular plate, so the generic name seems contradictory; furthermore if the eye is visible one assumes it is not blind!

Mexican Blind Lizard *Anelytropsis papillosus*

Anelytropsis see Family Anelytropsidae above; *papilla* (L) a pimple; -*osus* (L) suffix meaning full of; 'very pimply'; a reference to the rough scales on the body. Very rare and only found in Mexico. E. D. Cope (1840–1897) was an American zoologist who took a special interest in reptiles and wrote articles for the herpetological magazine *Copeia*; it was named in his honour (E. C. Jaeger).

Family CORDYLIDAE 33 species

kordulē (Gr) a club, a cudgel; not a reference to the shape of the tail but to its use as a weapon; there are large spines on the head, body and tail, and the latter can be lashed vigorously from side to side; the lizards in this genus have heavy protective armour.

Subfamily CORDYLINAE

Blue-spotted Girdle-tailed Lizard *Cordylus caeruleopunctatus*

Cordylus see Family Cordylidae above; *caeruleus* (L) dark blue; *punctum* (L) a hole, a prick; *punctatus* (L) spotted as with punctures; it has very marked bright blue spots on the sides of the body. Inhabiting the mountains in the southern part of Cape Province, South Africa.

Armadillo Lizard *C. cataphractus*

kataphraktos (Gr) covered, decked in; horses clad in full armour; also *cataphractus* (L) mail-clad; a reference to the heavy protective armour; the English name is from the mammal, Armadillo, which has protective bony scales. Inhabiting the western part of Cape Province, South Africa.

Common Girdle-tailed Lizard   *C. cordylus*
The name 'girdle-tailed' is a reference to the large spiked scales that encircle the tail and enhance its use as a weapon; it lashes vigorously with its tail if threatened. This lizard has a wider range than the other 22 species in the genus, inhabiting Ethiopia, Kenya and ranging south to Cape Province, South Africa.

Giant Girdle-tailed Lizard   *C. giganteus*
gigas (L) a giant; *giganteus* (L) gigantic; the largest lizard in this genus, it can grow to a length of about 38 cm (15 in). Inhabiting South Africa.

Spotted or Red-tailed Flat Lizard   *Platysaurus guttatus*
platus (Gr) flat; *saura* (Gr) a lizard; the head and body are unusually flat which enables it to hide in very narrow cracks in the rocky terrain where it lives; *gutta* (L) a drop (of a fluid); *guttae* (L) spots or marks on animals; *guttatus* (L) spotted, speckled. Inhabiting the Transvaal area of South Africa.

(No recognised English name)   *P. imperator*
imperator (L) a commander, a leader; an allusion to its size, being the largest of the 10 species in this genus, at 32 cm ($12\frac{1}{2}$ in). Inhabiting the north-east part of Zimbabwe and the neighbouring part of Mozambique.

Cape Snake Lizard   *Chamaesaura anguina*
khamai (Gr) on the ground, on the earth; *saura* (Gr) a lizard; the legs are much reduced, useless for crawling and barely visible, so the body must slide along on the ground like a snake; *anguis* (L) a snake; *-inus* (L) a suffix meaning like; not only is the movement snake-like but the body tapers down gradually to the tail which is more than twice the length of the body; only close examination would reveal where the tail actually starts. An inquisitive person, thinking it was a small snake and grabbing it by the tail, would quickly discover it was not a snake as the tail would break off and remain wriggling in his hand! Snakes are not capable of autotomy. Inhabiting South Africa.

Large-scaled Snake Lizard   *C. macrolepis*
makros (Gr) long; the word is not really suitable as strictly speaking it means long, not large; *lepis* (Gr) the scale of an animal; the legs are even more reduced than *C. anguina* (above) and are only vestigial. Inhabiting South Africa.

Subfamily   GERRHOSAURINAE

gerrhon (Gr) anything made of wicker work, especially an oblong shield; *saura* (Gr) a lizard; known as 'plated lizards' because of the special head shields, the bony cores in the body scales and their arrangement in longitudinal and cross rows giving the appearance of wicker work; this encases the lizard in a protective shell.

Yellow-throated Plated Lizard   *Gerrhosaurus flavigularis*
Gerrhosaurus see Subfamily Gerrhosaurinae above; *flavus* (L) yellow; *gula* (L) the throat; *-aris* (L) suffix meaning pertaining to. It inhabits Sudan, Ethiopia and ranges south through East Africa to the Cape.

Sudan Plated Lizard   *G. major*
major (L) greater; although indicating a large lizard, it does not mean the largest: *maximus* (L) greatest, would mean the largest lizard. At 56 cm (22 in) it is not so big as *G. validus* (below). It inhabits Sudan and Eritrea and ranges south through East Africa to South Africa.

South African Plated Lizard   *G. validus*
validus (L) strong, robust; at present, records show that this is the largest species in the genus at 69 cm (27 in). It inhabits Mozambique and ranges south to the eastern part of South Africa.

(No recognised English name)   *Cordylosaurus subtessellatus*
kordulē (Gr) see Family Cordylidae p. 95; *saura* (Gr) a lizard, *sub-* (L) under, can mean less than usual; *tessella* (L) a cube-shaped paving stone; *tessellatus* (L) set with small cubes; an allusion to the shields on the front part of the head, there being

less than those of other related species. Inhabiting Angola and ranging south to the western part of South Africa.

African Seps   *Tetradactylus africanus*
tetras (Gr) four; *daktulos* (Gr) a finger, can mean a toe; this genus shows a great variation in the number of toes on the feet so the generic name may be misleading; in this species, the fore legs are very small with only one toe on each foot. Inhabiting South Africa.

Short-legged Seps   *T. seps*
seps (Gr) a putrefying sore; a snake whose bite causes putrefaction; a kind of lizard; although the legs are very much reduced there are still five toes on each foot, so the generic name is again misleading. Inhabiting South Africa.

Long-tailed Seps   *T. tetradactylus*
tetradaktulos (Gr) four toes (see above under *T. africanus*). This species actually does have four toes, so the generic and specific names are correct; for an explanation of the tautonymous name see p. 9 under TAUTONYMS. Inhabiting Table Mountain, South Africa.

Family   XANTUSIIDAE   12 species

Named in honour of L. Jason Xantus (1825–1894), a Hungarian zoologist; he was chiefly known for his interest in birds and Xantus's Murrelet *Brachyramphus hypoleuca* is named after him, but he was an all-round naturalist and became Director of the Zoological Gardens in Budapest in 1866. The Night Lizards, as their English name suggests, are nocturnal and spend the day hidden under rocks, only appearing at night to hunt for food, mostly insects.

Cuban Night Lizard   *Cricosaura typica*
krikos (Gr) a ring, circular; *saura* (Gr) a lizard; a reference to the rounded shape of the body; *tupos* (Gr) a blow, a mark; can mean the general character of a thing, its kind, sort, e.g.

typical; it is typical of this family. A very rare lizard found only in Cuba and threatened with extinction.

Island Night Lizard   *Klauberina riversiana*
Named after Dr L. M. Klauber (born 1883), an American who was by profession an engineer but had a keen interest in reptiles and wrote several books on snakes; he was a member of the Zoological Society of San Diego; *riversiana*: this lizard was described by Cope in 1883, but the description was first published in the *American Naturalist* in 1879 by an unnamed zoologist who said that he wished to commemorate Mr Rivers of the University of California; further details about Mr Rivers are not recorded. It has less nocturnal habits than other lizards in this small family; it inhabits several small islands off the coast of California. E. D. Cope (1840–1897) was an American zoologist with a particular interest in herpetology; the journal *Copeia* was named in his honour (E. C. Jaeger).

Desert or Yucca Night Lizard   *Xantusia vigilis*
Xantusia see Family Xantusiidae, p. 98; *vigil* (L) genitive *vigilis* alert, watchful; an allusion to the eyes which have no eyelids but are covered by a transparent scale so they are never shut. Another lizard which can change colour; it is paler during the day than at night. Inhabiting desert areas of California, Nevada, Utah and Arizona; it is often found in Yucca trees or hiding amongst the litter beneath.

Family   TEIIDAE   200 species

teju (Portuguese), from the Tupi language, a lizard. These are typical lizards and in many ways resemble the Lacertidae of Europe and Africa, although they vary in size from about 7.5 cm (3 in) up to 140 cm (4 ft 8 in) and some have the legs much reduced.

Seven-lined Racerunner   *Cnemidophorus deppei*
knēmis (Gr) genitive *knēmidos* a greave, a legging, armour between knee and ankle; *phor* (Gr) a carrying, a bearing;

knēmidophorus (Gr) wearing greaves to protect legs; an allusion to the thick scales on the legs; F. Deppe (1794–1860) was a naturalist who collected in Mexico and Hawaii during the early part of the nineteenth century. The lizards in this genus are often known as 'racerunners' on account of their great speed when seeking safety; during a chase they can stop suddenly which may cause the predator to over-run; they then dash off at lightning speed in a completely different direction. Speeds of about 30 kph (18 mph) have been estimated. Inhabiting Mexico and ranging south to Costa Rica.

Six-lined Racerunner   *C. sexlineatus*
sex (L) six; *linea* (L) a linen thread, string; can mean a line drawn; *-atus* (L) suffix meaning provided with; an allusion to the pale stripes along the back and extending to the tail. Inhabiting a large area of southern North America in Nevada and Utah, and ranging south and east to include Florida and west to part of Mexico.

Chequered or Tessellated Racerunner   *C. tessellatus*
tessella (L) a cube-shaped paving stone; *tessellatus* (L) set with small cubes; an allusion to the shape of the scales on the back. Inhabiting the southern part of North America.

Common or Yellow-throated Runner   *Ameiva chrysolaema*
ameiva, a native name for a lizard from the Tupi language; *khrusos* (Gr) gold; *khruseos* (Gr) golden-yellow; *laimos* (Gr) the throat. Inhabiting rocky barren areas in Haiti.

Dwarf Runner   *A. lineolata*
linea (L) a linen thread, string; can mean a line drawn; *lineola* (L) a little line; *-atus* (L) suffix meaning provided with; a reference to the stripes on the back. A small lizard and, although called a 'dwarf runner', at 15 cm (6 in) it is not the smallest teiid. Inhabiting Haiti.

Striped Racerunner   *Kentropyx striatus*
kentron (Gr) a spike, spur; *pux* (Gr) the rump, buttocks (a later form of *pugē*, as used by Aristotle); an allusion to the large spiky

keeled scales on the belly; *stria* (L) a channel, a furrow; *striatus* (New L) striped; it has small granular scales which form stripes along the flanks. Inhabiting north-eastern Brazil.

(No recognised English name)   *Tupinambis teguixin*
The Tupinambas were a group of Tupian peoples, now extinct, of the Brazilian coast, from the mouth of the Amazon to São Paulo; *tegu = teju* (Portuguese) from the Tupi language, a lizard; *ixia* (Gr) the chamaeleon plant; a reference to its liking for juicy fruits and leaves, although its diet is very varied, including small mammals and birds, their eggs, amphibians, insects and worms. This is a big lizard and can grow to a length of 140 cm (about 4 ft 6 in); it inhabits a large area of eastern South America from north of the Amazon to Uruguay.

Red Tegu   *T. rufescens*
rufus (L) red; *-escens* (L) suffix meaning nearly, approaching, i.e. 'reddish'; this is a big lizard but not attaining the size of *T. teguixin* (above). Inhabiting Argentina.

False Monitor   *Tejovaranus flavipunctatus*
tejo = teju (Portuguese) from the Tupi language, a lizard; *varanus* (New L) from *waran* (Ar) a monitor lizard; *flavus* (L) yellow; *punctum* (L) a hole, a prick; *punctatus* (L) spotted as with punctures; a reference to the yellow spots on the body. A big lizard measuring about 100 cm (3 ft 4 in) and certainly having the appearance of a monitor lizard, but known as the False Monitor because it is not a true monitor of the family Varanidae. It is a voracious carnivore and something of a cannibal as it often eats small lizards. Inhabiting Peru.

Caiman Lizard   *Dracaena guianensis*
drakōn (Gr) fem. *drakaina* a dragon; *-ensis* (L) suffix meaning belonging to; named from Guiana, it inhabits a large area of north-eastern South America. It is known as a Caiman from the Spanish *caiman*, an alligator; it has a vertically flattened tail for swimming and spends most of the day in the water, but it is not an alligator of the family Alligatoridae. Rather bigger, at about 125 cm (4 ft 2 in), than the False Monitor (above).

Dragon Lizardet *Crocodilurus lacertinus*
krokodeilos (Gr) a kind of lizard; actually an Ionic Greek word
and can mean the Nile crocodile; *oura* (Gr) the tail; it has a
flattened tail similar to a crocodile; *lacerta* (L) a lizard; *-inus* (L)
suffix meaning like. A good swimmer, spending much of the
day in the water, it eats fish and frogs. Inhabiting Central
America and northern South America.

Water Teiid *Neusticurus bicarinatus*
neustikos (Gr) able to swim; *oura* (Gr) the tail; *bi-* (L) prefix
meaning two; *carina* (L) the keel of a ship; *-atus* (L) suffix
meaning provided with; it has two parallel keels of spiny scales
along the top of the tail, which is flattened and well adapted for
swimming. It eats mostly tadpoles and small fish. Inhabiting
Venezuela and ranging east to north-eastern Brazil.

Spectacled Teiid *Gymnophthalmus speciosus*
gumnos (Gr) naked; *ophthalmos* (Gr) the eye; the lower eyelid is
transparent and so forms a sort of spectacle when closed;
speciosus (L) showy, brilliant; a reference to the brilliant colours;
it has a blue line on the side of the head, a brownish head and
body with a metallic sheen, and an orange tail. A small lizard,
only 15 cm (6 in), inhabiting Mexico and ranging south to
Colombia.

Earless Teiid *Bachia cophias*
bachia; Gray listed this name in his 1945 *Catalogue of Lizards* but,
as frequently happens regarding his names, he did not explain
it; one assumes that it commemorates a naturalist named Bach;
cōphos (Gr) blunt, obtuse; can mean deaf; the lizard is not deaf
but does not have a visible tympanum like most lizards. It is a
strange-looking creature, worm-like, with tiny legs that are
almost useless for locomotion, so it moves about with the action
of a snake. It inhabits northern South America, ranging south
to Bolivia and Chile. Dr J. E. Gray FRS (1800–1875) was a
zoologist at the British Museum (Natural History) in 1840.

Rough Teiid *Echinosaura horrida*
ekhinos (Gr) a hedgehog; *saura* (Gr) a lizard; *horridus* (L) rough,

prickly; a reference to the rows of large spiky scales on the back. Inhabiting Panama, Colombia and Ecuador.

Family LACERTIDAE over 200 species

lacerta (L) a lizard. It is quite reasonable to consider the lizards in this family as 'typical lizards'; they do not have any special features to distinguish them like the geckos with their toes specially adapted for climbing smooth surfaces, the anoles with the expanding dewlap, or the chameleons with their unusual eyes, feet and ability to change colour, not to mention the extraordinary tongue.

Chameleons are not the only lizards that can change colour and some lizards can do this as quickly as the chameleons, but not the lacertids. They do all have the ability to shed their tails, known as autotomy (see p. 17), but this is not the case with all the Sauria.

Among the 200 or so species there are many small variations in diet, habitat, colour and scale formation, and this has caused taxonomists to divide them into many genera, species and subspecies; opinions about these divisions are always changing and have been doing so since the late nineteenth century. Herpetologists have spent many hours in the field and in the laboratory trying to establish satisfactory divisions and have even divided the genera into subgenera in an attempt to solve the problem; I am not including these as the whole subject is still under discussion and anything that appears now would soon be out of date.

Sand Lizard *Lacerta agilis*

lacerta see Family Lacertidae above; *agilis* (L) agile, busy; it seems hardly necessary to explain these Latin names; almost all the lacertids are very active and agile when their body temperature is raised by the warmth of the sun, although *L. agilis* is not actually the most agile. In spite of the English name it is by no means always found in sandy areas. It is widespread

in Eurasia, including southern England, southern Sweden and
Spain in the west, and ranging east as far as Lake Baikal.

Lagarto   *L. atlantica*
atlantica (L) of the Atlantic; this lizard inhabits two of the
islands in the Canary Islands group in the Atlantic. Lanzarote
and Fuerteventura. The diet is unusual for a lacertid as instead
of the usual insects it seems to prefer snails, worms, carrion and
even the droppings of some animals; this is not surprising if they
are rabbit droppings as rabbits always evacuate a certain
amount of pellets, which differ from ordinary pellets in being
rich in protein and which are eaten and redigested (R. M.
Lockley). *Lagarto* is Spanish for a lizard.

Derjugin's Lizard   *L. derjugini*
Named by Nikolski in 1898 after Dr K. N. Derjugin (1878–
1938) who was a Professor at the Leningrad State University.
It inhabits the Krym (Crimea) Peninsula and the border of
northern Georgia and southern Russia in the Caucasus Mountains. A. M. Nikolski (1858–1942) was a Russian herpetologist
and Professor at Kharkov University.

Eyed or Jewelled Lizard   *L. lepida* (or *ocellata*)
lepida (L) graceful; at the opposite end of the scale to the little
Dwarf Lizard (below), this is the largest in the family, sometimes reaching a length of 80 cm (2 ft 8 in). The English name
is an allusion to the blue eyelike spots, usually bordered by a
black ring, along the flanks; the body is a brilliant green.
Inhabiting Italy, southern France, Spain, Portugal and north-
west Africa.

Wall Lizard   *L. muralis muralis*
murus (L) a wall; usually meaning a city wall; *-alis* (L) suffix
meaning relating to; this is the nominate subspecies (see
Chapter 1, p. 10). There are many subspecies and three are
given here; this one inhabits a large area in central, southern
and eastern Europe.

Albanian Lizard *L. m. albanica*
-icus (L) suffix meaning belonging to; although named from
Albania, it is also found in Yugoslavia, Macedonia and
Peloponnesos. It lives in mountains up to a height of about
1,800 m (6,000 ft).

(No recognised English name) *L. m. maculiventris*
macula (L) a mark, a spot; *venter* (L) genitive *ventris* the belly,
stomach; it has dark spots on the belly. Inhabiting northern
Italy and an area along the east coast.

Dwarf Lizard *L. parva*
parvus (L) small; usually not more than 15 cm (6 in) in length.
Inhabiting Asian Turkey.

Rock Lizard *L. saxicola*
saxum (L) a rock, a large stone; *colo* (L) I inhabit; it lives on the
rocky slopes of the Caucasus Mountains, which form the border
between Russia and Georgia.

Ruin Lizard *L. sicula sicula*
siculus (L) belonging to Sicily; this is the nominate subspecies
(see Chapter 1, p. 10). Although named from Sicily, it has a
wide distribution in Italy south of Rome, in Corsica and
Sardinia, and in the eastern part of Sicily. There are even more
subspecies named than with *L. muralis*, and 5 of these are given
here; they inhabit various islands in the Adriatic and
Tyrrhenian Seas and each island seems to have developed its
own form and colour patterns; often found living in the ruins of
old buildings.

(No recognised English name) *L. s. adriatica*
Considering the enormous number of species and subspecies of
Lacerta it is not surprising that many of them have no
vernacular name; to most Europeans, and certainly to most
visitors to Europe, they are just 'lizards'; they can be seen
almost everywhere in southern Europe scuttling away to hide
as one approaches. Inhabiting Pelagosa Picciola in the Adriatic; this species is inclined to be melanistic.

(No recognised English name)   *L. s. coerulea*
coeruleus = caeruleus (L) blue, sky-blue, sometimes dark blue; it is
greyish black on the back changing to blue flanks and sky-blue
throat and belly. Inhabiting Capri.

Yellow-throated Lacertid   *L. s. flavigula*
flavus (L) yellow; *gula* (L) the gullet, throat; it lives on San
Giovanni Faro in the Adriatic Sea.

San Stephano Lacertid   *L. s. sanctistephani* (formerly
sancti-stephani)
Bolder markings distinguish it from other similar subspecies.
Inhabiting San Stephano in the Tyrrhenian Sea. Although
originally named *sancti-stephani*, the Code now forbids the use of
hyphens in scientific names.

Simony's Lizard   *L. simonyi*
Living on Hierro, one of the Canary Islands (though possibly
not today), is this lizard named by Steindachner in 1889, after
a Mr Simony who discovered it; further details of this naturalist
are not known. It has not been seen and recorded since 1930,
and later searches have proved fruitless so it is probably extinct.
Dr F. Steindachner (1834–1919) was a German zoologist and
Director of the Vienna Museum in 1882.

Three-lined Green Lizard   *L. trilineata*
tria (L) three; *linea* (L) a linen thread, string; can mean a line
drawn; *-atus* (L) suffix meaning provided with; in some cases
there are five lines but there is always a central one along the
backbone. Inhabiting Bulgaria, Greece and Turkey.

Green Lizard   *L. viridis*
viridis (L) green; one of the larger lizards in this family it may
grow to a length of 45 cm ($17\frac{1}{2}$ in). Inhabiting the warmer parts
of Europe, from Spain ranging east to Asia Minor.

Common or Viviparous Lizard   *L. vivipara*
vivus (L) alive; *pareo* (L) I bring forth, I beget; this lizard should
really be known as ovoviviparous, from *ovum* (L) an egg; it has
no placenta and the young are born alive *in the egg*; they have

received no nourishment from the mother. It has the advantage that the eggs are kept to a moderate temperature even in Arctic areas where this lizard is sometimes found; it can make use of the sun and move the eggs, still in its body, from place to place; it could not do this if the eggs were laid and buried. The young, normally black, soon break out of the egg membrane, which is very thin, and are immediately independent, there being no parental care.

This lizard has a wider distribution than any other lizard, inhabiting north and central Europe, including the British Isles, and ranging north in Sweden to the Arctic Circle and east to Mongolia. It is seldom seen, if ever, in southern Spain, Italy and Greece, but this depends on the local climate; preferring rather damp areas near water, it is a good swimmer and even hunts for prey in the water.

African Sand Lizard *Psammodromus algirus*
psammos (Gr) sand; *dromos* (Gr) running, escape; *algirus* is a coined word and supposed to mean 'of Algiers'; it is a much larger lizard than *hispanicus* (below) at about 30 cm (12 in) in length. In addition to north-west Africa, it inhabits Spain and Portugal and can often be seen in parks and gardens.

Spanish Sand Lizard *Ps. hispanicus*
hispanicus (L) Spanish; in a case like this the scientific name becomes very important; if the English name is Sand Lizard we must be able to distinguish it from the Sand Lizard inhabiting southern England, Europe and ranging east to Lake Baikal, which is named *Lacerta agilis*. They must be related because they are in the same family, but they are not in the same genus. *Ps. hispanicus* inhabits the French and Spanish Mediterranean coasts. The abbreviation of the generic name to *Ps.* is better than the initial *P.* because the Greek letter *psi* combines the two (see transliteration on p. 153).

Snake-eyed Lacertid *Ophisops elegans*
ophis (L) a snake; *ops* (Gr) the eye; the eyelids are permanently closed and have a transparent window like that of snakes;

elegans (L) neat, elegant. Inhabiting north-eastern Africa and Asian Turkey.

Desert Racerunner   *Eremias arguta*
erēmia (Gr) desert, wilderness; *argutus* (L) lively; inhabiting mostly semi-desert areas in southern Ukraine, Moldavia and Romania.

(No recognised English name)   *E. velox*
velox (L) rapid, swift; inhabiting semi-desert areas of southern Kazakhstan bordering the Caspian Sea and ranging east to central Asia.

Fringe-toed Lizard   *Acanthodactylus erythrurus*
akantha (Gr) a thorn, a prickle; *daktulos* (Gr) a finger or a toe; an allusion to the scales on the borders of the toes, which increase the surface area; the feet are thus better adapted for running on loose sand; *eruthros* (Gr) red; *oura* (Gr) the tail; strangely, the red colour at the tip of the tail gradually fades in the male as he reaches maturity and finally disappears. Inhabiting sandy areas in Spain and Portugal.

African Fringe-toed Lizard   *Aporosaura anchietae*
a- (Gr) prefix meaning not, or there is not; *poros* (Gr) a passage through the skin, a pore; *saura* (Gr) a lizard; a reference to the absence in the male of the femoral pores; some doubt exists regarding the function of the pores on the under surface of the male femur, but herpetologists think that they may excrete a substance that gives the male a better grip of the female during copulation. This lizard appears to have been named after a comparatively unknown Portuguese naturalist, J. de Anchieta, who died in 1897; presumably a woman because of the feminine genitive ending -*ae*; at one time she was resident in Angola (Portuguese West Africa), where this lizard is found living in sandy desert areas. The English name 'fringe-toed' is explained under *Acanthodactylus* (above).

Long-tailed or Six-lined Grass Lizard *Takydromus sexlineatus*
takhus (Gr) quick, swift; *dromos* (Gr) running, escape; a very nimble small lizard measuring about 36 cm (14 in), but most of this is tail; probably the lizard with the longest tail in proportion to the length of the body; of the total length only about 6 or 7 cm (2¼ to 2¾ in) consists of the body, about one fifth of the total length: *sex* (L) six; *linea* (L) a linen thread, string; can mean a line drawn; -*atus* (L) suffix meaning provided with. It lives among grasses and small plants in the Vietnam–Kampuchea area, Malaysia and Indonesia.

(No recognised English name) *Tropidosaura montana*
tropis (Gr) genitive *tropios* later to become *tropidos* a keel; *saura* (Gr) a lizard; an allusion to the noticeably keeled scales of the back which are also imbricated; *mons* (L) genitive *montis* a mountain; *montanus* of a mountain. Inhabiting the mountains of Cape Province, South Africa, up to an altitude of about 2,000 m (6,500 ft).

(No recognised English name) *Ichnotropis capensis*
ikhnos (Gr) a track, trace; *tropos* (Gr) a turn, direction; a reference to this lizard's peculiar method of escape from danger, running in wide zig-zags and making use of any available clumps of grass to hide in, at each change of direction; *capensis* (L) of the Cape. It inhabits Kalahari, Transvaal and Mozambique.

Family   ANGUIDAE   about 70 species
anguis (L) a snake; although many of the lizards in this family (known as Lateral Fold Lizards) have no legs and so are snake-like, some have four perfectly good legs; also they do not all have the lateral fold, but are grouped together for other anatomical reasons, chiefly characteristics of the teeth, tongue, and skull.

Subfamily   DIPLOGLOSSINAE

diploos (Gr) two-fold, double; *glōssa* (Gr) the tongue; a reference to the peculiar form of the tongue, the end being retractable into the basal portion, which forms a sort of sheath.

West Indies Galliwasp   *Diploglossus costatus*
Diploglossus see Family Diploglossinae above; *costa* (L) a rib; *costatus* (L) having ribs; can mean having rib-like lines; this refers to lines that run across the body and partly down the sides, as though indicating ribs. The lizards in this genus do not have the lateral fold. Inhabiting Hispaniola, one of the larger islands of the Greater Antilles. The origin of the name galliwasp is obscure.

Galliwasp   *D. tenuifasciatus*
tenuis (L) thin, slender; *fascia* (L) a band or girdle; *fasciatus* (L) banded, can mean striped; an allusion to the thin dark lines round the body similar to those of *costatus*, above. Inhabiting the eastern part of Central America.

Worm Lizard   *Ophiodes striatus*
ophis (Gr) a snake; *-odes* (New L) derived from *eidos* (Gr) apparent shape, form; in appearance it is similar to the Slow-worm, but has a pair of diminutive hind legs that are useless for crawling, but retain some muscular movement; *striatus* (New L) striped; an allusion to two brown stripes that run the length of the body and the tail. It inhabits Brazil and Argentina.

Subfamily   GERRHONOTINAE

gerrhon (Gr) a type of shield, anything made of wicker work; *nōton* (Gr) the back; a reference to the pattern of the scales; this, and the apparent stiffness of the body, gave rise to the name Alligator Lizards. This subfamily have the lateral fold, a kind of pleat along the flanks which compensates for the rigidity of the hard scales; it assists movement of the body, expansion for breathing and for pregnant females.

Scheltopusik or Pallas's Glass Lizard *Ophisaurus apodus*
ophis (Gr) a snake; *saura* (Gr) a lizard; *a-*(Gr) prefix meaning not, or there is not; *pous* (Gr) genitive *podos*, the foot; 'snake-like lizard with no feet'; it has in fact two tiny vestigial hind legs only about ($\frac{1}{10}$ in) long, little more than pimples. It is quite a big lizard and may grow to a length of 1.3 m (over 4 ft). The name scheltopusik is from the Russian word zheltopuzik, which means 'yellow belly'. Inhabiting a large area ranging from Greece and the Adriatic coast, through Iraq and Iran, to central Russia. Named after Peter Simon Pallas (1741–1811), a German zoologist and explorer and an authority on Russian wildlife. He was a Professor at St Petersburg University in Russia and made contributions to most of the natural sciences. The reason for the name Glass Lizard is given below under *O. gracilis*.

Slender Glass Lizard *O. attenuatus*
attenuo (L) I make thin, weak; *attenuatus* (L) weakened, enfeebled; this is not a well-chosen specific name, as it is supposed to mean slender and not enfeebled. It was named by Professor S. F. Baird (1823–1887), the American zoologist: 'Baird did more than any other man of his time to advance the study of ornithology and zoology' (T. S. Palmer). This lizard has a wide distribution in the River Mississippi area, USA.

Burman Glass Lizard *O. gracilis*
gracilis (L) thin, slender; can mean plain, unadorned; like all the Glass Lizards it has no legs and the layman would almost certainly think it was a snake; even if he saw it blink its eyes he would not realise that it was not a snake. It can break off its tail (autotomy) to escape from a predator and the tail constitutes a large proportion of the whole animal; this may break into several pieces, which gives the impression that the whole animal has fallen to bits! Hence, a 'glass lizard'. Named from

Burma, it ranges from north-eastern India to south-western China.

Northern Alligator Lizard   *Gerrhonotus coeruleus*
Gerrhonotus see Subfamily Gerrhonotinae, p. 110. *coeruleus* = *caeruleus* (L) dark blue, can mean dark-coloured. This is one of the species in this family that has four normal legs and five toes; it inhabits the north-western part of the USA, ranging south through California.

Popocatepetl Alligator Lizard   *G. imbricatus*
imbrico (L) I cover with tiles; *imbricatus* (L) tiled; it usually means overlapping tiles like those on a roof; a reference to the type of scales. It lives high up on the volcanic mountain Popocatepetl, Mexico, at about 4,000 m (13,000 ft). There has not been a serious eruption since 1664; the name is an Aztec word meaning 'smoking mountain'.

Subfamily   ANGUINAE

anguis (L) a snake; the Slow-worm is really a lizard, but Linnaeus gave it this name because it has no legs and he thought it was a snake (for details see Chapter 2, p. 17).

Blue-spotted Slow-worm   *Anguis fragilis colchicus*
Anguis see Subfamily Anguinae above; *fragilis* (L) fragile; an allusion to the tail, which easily breaks off if seized by a predator (autotomy); -*icus* (L) suffix meaning belonging to; Colchis is an ancient territory in Asia situated between the Black Sea and the Caspian Sea; it does not appear on modern maps and only exists as a Greek legend, once famous as a home of sorcery. This subspecies has small blue spots on the back; it inhabits eastern Europe and parts of Asia.

Slow-worm   *A. f. fragilis*
Anguis fragilis (L) see above. It is widespread in Europe including the British Isles, but not northern Scandinavia; it can also be found in part of northern Africa and in Asia Minor. This is the nominate subspecies (see Chapter 2, p. 16).

desert areas in south-east Europe, Asia Minor and northern Africa.

Boa Constrictor *Boa constrictor*

Boa see Subfamily Boinae, p. 127; *constringo* (L) I bind together, confine. The snakes in the family Boidae are not venomous; they seize their prey with powerful teeth and then coil round the animal's body; they do not crush it to death, but constrict it enough to stop it breathing; thus it dies from suffocation. They are big snakes, though the Boa Constrictor is not the longest at about 4 m (13 ft). Inhabiting Mexico, Central America and ranging south to central Argentina.

Anaconda *Eunectes murinus*

eu- (Gr) prefix meaning well, nicely; *nēktēs* (Gr) a swimmer; 'a good swimmer'; *murinus* (L) mouse-like, mouse-coloured; although not so brightly coloured as some of the other big snakes the name does not seem really suitable. This big snake is largely aquatic and is usually seen in the water. There is some competition between the Anaconda and the Reticulated Python as to which can be called the longest reptile in the world; some herpetologists give the length of the Anaconda as up to 9.5m (31 ft) and say it is the longest, while others say that the Reticulated Python has been recorded as measuring 10 m (32 ft 6 in). The Anaconda inhabits South America east of the Andes from Colombia ranging south to Paraguay.

Subfamily BOLYERIINAE

The genus was created by Gray, who gave no reason for the name. It seems likely that it refers to a little known collector named Bolyer.

Round Island Snake *Bolyeria multicarinatus*

Bolyeria see Subfamily Bolyeriinae above; *multus* (L) many; *carina* (L) a keel; *carinatus* (L) keeled; a reference to spines on the underside of the vertebrae. Originally living on Mauritius but now found only on the nearby Round Islet; it is considered to be an endangered species and may soon be extinct.

Family   COLUBRIDAE   about 1,200 species

coluber (L) fem. *colubra* a serpent. Known as the Typical Snakes.

Subfamily   XENODERMINAE

xenos (Gr) a stranger; can mean strange, unusual; *derma* (Gr) skin, hide; there are several unusual features concerning the scales, for example the lip scales have upturned edges and the body scales are similar to those in some lizards, which do not overlap.

Javan Xenodermin   *Xenodermis javanicus*
Xenodermis see Subfamily Xenoderminae above; *-icus* (L) suffix meaning belonging to; inhabiting Java.

Stoliczka's Xenodermin   *Stoliczkaia khasiensis*
Named after Dr F. Stoliczka (1838–1874) who carried out a geological survey in India; *-ensis* (L) suffix meaning belonging to, usually a place; it was probably first found by Dr Stoliczka on the Khasi Hills in north-eastern India where this snake inhabits a large area of mountainous terrain.

Subfamily   SIBYNOPHINAE

sibynē (Gr) a spear; *ophis* (Gr) a snake; a reference to the shape of the head, hence the English name Spear Snakes.

Asian Spear Snake   *Sibynophis chinensis*
Sibynophis see Subfamily Sibynophinae above; *-ensis* (L) suffix meaning belonging to, usually a place; inhabiting eastern Asia including China and surrounding areas.

(No recognised English name) *Scaphiodontophis annulatus*
skaphē (Gr) anything dug out, or scooped out; *odous* (Gr)
genitive *odontos* a tooth, fang; *ophis* (Gr) a snake; a reference to
the widened tips of the maxillary teeth; *annulatus* (L) having a
ring; this is a reference to the striking pattern of alternating
rings of red, black and yellow on the body. Inhabiting Central
America and the north-western part of South America.

Subfamily XENODONTINAE

xenos (Gr) a stranger; can also mean strange, unusual; *odōn*
(Ionic Gr) a tooth, fang; a reference to the unusual dentition;
they have enlarged *solid* and *ungrooved* fangs at the back of the
upper jaw and yet some are known to produce venom. Into this
subfamily come the American Hog-nosed Snakes.

Eastern Hog-nosed Snake *Heterodon platyrhinos*
heteros (Gr) different; can mean other than usual; *odōn* (Ionic
Gr) a tooth, fang, see Subfamily Xenodontinae above; *platus*
(Gr) flat, wide; *rhis* (Gr) genitive *rhinos* the nose; a reference to
the peculiar shape of the nose which is adapted for burrowing.
Inhabiting eastern North America.

Subfamily NATRICINAE

nato (L) I swim; *natrix* (L) genitive *natricis* a water-snake; the
name Water Snakes may be misleading as they spend a lot of
their time on land and hence are sometimes known as Grass
Snakes; they are good swimmers, living near water, and frogs
form an important part of their diet.

Ringed Snake or Grass Snake *Natrix natrix natrix*
Natrix see Subfamily Natricinae above. This is the nominate
subspecies; for an explanation of the generic name *Natrix*
appearing three times see TAUTONYMS, p. 9. The colour of this
snake varies in different individuals from greyish brown to
green, and the name Ringed Snake arises from two half-moon
yellow patches just behind the head which almost completes a

ring; in some countries it is called 'The Snake with the Golden Crown' and is supposed to bring good luck. Inhabiting Europe, though not Ireland, northern Scotland, Iceland, or northern Scandinavia, but ranging east to part of Russia and south to northern Africa.

Collarless Grass Snake   *N. n. astreptophora*
a- (Gr) prefix meaning not, or there is not; *streptos* (Gr) a kind of collar; *phora* (Gr) a carrying, bearing; 'not having a collar'; the marking on the neck is not so distinct as with the Ringed Snake, see above. Inhabiting the Iberian Peninsula and north-west Africa.

Sicilian Grass Snake   *N. n. sicula*
siculus (L) a Sicilian. This subspecies is found only in Sicily and other subspecies are found on other islands such as Corsica and Sardinia.

Red-bellied Water Snake   *N. erythrogaster*
eruthros (Gr) red; *gaster* (Gr) the belly; inhabiting a large area in the south-eastern part of the USA, but not as far south as Florida.

Viperine Snake   *N. maura*
mauros (Gr) dark; the pattern of marking on the back is similar to a viper, but it is a harmless snake; people have been known to get bitten by picking up a viper thinking it was the harmless *N. maura*. Inhabiting the Iberian Peninsula and the south-eastern part of France.

Fishing Snake   *N. piscator*
piscator (L) a fisherman; an aquatic snake, it spends a lot of time in the water and the diet is mostly fish and frogs. Inhabiting a wide area in southern and south-east Asia.

Common Water Snake   *N. sipedon*
sēpedōn (Gr) rottenness, decay; can mean a snake whose bite causes putrefaction, but it is not venomous. Inhabiting a large area on the eastern side of North America ranging from the Great Lakes south to Florida.

Diced Snake   *N. tessellata*
tessellatus (L) set with small cubes; the body is marked with a diced pattern in rows. Inhabiting a range from West Germany across eastern Europe to central Asia.

(No recognised English name)   *N. trianguligera*
triangulum (L) a triangle; *gero* (L) I carry; a reference to the red triangular marks on the side of the body. Inhabiting Malaysia and Indonesia.

Kirtland's Water Snake   *Clonophis kirtlandi*
klonos (Gr) violent confused motion, persons fleeing in confusion; presumably a reference to persons who flee when seeing this snake; Liddell and Scott's *Lexicon* adds: 'and, comically, a turmoil in the bowels'; doubtless similar to our modern saying 'butterflies in the stomach'! *ophis* (Gr) a snake; it is a harmless snake. Named after Dr J. P. Kirtland (1793–1877), an American physician and zoologist, who founded the Cleveland Medical College, Ohio. This snake ranges from Ohio through Pennsylvania to New Jersey.

Common Garter Snake   *Thamnophis sirtalis*
thamnos (Gr) a bush, shrub; *ophis* (Gr) a serpent; it may be found in marshy areas, or where there are shrubs, and even near houses but it is not known to live mostly in shrubs; the colourful striped pattern is supposed to resemble a woman's garter. Ranging from southern Canada to the eastern part of the USA.

Subfamily   COLUBRINAE

coluber (L) fem. *colubra* a serpent.

Smooth Snake   *Coronella austriaca*
corona (L) a crown; *-ellus* (L) diminutive suffix; no reason is given for naming this snake 'a little crown'; *auster* (L) genitive *austri* the south wind; *-acus* (L) suffix meaning relating to, hence *austriaca*, of the south, southern. It is widespread in Europe including southern Scandinavia and southern Britain; the

scales are smooth, in contrast with most other snakes that have keeled scales.

Milk Snake   *Lampropeltis getulus*

lampros (Gr) shining, beautiful; *peltē* (Gr) a small shield; in this case taken to mean the scales, skin, as in the English pelt, 'shining pelt', a reference to the bright colouring specially noticeable after shedding the skin – 'Among the most beautiful colubrid snakes in the world' (Grzimek); *getulus* (L) belonging to the Getulians, a people inhabiting north-west Africa in ancient times; this is a mistake, as the snake was thought to have been found in the Morocco area, whereas it lives in the southern part of the USA and Mexico. It acquired the name Milk Snake because of a story that it sucked milk from cows while they slept; it is unlikely to be true.

Smooth Green Snake   *Opheodrys vernalis*

opheo (New L) from *ophis* (Gr) a snake; *drus* (Gr) a tree, usually an oak tree; *verno* (L) I flourish, I become green; *-alis* (L) suffix meaning relating to; it inhabits shrubs and grassland. The scales are smooth like those of *Coronella austriaca* p. 133; it is widespread in the USA.

Balkan Racer   *Coluber gemonensis*

coluber (L) a snake; *-ensis* (L) suffix meaning belonging to; named from Gemona, in north-east Italy, it also inhabits the adjacent part of Yugoslavia, the Balkan coast and some Greek islands such as Crete. Known as a 'racer' from its rapid movement when disturbed – 'On a wooded rocky slope they can disappear with lightning speed' (Schmidt & Inger).

Horseshoe Racer   *C. hippocrepis*

hippos (Gr) a horse; *krepis* (Gr) a shoe; a reference to a horseshoe-like mark on the head. Inhabiting the Iberian Peninsula, north-western Africa and the small island of Pantellaria off the north-east coast of Tunisia.

Slender Racer   *C. najadum*

naja (New L) from *nāga* (Sanskrit) a serpent; a very slender snake, little more than 7 mm ($\frac{5}{16}$ in) in diameter, with a length of about 1.3 m (4 ft 2 in). Inhabiting the Balkan countries and ranging east through Asia Minor.

Coachwhip Snake   *Masticophis flagellum*
mastic (New L) from *mastix* (Gr) a whip; *ophis* (Gr) a snake; *flagellum* (L) a small whip; there is a legend which says that this snake can coil round a man and bind him to a tree, and then whip him to death with its tail; it is, of course, no more than a legend, as the snake is not a constrictor and is far too small to perform such a feat. It is widespread along the southern part of the USA including Florida and ranging south to Mexico.

Aesculapian Snake   *Elaphe longissima*
elaphos (Gr) a deer; the reason for the name is obscure. Linnaeus gave no explanation when he created it in 1758. *longus* (L) long; *longissima* (L) very long; in spite of the name, it is not the longest snake in this genus, at about 2 m (6 ft 6 in). Inhabiting south-eastern Europe and Asia Minor. In ancient times, this snake was associated with the snake symbol of Aesculapius, the god of medicine, and hence enjoyed protection; it is depicted on the badge of the Royal Army Medical Corps.

Sharp-headed Rat Snake   *E. oxycephala*
oxus (Gr) sharp, pointed; *kephalē* (Gr) the head. An arboral snake inhabiting Burma, Malaysia, Indonesia and the Philippines. Some species are known as Rat Snakes because rats form a large part of the diet.

Four-lined Rat Snake   *E. quattuorlineata*
quattuor (L) four; *linea* (L) a line; *lineata* (L) lined; the four lines along the body are usually seen best in the older snakes. The single 't' in the specific name is not correct Latin. Inhabiting Italy, Sicily, the Balkan Peninsula and ranging east through Turkey to the Caucasus.

Ladder Snake   *E. scalaris*
scala (L) a ladder; *-aris* (L) suffix meaning pertaining to; there

are two lines forming a ladder-like pattern along the back which is most noticeable in older animals. Inhabiting the Iberian Peninsula.

Oriental Rat Snake *Ptyas mucosus*
ptuas (Gr) the spitter, a kind of serpent which is supposed to spit poison into the eye of an aggressor; *mucus* (L) the mucous matter of the nose; *mucosus* (L) full of mucous; it is not recorded that this snake actually spits, like the Spitting Cobra, but it makes a peculiar coughing noise, as though it has a sore throat, in addition to the usual hissing. Inhabiting a large area of south-east Asia, including India and China, but not Kampuchea, Vietnam, and Malaysia, although it is found further south in Java. Known as a Rat Snake because rats form an important part of the diet.

Keeled Rat Snake *P. carinatus*
carina (L) the keel of a ship; *-atus* (L) suffix meaning provided with; a reference to the keeled scales of the under-belly. Inhabiting eastern Indian, Malaysia and Indonesia.

Black Tree Snake *Thrasops flavigularis*
thrasos (Gr) boldness, impudence; *opsis* (Gr) appearance, aspect; a harmless snake, but on account of its colour and size it is easily mistaken for the Black Mamba, a very dangerous venomous snake; *flavus* (L) yellow; *gula* (L) the throat, gullet; *-aris* (L) suffix meaning relating to. Inhabiting western Africa.

Subfamily   CALAMARINAE

calamus (L) a reed; *-aria* (L) suffix meaning like or connected with; the reason for the name Reed Snakes is not explained in zoological records, but they are often found in marshy places.

Linné's Reed Snake *Calamaria linnaei*
Calamaria see Subfamily Calamarinae above. Named after Carl von Linné (1707–1778), the famous Swedish botanist; he studied and named many animals, in addition to plants. Inhabiting Java.

Subfamily   LYCODONTINAE

lukos (Gr) a wolf; *odous* (Gr) genitive *odontos* a tooth; a reference to the long upper jaw teeth, the Wolf Snakes.

Indian Wolf Snake   *Lycodon aulicus*
Lycodon see Subfamily Lycodontinae above; *aluix* (L) genitive *aulicis* a furrow; probably an anatomical mistake as the long upper teeth are not grooved. Widespread in south-eastern Asia, including India, Sri Lanka, the Burma-Vietnam area, Malaysia, Indonesia and the Philippines.

Cape Wolf Snake   *Lycophidion capense*
ophis (Gr) a snake; diminutive *ophidion* a small snake; the length is about 45 cm (1 ft 5½ in) and should be compared with that of the Indian Wolf Snake (above) which is usually more than 50 cm (about 1 ft 8 in); *-ensis* (L) suffix meaning belonging to; 'of The Cape'. Inhabiting the southern part of South Africa.

African Striped Ground Snake   *Bothrophthalmus lineatus*
bothros (Gr) a hole, a trench; *ophthalmus* (Gr) the eye; a reference to the small heat-sensitive pits in front of the eyes (see Pit Vipers, p.oo) *linea* (L) a line; *lineatus* (L) lined; a reference to the black and red stripes. Inhabiting the Ivory Coast and ranging south through Nigeria, to Congo and Zaire.

Subfamily   DIPSADINAE

dipsa (Gr) thirst; *dipsas* (Gr) genitive *dipsados* a venomous snake whose bite causes intense thirst, hence the English name Thirst Snakes.

Indonesian Thirst Snake   *Dipsas carinatus*
Dipsas see Subfamily Dipsadinae above; *carina* (L) a ship's keel; *carinatus* (L) keeled; a reference to the keeled scales of the belly. Inhabiting Sumatra and Java.

(No recognised English name)   *Sibynomorphous ventrimaculatus*
sibynē (Gr) a spear; *morphē* (Gr) form, shape; an allusion to the shape of the head; *venter* (L) genitive *ventris* the belly; *macula* (L)

a mark, a spot; *maculatus* (L) spotted; a reference to the marks
on the under-belly. Inhabiting North America.

Subfamily DASYPELTINAE

dasus (Gr) hairy, shaggy, can mean rough; *peltē* (Gr) a small
shield, in this case taken to mean the scales, skin, as in the
English word 'pelt'; a reference to the rough scales of the body.
Known as the Egg-eating Snakes.

African Egg-eating Snake   *Dasypeltis scabra*
Dasypeltis see Subfamily Dasypeltinae above; *scaber* (L) fem
scabra, rough. The egg-eating snakes have only small weak
teeth which are of little use except perhaps to assist in
swallowing the egg; however the vertebrae of the neck have
sharp processes which penetrate the oesophagus, almost like a
saw, and this cuts open the egg as it is being swallowed; the
shell is regurgitated. This species is widespread in Africa.

Indian Egg-eating Snake   *Elachistodon westermanni*
elakhus (Gr) small, short; *elakhistos* (Gr) smallest, shortest; *odōn*
(Ionic Gr) fang, tooth; it has only small, weak teeth (see *D.
scabra* above). Dr G. F. Westerman (1807–1890) was for many
years the Director of the Zoological Gardens in Amsterdam.
This snake inhabits a small area in north-eastern India.

Subfamily HOMALOPSINAE

homalos (Gr) smooth, even; *opsis* (Gr) aspect, appearance; an
allusion to the smooth scales. The species in this subfamily are
largely aquatic, inhabiting both inland waters and the sea.

(No recognised English name)   *Homalopsis buccata*
Homalopsis see Subfamily Homalopsinae above; *bucca* (L) the
cheek, especially when puffed out as in eating; *-atus* (L) suffix
meaning provided with. Inhabiting south-east Asia, including
Burma, Sumatra, Java and neighbouring small islands, parti-

cularly along the coast; the anatomy is adapted for an aquatic life.

Tentacled Snake   *Erpeton tentaculatum*
herpeton (Gr) a reptile; *tentaculum* (L) a feeler; *-atus* (L) suffix meaning provided with; it has a peculiar feeler-like process on each side of the snout. Inhabiting Kampuchea and the southern part of Vietnam.

Subfamily   BOIGINAE

The name Boiga was coined, with no explanation given, by the Austrian zoologist Dr Fitzinger (1803–1862).

Mangrove Tree Snake   *Boiga dendrophila*
Boiga see Subfamily Boiginae above; *dendron* (Gr) a tree; *philos* (Gr) loved, dear. Inhabiting southern Asia, Indonesia and the Philippines.

Hooded Snake   *Macroprotodon cucullatus*
makros (Gr) long; *prōtos* (Gr) first; *odōn* (Gr) a tooth; an allusion to the elongated upper front teeth; *cucullus* (L) a hood; *cucullatus* (L) hooded; this name is an allusion to the dark marking on the head and neck. Inhabiting southern Spain, the Balearic Islands and the north-western part of northern Africa.

(No recognised English name)   *Dendrophis mycterizans*
dendron (Gr) a tree; *ophis* (Gr) a snake; this is a leaf-green arboreal snake; *mycterizō* (Gr) I turn up the nose; *mycterizans* (New L) a turning up of the nose; this refers to the tip of the snout, which is a moveable trunklike structure. Inhabiting the southern half of the Malay Peninsula.

Grey Vine Snake   *Oxybelis acuminatus*
oxus (Gr) sharp, pointed; *belos* (Gr) a dart, a sting; *acumen* (L) genitive *acuminis* a point to sting with; *-atus* (L) suffix meaning provided with; although mildly venomous the poison is not usually strong enough to be dangerous to human beings. The

slender body has a long drawn-out snout; it is an arboreal snake and often lives in vine trees. Inhabiting South America.

Green Vine Snake   *O. fulgidus*

fulgidus (L) shining; a reference to the bright green and yellow colour, which is particularly noticeable after the snake has shed its skin. Inhabiting Central America and the adjacent part of South America.

Flying Snake   *Chrysopelea ornata*

khrusos (Gr) gold; *pēlēx* (Gr) a crown, helmet; *ornatus* (L) ornament, decoration; a reference to the bright green and yellow colours of the head and body. Certainly this snake cannot fly, although an ancient legend says that it turns into a bird when moving from tree to tree! Even its ability to glide a short distance has rarely been seen and recorded, although some unusual anatomical features suggest that short glides are possible. It inhabits Sri Lanka and ranges through south-eastern Asia including China, the Thailand–Vietnam area, Malaya, Indonesia and the Philippines.

Boomslang   *Dispholidus typus*

dus- (Gr) prefix meaning bad, ill, not normal, as in e.g. dyspepsia; *pholis* (Gr) genitive *pholidos* a horny scale, especially of reptiles; a reference to the unusual formation of the dorsal scales on the forepart of the body, being spread out on the sides and strongly overlapping near the spine; *tupos* (Gr) a blow, mark, or impression; can mean a type, and may be a reference to this unusual scale formation. Widespread in the southern half of Africa.

Family   ELAPIDAE   150 species

elops (Gr) mute, the mute one, the name of a type of fish; also a type of serpent, giving rise to *elaps* (New L) a serpent. The Cobras.

King Cobra   *Ophiophagus hannah*

ophis (Gr) a snake; *phagein* (Gr) to eat; it feeds almost entirely on snakes, even poisonous snakes; the name *hannah* is taken to mean a giant; it is the largest venomous snake known and may reach a length of 5 m (16 ft 3 in) though 4 m (13 ft 1 in) is more usual. Inhabiting India, though not Sri Lanka, and ranging to southern China, Malaysia, the Sunda Islands, the Andaman Islands and the Philippines.

Indian Cobra   *Naja naja*
naja (New L) derived from Sanskrit *nāga*, a snake; in Hindu mythology this is a divine snake. The snake in one of Kipling's stories was called Nag. Inhabiting India and ranging through Asia to southern China, the Sunda Islands and the Philippines.

Egyptian Cobra   *N. haje*
hajj or *hadj* means a Mohammedan pilgrimage to Mecca. Widespread in northern Africa but not the Sahara and ranging south on the eastern side to Mozambique.

Spitting or Black-necked Cobra   *N. nigricollis*
niger (L) black; *collum* (L) the neck. It only spits the venom at intruders, not at its prey; it does this by means of the fangs, which have a hole in the front, so that pressure from the poison gland forces the venom directly forward; it does not spit in the ordinary sense of the word. Inhabiting Africa south of the Sahara, but not Madagascar or the most southern part of Africa.

Shield-nosed Snake   *Aspidelaps scutatus*
aspis (Gr) genitive *aspidos* a shield; *elaps*, see Family Elapidae, p. 140; *scutum* (L) an oblong shield, *scutatus* (L) armed with a shield; an allusion to the broad snout plate which is used for digging. This burrowing snake lives in the sandy deserts of South Africa.

(No recognised English name)   *Elaps corallinus*
elaps (New L) see Family Elapidae, p. 140; *corallinus* (L) coral-red; a reference to the bright red bands round the body that alternate with black bands; 'One of the prettiest in this genus' (H. Gadow). Inhabiting the forests of tropical South America

and the Lesser Antilles. Dr H. F. Gadow FRS (1855–1927) was at one time Curator at the Cambridge University Museum.

Water Cobra   *Boulengerina annulata*
Named after George Albert Boulenger, the famous Belgian-British herpetologist, who did a lot of work for the British Museum (Natural History) relating to reptiles during the years 1882 to 1896; *annulus* (L) (or *anulus*) a ring; *annulata* (L) having a ring; a reference to the black and brown bands on the body. It inhabits shallow water and lives in the large lakes of Central Africa.

Black Mamba   *Dendroaspis polylepis*
dendron (Gr) a tree; *aspis* (Gr) a type of snake, an asp; *polus* (Gr) many; *lepis* (Gr) a scale; a reference to the smooth scales arranged in diagonal rows. Although the generic name indicates a tree-snake it lives mostly on the ground but sometimes climbs into bushes; it is not really black but dark brown or dark grey. Inhabiting Africa south of the Sahara but not the extreme southern part.

Banded Krait   *Bungarus fasciatus*
bungarus (New L) from *bangāru* (Telugu); this is the language of a large group of people living in Andhra Pradesh State, India; *fascia* (L) a band or girdle; *fasciatus* (L) banded; it has yellow bands on a shining black body. Inhabiting south-eastern Asia and the Sunda Islands.

Many-banded Krait   *B. multicinctus*
multus (L) many; *cinctus* (L) a girdle; it has closely set narrow black and white rings. Inhabiting southern China.

South American Coral Snake   *Micrurus corallinus*
mikros (Gr) small; *oura* (Gr) the tail; *korallion* (Gr) red coral; *corallinus* (New L) coral red; an allusion to the broad red bands; these are interspersed with narrow bands of yellow and black. The Coral Snakes are brightly coloured and venomous, some having a very dangerous poisonous bite. Inhabiting Brazil.

Eastern or Common Coral Snake   *M. fulvius*
fulvus (L) tawny, yellowish brown; 'tawny' does not do justice
to this brightly coloured snake; it has wide red and black bands
interspersed with narrow yellow bands. Inhabiting south-
eastern USA and Mexico.

Arizona Coral Snake   *Micruroides euryxanthus*
-*oides* (New L) from *eidos* (Gr) apparent shape, form; this snake,
similar to *Micrurus*, has to be placed in a separate genus because
the dentition is different; *eurus* (Gr) wide; *xanthos* (Gr) yellow;
an allusion to the yellow bands which are wider than those of
Micrurus. Inhabiting the western part of Arizona.

Taipan   *Oxyuranus scutulatus*
oxus (Gr) sharp, pointed; *oura* (Gr) the tail; -*anus* (L) suffix
meaning belonging to; it has a long pointed tail; *scutulata* (L) a
chequered garment; an allusion to the type of scales on the
body. Inhabiting coastal areas of northern Queensland and
New Guinea, and islands in the Torres Strait, which is the
name of the sea between New Guinea and Australia.

Death Adder   *Acanthophis antarcticus*
akantha (Gr) a thorn, a prickle; *ophis* (Gr) a serpent; it has a
short tail with a spiked tip and some people believed it could
sting with its tail; -*icus* (L) suffix meaning belonging to; it does
not live in the Antarctic; it inhabits central and western
Australia and New Guinea. The name Death Adder is justified;
it has a head similar to an adder and the poison is deadly, more
deadly than the cobra; records suggest that about 50% of
people bitten by this snake will die.

Family   HYDROPHIIDAE   50 species
hudōr (Gr) water; *ophis* (Gr) a serpent. The Sea Snakes.

Subfamily   LATICAUDINAE
latus (L) broad, wide; *cauda* (L) the tail.

Black-banded Sea Krait   *Laticauda laticauda*
Laticauda see Subfamily Laticaudinae above; the tail is rudder-
shaped and flattened vertically, an adaptation for swimming;
however Sea Kraits are often seen ashore sunning themselves
and the females come ashore to lay and bury their eggs.
Inhabiting coastal waters from the Bay of Bengal and Japan
and ranging south-east to northern Australia and New Guinea.
For an explanation of the specific name being the same as the
generic name see TAUTONYMS, p. 9.

(No recognised English name)   *L. semifasciata*
semi- (L) half; *fascia* (L) a band or girdle; *fasciatus* (L) banded;
the young have distinct dark bands on the body but adult
animals gradually lose the bands, so at one stage they are 'half-
banded'. Inhabiting the coastal waters of the Ryukyu Islands,
the Philippines and the Moluccas.

Subfamily   HYDROPHIINAE

hudōr (Gr) water; *ophis* (Gr) a serpent; the Sea Snakes.

Blue-banded Sea Snake   *Hydrophis cyanocinctus*
Hydrophis see Subfamily Hydrophiinae above; *kuaneos* (Gr) dark
blue; *cinctus* (L) a girdle; these are genuine water animals, much
more so than those in the subfamily Laticaudinae. Their
anatomy is adapted for a marine life, they bear live young and
never come ashore; indeed if washed ashore by accident, or
caught and put on land, they are almost helpless, and the rib
cage, normally supported by the buoyancy of the water, is
liable to collapse under its own weight and they suffocate; in
fact just like a stranded whale. This snake is about 2m (6 ft 6 in)
long and is found in a large area of eastern Asia, inhabiting
coastal waters from the Persian Gulf to Japan and New Guinea.

Luzon Sea Snake   *H. semperi*
Dr C. G. Semper (1832–1893) explored the Philippines in 1858
and published his book *Travels in the Philippine Archipelago* in
1886. This snake inhabits Lake Taal, in Luzon; perhaps not

strictly a 'sea snake', it is the only species known in the Family Hydrophiidae to live in fresh water.

Hardwicke's Sea Snake   *Lapemis hardwickii*
Lapemis has no real meaning, it is simply an anagram of *Pelamis* (below). Major General T. Hardwicke FRS (1756–1835) was a naturalist who served in the Indian Army. This snake inhabits coastal waters in south-east Asia ranging from the Burma-Vietnam area through Malaysia, Indonesia and the Philippines, to New Guinea and northern Australia.

Yellow-bellied Sea Snake   *Pelamis platurus*
pēlamus (Gr) the tunny fish; this seems a peculiar name for a snake, but with its flattened, quite bulky body, it does resemble a typical fish; *platus* (Gr) wide, flat; *oura* (Gr) the tail; the rudder-like tail is flattened vertically and thus has a similar action to the tail of a fish. Inhabiting the warm areas of the Indian and Pacific Oceans; it does not always remain near the coast.

Small-headed Sea Snake   *Microcephalophis gracilis*
mikros (Gr) small; *kephalē* (Gr) the head; *ophis* (Gr) a serpent; with a thick body possibly 4 cm ($1\frac{1}{2}$ in) in diameter the unusually thin neck and head are very noticeable; *gracilis* (L) thin, slender. Inhabiting the warm areas of the Indian and Pacific Oceans.

Family   VIPERIDAE   80 species

vipera (L) a viper, possibly derived from *vivus* (L) alive, and *pario* (L) I bear, bring forth, i.e. 'born alive'; most vipers do not lay eggs, they bear live young and are referred to as being viviparous.

Sand Viper   *Vipera ammodytes*
Vipera, see Family Viperidae above; *ammos* (Gr) sand; *dutes* (Gr) a burrower, a diver; it is not well named as on the whole it prefers a rocky or stony habitat. Inhabiting south-eastern Europe including Yugoslavia and Greece and ranging east to

Asia Minor. It is the most dangerous European snake, although the venom is not so powerful as the cobra, or the rattlesnake.

Asp Viper   *V. aspis*
aspis (Gr) a viper, an asp. Inhabiting the Mediterranean area and ranging north to Switzerland and the southern part of Germany.

Adder or Common European Viper   *V. berus*
berus (New L) a name that was at one time used for a snake, possibly *Natrix natrix*, the Water Snake. Inhabiting Europe as far north as the Arctic Circle and ranging east to the Caucasus Mountains.

Caucasus Viper   *V. kaznakovi*
A. N. Kaznakow was a Russian naturalist but little is known about him; the name was given by Nikolski in 1909. Inhabiting the western Caucasus and Turkey. Prof A. M. Nikolski (1858–1942) was a herpetologist at Kharkov University.

Radde's Viper   *V. raddei*
Prof G. F. R. Radde (1831–1903) was a Director at the Caucasian Museum, Tbilisi, in Georgia. This viper inhabits Turkey, Iran and Georgia.

Russell's Viper   *V. russelli*
Named after Dr Patrick Russell (died 1805), a British physician and naturalist. This viper possesses a powerful venom and has a reputation for causing many deaths; it inhabits India and Burma, southern China and some Australasian islands.

Mountain Viper   *V. xanthina*
xanthos (Gr) various shades of yellow; *-inus* (L) suffix meaning like; it is a reddish brown colour. Inhabiting the mountains of northern Asia Minor.

Saw-scaled Viper   *Echis carinatus*
ekhis (Gr) a viper, an adder; *carina* (L) a keel; *-atus* (L) suffix meaning provided with; an allusion to the scales which have prominent keels along the back and transverse keels on the

sides. It has a wide distribution ranging from desert areas in North Africa, through Saudi Arabia, Iraq and Iran to India and Sri Lanka.

Horned Viper   *Cerastes cerastes*
cerastes (L) a horned serpent; it has a sharp horn-like scale above each eye. Inhabiting sandy desert areas in North Africa and Arabia. For an explanation of the specific name being the same as the generic name, see TAUTONYMS, p. 9.

Common Sand Viper   *C. vipera*
In this case the generic name is misleading as it does not have the two horns. Inhabiting a similar area to *C. cerastes*, see above.

Puff Adder   *Bitis arietans*
bitis (New L) to bite; *arieto* (L) I butt like a ram; can mean I strike violently; *arietans* (L) striking violently; 'to bite striking violently'. Widespread in Africa from southern Morocco to the Cape of Good Hope and ranging east into Arabia. The name Puff Adder arises from its unusual form of hissing, which is alarmingly loud and caused by forcing air in and out of the lungs; i.e. 'puffing'.

Gabon Viper   *B. gabonica*
Named from Gabon, in western Africa, it inhabits a large area in western and central Africa and is especially common in Cameroon. Because of its widespread distribution it is reputed to have caused more deaths than any other African snake. In addition to 'puffing', some adders are able to inflate themselves to much more than normal size when in the mood for aggression, which may also account for the name 'puff adder'.

Rhinoceros Viper or River Jack   *B. nasicornis*
nasus (L) the nose; *cornu* (L) the horn of animals; the scales form two horn-like projections on the snout. The name River Jack arises from its liking for marshy areas near rivers; it is a good swimmer and widespread in Africa south of the Sahara.

Dwarf Puff Adder   *B. peringueyi*
Dr L. A. Peringuey (1855–1924) was a French naturalist and a

Director of the Natural History Museum in Cape Town from 1906 until his death in 1924. This small puff adder is only about 30 cm (1 ft) long; it inhabits the south-western part of Africa.

Burrowing or Mole Viper   *Atractaspis microlepidota*
atraktos (Gr) a thin shaft, an arrow; *aspis* (Gr) a viper, an asp; an allusion to the body being more slender than other vipers; the head is not triangular and not really distinct from the body, which assists in the burrowing activity; *mikros* (Gr) small; *lepis* (Gr) genitive *lepidos* a scale; *-ota* (New L) a suffix used to mean provided with; it has small granular scales. Inhabiting Africa south of the Sahara.

Family   CROTALIDAE   about 130 species
krotalon (Gr) a little bell, a rattle; this family owes its scientific name to the rattlesnakes, known as Pit Vipers, see *Bothrops atrox*, p. 150.

Eastern Diamond-back Rattlesnake   *Crotalus adamanteus*
adamanteus (L) hard as steel; comparing the hardness of steel to that of a diamond; this snake has a pattern of diamond-shaped marks along the back. Inhabiting the south-eastern part of the USA including Florida.

Western Diamond-back Rattlesnake   *C. atrox*
atrox (L) fearful, cruel; all rattlesnakes are venomous, with a powerful venom, and much feared by Man. Inhabiting a large area of desert and arid country in the south western USA.

Santa Catalina Rattlesnake   *C. catalinensis*
-ensis (L) suffix meaning belonging to; it lives on Santa Catalina Island, in the gulf of California and is unique in having no rattle; this is because the terminal scales which in normal rattlesnakes form the rattle are shed when it moults.

Sidewinder or Horned Rattlesnake   *C. cerastes*
cerastes (L) a horned serpent; the scales on the head form a small horn above each eye. A small rattlesnake, length only about 65

cm (2 ft 2 in) it inhabits desert areas in the south-western USA. The name 'sidewinder' refers to its peculiar method of movement on loose sand by throwing loops of its body forward, which gives the impression that it faces sideways to the actual direction of travel.

Timber Rattlesnake   *C. horridus*
horridus (L) rough, prickly; a reference to the type of scales. Inhabiting the south-eastern part of the USA, but not Florida.

Prairie Rattlesnake   *C. viridis viridis*
viridis (L) various shades of green; it is an olive colour with rows of brown spots. Inhabiting the north-western part of the USA and the neighbouring part of Canada. There are a number of subspecies in the western part of North America; this is the nominate subspecies and three other subspecies are given below. For an explanation of subspecies see Chapter 2, p. 16.

Arizona Black Rattlesnake   *C. v. cerberus*
Named after Cerberus, the mythical 3-headed monster. It is not really black but a very dark brown or blue colour. Inhabiting Arizona.

Utah Rattlesnake   *C. v. concolor*
concolor (L) of one colour; it is a pale brown colour without the conspicuous markings of the other rattlesnakes. Inhabiting eastern Utah.

Oregon Rattlesnake   *C. v. oreganus*
-anus (L) suffix meaning belonging to; named from Oregon, it inhabits California, Oregon and British Columbia.

Massasauga   *Sistrurus catenatus*
sistrum (L) derived from *seistron* (Gr) a small rattle used in religious worship, a child's rattle; *oura* (Gr) the tail; 'a tail-rattle'; *catena* (L) a chain, a shackle; can mean a gold or silver chain worn by women as an ornament; a reference to the chain-like coloured pattern along the back. It inhabits Illinois, Indiana, Wisconsin and Michigan and ranges east to the southern part of Ontario and central New York State. Known

as the Massasauga Rattler, the name is a corruption of Missisauga, the name of a river in Ontario.

Mexican Pygmy Rattlesnake *S. ravus*
ravus (L) tawny; although known as a 'pygmy rattlesnake', measuring about 86 cm (2 ft 10 in) it is not so small as the Sidewinder (p. 148). Inhabiting Mexico.

Fer de Lance *Bothrops atrox*
bothros (Gr) a hole, a pit; *ops* (Gr) the eye, face; *atrox* (L) hideous, savage; the generic name refers to a small depression or pit on the head between the eye and the nostril. A membrane in the pit is richly supplied with nerve endings which are so sensitive to heat that the warmth of a small warm-blooded animal can be detected 30 cm (1 ft) or more away; obviously of great benefit in the dark. Inhabiting Central America and the northern half of South America. Fer de Lance is French for a spearhead.

Island Viper *B. insularis*
insula (L) an island; *aris* (L) suffix meaning pertaining to; it is confined to the small island of Queimada Grande, off the coast of Brazil. The island has no human inhabitants and the number of these snakes has been steadly decreasing during the past few decades, possibly because the continued interbreeding causes a deterioration in health; they may be in danger of extinction.

Jararaca *B. jararaca*
Jararaca is a native name for this snake derived from the tupi language; the Tupi are a group of people living in the Amazon valley. This viper inhabits southern Brazil and Argentina.

White-lipped Tree Viper *Trimeresurus albolabris*
The meaning of *Trimeresurus*, which suggests 'three-part tail', is obscure. (Further research was intended by the Author.) *albus* (L) white; *labrum* (L) a lip. Inhabiting India.

Okinawa Habu or Yellow-spotted Lance-head *T. flavoviridis*
flavus (L) yellow; *viridis* (L) green. Inhabiting Okinawa and the

Ryukyu Islands; Habu is a native name for this snake in these islands.

Large-scaled Lance-head   *T. macrolepis*
makros (Gr) long; *lepis* (Gr) a scale; a reference to the unusually large scales on the head. Inhabiting Sri Lanka.

Chinese Mountain Viper   *T. montecola*
mons (L) genitive *montis* a mountain; *colo* (L) I inhabit, I dwell in. Inhabiting the mountains of southern China.

Chinese Habu   *T. mucrosquamata*
mucro (L) a sharp point; *squamatus* (L) scaly; a reference to the sharply keeled scales. Inhabiting southern China. Habu see Okinawa Habu above.

Bushmaster   *Lachesis mutus*
Lachesis was one of the three Fates in Greek mythology and was supposed to assign to Man his term of life, a macabre thought by Linnaeus who named this snake as it can certainly do this; it is the largest venomous snake in North or South America. *mutus* (L) dumb, mute; related to the rattlesnakes and similar in appearance, it shakes its tail vigorously when alarmed, but has no rattle so it was named *mutus*. However, when in the undergrowth, the tail actually makes quite a loud rustling noise. Inhabiting almost the entire north-eastern half of South America and the southern part of Central America.

Chinese Copperhead   *Agkistrodon acutus* (= *Ancistrodon*)
agkistron (Gr) a fish-hook; *odon* (Gr) a tooth; a reference to the curved fangs, though of course they are not barbed; *acutus* (L) sharp, pointed. Inhabiting the Shanghai area of China and ranging west to North Vietnam.

Tropical Moccasin   *A. bilineatus*
bis (L) two, double; *linea* (L) a line; *-atus* (L) suffix meaning provided with; an allusion to the yellow lines, one above the eye and one below, along the side of the head. Inhabiting Mexico.

Copperhead   *A. contortrix*
contorqueo (L) I twist, turn; *contortus* (L) full of turns, twisted;
contortrix (L) one that is able to turn, twist. Inhabiting the
south-eastern part of the USA including Florida. The top of the
head is reddish brown.

Halys Viper   *A. halys*
halusis (Gr) a chain; a reference to the chain-like pattern along
the back; this species, together with several subspecies, is very
widespread in south-east Asia.

Himalayan Viper   *A. himalayanus*
Inhabiting the mountains of the Himalayan region and sometimes found at an altitude of about 2,800 m (9,100 ft).

Cottonmouth or Water Moccasin   *A. piscivorus*
piscis (L) a fish; *voro* (L) I eat, devour; although known as the
Water Moccasin it is not really an aquatic animal, but is a good
swimmer; the diet is mostly fish and frogs. Inhabiting the south-
eastern part of the USA but not Florida. The name Cottonmouth refers to the interior of the mouth, which is white and
very conspicuous when the mouth is opened wide in a defensive
or attacking posture.

Appendix

Transliteration of Greek Alphabet

Greek		Name	Modern System	Latin System
A	α	alpha	a	a
B	β	bēta	b	b
Γ	γ	gamma	g	g
Δ	δ	delta	d	d
E	ε	epsilon	e	e
Z	ζ	zēta	z	z
H	η	ēta	ē	e
Θ	θ	thēta	th	th
I	ι	iōta	i	i
K	κ	kappa	k	c
Λ	λ	lambda	l	l
M	μ	mū	m	m
N	ν	nū	n	n
Ξ	ξ	xi	x	x
O	o	omicron	o	o
Π	π	pi	p	p
P	ρ	rhō	r	r
Σ	σ ς	sigma	s	s
T	τ	tau	t	t
Y	ν	upsilon	u	y
Φ	φ	phi	ph	ph
X	χ	chi	kh	ch
Ψ	ψ	psi	ps	ps
Ω	ω	ōmega	ō	o

Bibliography

Clarke, R. B. & Panchen, A. L. *Synopsis of Animal Classification* Chapman and Hall, London.

Darwin, C. *The Origin of Species*

Gotch, A. F. *Mammals – Their Latin Names Explained* Blandford Press, Poole.

Gotch, A. F. *Birds – Their Latin Names Explained* Blandford Press, Poole.

Jaeger, E. C. *A Source Book of Biological Names and Terms* Charles C. Thomas, Illinois.

Jeffrey, C. *Biological Nomenclature* Edward Arnold, London.

Lerwill, C. J. *An Introduction to the Classification of Animals* Constable, London.

Liddell, H. G. & Scott, R. *Greek-English Lexicon* Oxford University Press.

Lockley, R. M. *The Private Life of the Rabbit* Deutsch, London.

Mayr, E. *Principles of Systematic Zoology* McGraw-Hall.

Rothschild, Lord L. W. *A Classification of Living Animals* Longman, London.

Savory, T. H. *Latin and Greek for Biologists* Merrow.

Schmidt & Inger *Living Reptiles of the World*.

Glossary

Acrodont With teeth set at the top of the jaw bone (see p. 32).

Aestivate To sleep for a long period to escape the heat in summer; similar to hibernation in winter (see p. 46).

Aglypha Fangs of snakes lacking the groove or channel for conducting venom; i.e. non-venomous (see p. 32).

Autotomy A voluntary 'cutting off' of the tail in order to escape from a predator when seized by the tail (see p. 9).

Carapace Upper part of the shell of a tortoise or turtle (see p. 40).

Cloaca The common chamber into which the intestinal, urinary and generative canals open in reptiles, birds, amphibians and many fishes; from *cloaca* (L) a sewer or drain.

Code The Rules of the International Commission on Zoological Nomenclature are now known as the Code (see pp. 10 and 12).

Crepuscular Appearing at dusk, twilight.

Cryptodira Tortoises in which the head and neck are withdrawn and bent in a vertical plane, thus being completely hidden (see pp. 38 and 39).

Dewlap Pendulous fold of skin under the throat of some lizards and some other animals such as cattle (see p. 103).

Herpetology The study of reptiles, from *herpeton* (Gr) a reptile.

Hibernaculum A place where animals hibernate.

Hibernate To sleep for a long period in a protected place to escape the cold of winter.

Homeothermic Scientific term for 'warm-blooded' (see p. 29).

Imbricate With overlapping scales like the tiles on a roof (see pp. 47, 109 and 112).

Jacobson's Organ A structure in the roof of the mouth of most reptiles that is, or augments, the sense of smell (see p. 33).

Nictitating Membrane A third eyelid, more or less transparent, at the inner corner of the eye, which can sweep rapidly across the cornea cleaning and lubricating the surface.

Nuchal Pertaining to the nape of the neck.

Opisthoglypha The poison fangs of a snake that are situated at the back of the mouth (see p. 32).

Ovoviviparous A term to describe animals in which the young are born alive, but in the egg, which is really only a thin membrane and easily broken open (see p. 106).

Placenta The structure that unites the foetus to the mother's womb, and supplies it with nourishment and oxygen.

Plastron The lower part of the shell of a tortoise or turtle.

Pleurodira Tortoises in which the head and neck, when withdrawn, are bent sideways, and part of the neck remains visible (pp. 38 and 50).

Pleurodont With teeth set on the side of the jaw bone (see p. 32).

Poikilothermic A 'cold-blooded' animal; the temperature of the blood varies according to the surroundings and is not controlled by the animal's nervous system (see p. 29).

Pores, Femoral Pores on the under surface of the femur of some lizards, usually only the male, the purpose of which is not known for certain (see p. 108).

Process (Biol) Projecting part, especially on bone (see p. 138).

Proteroglypha The poison fangs of a snake that are situated at the front of the mouth (see p. 32).

Solenoglypha The poison fangs of a snake that are actually hollow, like a hypodermic needle (see p. 32).

Viviparous A term to describe animals in which the young are born alive (see p. 145).

General Index

This index includes only technical terms, names of zoologists and animals other than those reptiles included in Chapters 7 to 11. Some individual species of animals are listed with their names in *italics*. Phyla, subphyla and classes are listed THUS.

Index of English Names

This index includes the English names of all reptiles mentioned in this book. In general, only the page number of the main reference is given but, where there is an important reference of a general or less important nature, then this page number is indicated in *italic*.

Index of Latin Names

This index contains the Latin names of all reptiles mentioned in this book. The Phyla, Subphyla, Classes, Subclasses, Orders, Suborders, Families and Subfamilies are indicated THUS. In general, only the page number of the main reference is given but, where there is an additional reference of a general or less important nature, then this page number is indicated in *italic*.